Roman Catholics & Shi'i Muslims

Roman

PRAYER, PASSION, & POLITICS

Catholics

JAMES A. BILL & JOHN ALDEN WILLIAMS

&

THE UNIVERSITY OF NORTH CAROLINA PRESS

Shiʻi

CHAPEL HILL & LONDON

Muslims

© 2002
The University of North Carolina Press
All rights reserved
Manufactured in the United States of America
Designed by Richard Hendel
Set in Cycles type
by Tseng Information Systems, Inc.
The paper in this book meets the guidelines for
permanence and durability of the Committee on
Production Guidelines for Book Longevity of the
Council on Library Resources.

Library of Congress
Cataloging-in-Publication Data
Bill, James A.
Roman Catholics and Shi'i Muslims : prayer,
passion, and politics / James A. Bill and
John Alden Williams.
     p. cm.
Includes bibliographical references and index.
ISBN 0-8078-2689-8 (cloth: alk. paper)
1. Shī'ah—Relations—Catholic Church.   2. Catholic
Church—Relations—Shī'ah.   3. Islam—Relations—
Catholic Church.   4. Catholic Church—Relations—
Islam.   I. Williams, John Alden.   II. Title.
BP194.18.C383   2002
261.2'7—dc21   2001053233

06 05 04 03 02   5 4 3 2 1

Frontispiece:
Iranian president Muhammad Khatami talks with
Pope John Paul II during a meeting at the Vatican on
March 11, 1999. Reuters/Pool/Archive Photos; photo
by Sabucetti.

To the memory of
Monsignor Charles A. Kelly Jr.
and
Professor Wilfred Cantwell Smith,

Probing minds,
Great mentors,
Unforgettable men

CONTENTS

ACKNOWLEDGMENTS

Many scholars assisted and advised us as we prepared this comparative study of two religions. Seyyed Hossein Nasr, internationally recognized as the dean of Shi'i scholars, encouraged us from the beginning. The work of Dr. Nasr provided much of the inspiration for our book. Two of our colleagues at the College of William and Mary, Thomas Finn and James Livingston, both authorities on the history and philosophy of Roman Catholicism within the Christian tradition, helped explain to us some of the intricacies of Catholic thought. The late Monsignor Charles Kelly and Father Joseph Tetlow S.J. also read sections of the manuscript and commented constructively. Among other scholars of Islam and Shi'ism who provided invaluable assistance are John Esposito, William Graham, Hossein Modarressi Tabataba'i, Mehdi Noorbaksh, Kevin Reinhart, Abdul Aziz Sachedina, Tamara Sonn, Antony Sullivan, and John Voll. Natural law scholar J. Budziszewski helped us understand this complex subject. Herbert Mason provided insights into Sufism and shared his vast knowledge of the late Louis Massignon.

Others who encouraged us in this endeavor include Mumtaz Ahmad, Said Amir Arjomand, Betty Ann Bill, Ralph Braibanti, Rebecca Bill Chavez, Paul Chellgren, Robert Crane, James Deffenbaugh, Marlan Downey, Dale Eickelman, Kail Ellis, Shafeeq Ghabra, Muhammad and Soussan Koochekzadeh, Frank Korn, Leonard Liggio, Bruce Mazlish, Richard Norton, Willard Oxtoby, A. K. Rafeq, Frank Shatz, Robert Springborg, Bishop Walter Sullivan, John Washburn, and Amir Zinat. We also thank the Earhart Foundation for providing a generous research grant that enabled us to complete this project. Charles Grench and Paula Wald at the University of North Carolina Press have enthusiastically supported us throughout the preparation of this book.

Finally, we thank our wives, Caroline Williams and Ann Marie Bill, for their indispensable assistance.

On September 11, 2001, several unprecedented acts of terrorism shook the United States to the core. Working in close coordination, nineteen hijackers boarded four commercial aircraft. The hijackers forced two of the planes to fly into the World Trade Center in New York City; a third plane crashed into the Pentagon; and a fourth exploded upon impact in the Pennsylvania countryside. These atrocious acts resulted in the deaths of more than 5,000 people. Because the perpetrators were reported to be practicing Muslims of Middle Eastern origin, a glaring international spotlight was shown on Islam, one of the world's three great monotheistic religions. Many thoughtful commentators emphasized that Islam was a religion of peace. Others were not so sure. The latter group viewed Islam as an alien, militant, anti-Western force that was fundamentally different from Christianity and Judaism. Whatever their conclusions, most serious observers agree that it is in everyone's interest to develop a greater understanding of Islam. This book attempts to take an important step on that path by comparing two enormously important faith systems embedded within Christianity and Islam, the Roman Catholic and the Twelver Shiʿi Muslim faiths.

NOTE ON TRANSLITERATION

The system of transliteration in this book generally follows the formats used in the *International Journal of Middle East Studies* and the *Encyclopaedia of Islam*. Other than the ayn (ʿ) and hamza (ʾ), we have omitted diacritical marks. Examples include ʿAli, Hasan, Husayn, Qurʾan, Shiʿi, ʿUmar, ʿUthman, *shariʿa*, and Ismaʿili. Arabic, Persian, and Turkish words commonly used in English are spelled as they appear in *Webster's Third International Dictionary*, for example, Qum, Madina, Mecca, and Sufi. Well-known names are presented as they generally appear in English, for example, Muhammad, Fatima, Ayatollah Ruhollah Khomeini, and Abu Bakr.

Roman Catholics & Shi'i Muslims

INTRODUCTION:
TWO GREAT RELIGIOUS
CIVILIZATIONS

On March 11, 1999, Pope John Paul II, the leader of 1 billion Roman Catholics, received a special guest in his private library in the Vatican. In the extraordinary meeting that ensued, Hojjat ol-Islam Muhammad Khatami, president of the Islamic Republic of Iran, the leading Shiʻi Islamic country in the world, spoke with the Catholic leader about violence, injustice, and the desperate need for humankind to communicate across national, ethnic, and religious divides. Stooped with age and disease and dressed completely in white, the seventy-eight-year-old pontiff spoke earnestly with his fifty-six-year-old guest. The bearded Iranian religious and political leader wore a black turban and dark gray and black robes. This was the pope's first meeting with a Shiʻi Muslim national leader. The world press described the exchange as "ground-breaking," "a landmark," and "a water-shed moment" in Christian-Muslim relations.

This highly symbolic encounter represented an attempt by the Shiʻi Muslim leader and the Roman Catholic pontiff to emphasize the need to open channels of communication between members of different faith systems. Each man showed a quiet respect for the other. President Khatami told the pope that there was hope for the victory of monotheism, ethics, and morality. Peace and reconciliation were eminently possible. Searching for common ground, Khatami stated that all religions are "not quintessentially different." He referred to the "spirit of Assisi," a program of interreligious prayer meetings begun in the 1980s by the pope. The Shiʻi cleric indicated that he had come to open the doors of dialogue and détente. He asked the pontiff to pray for him.

Pope John Paul II blessed the Iranian religious leader and described the meeting as "important and promising." In an official communique following their session, the Vatican emphasized the importance of the meeting in promoting a true spirit of dialogue between Muslims and Christians.[1]

After an exchange of gifts, the two religious leaders spoke hopefully about the future. The warmth and emotion of the moment were captured when one of the clerics accompanying Khatami spontaneously ran to the pope and embraced him, kissing him on both cheeks. Muslim Shiʿis and Roman Catholics had established friendly personal contact at the highest ecclesial level. The pope further demonstrated his concern for maintaining cordial relations with Muslims by visiting Damascus, Syria, in May 2001.

Encounters between Christians and Muslims have not always been so cordial. According to one pre–Vatican II Catholic source, "[Muhammad] commanded his followers to conquer all nations and either kill or enslave or convert them. The name of Allah became known as the Prince of War. Our Lord and Savior Jesus Christ has always been the Prince of Peace. Mohammedanism was a religion of the sword."[2] A medieval Muslim source, however, states: "Mysterious are the works of the Creator, the author of all things! When one comes to recount cases regarding the Franks [Western Christians], he cannot but glorify Allah . . . and sanctify him, for he sees them as animals possessing the virtues of courage and fighting, but nothing else; just as animals have only the virtues of strength and carrying loads."[3]

With the rise of what is known as "religious fundamentalism," it is important that universal religious movements such as Christianity and Islam embark on a major effort to understand one another's histories and beliefs. Myths and misunderstandings prevail, and observers tend to focus on the differences between the two faith systems. In the Western world, many observers continue to view Islam as a violent, uncivilized, fanatical force lacking in civility and morality. The Muslim perspective, however, tends to see the West as an amoral and confused world in which technology has run amok. In the words of Sadeq al-Mahdi of Sudan: "Today backward and deprived, we face an economic and military giant with the moral and spiritual scruples of a flea. It is not a pleasant encounter."[4]

In this book, we focus on the similarities that mark the two faith systems. We are, of course, well aware that each has generated a distinctive civilization and that confrontations have occurred between these civilizations. We have no intention of understating their differences. Enough has been written about "the clash of civilizations." It is time to address the more interesting question of the community of civilizations. Because the differences are commonly known and heavily emphasized, we choose to uncover the roots that remain deeply entangled and intertwined in the histories and philosophies of Christians and Muslims. In pursuing this complex task, we compare two primary sects of both traditions: Roman Catholicism within the Christian heritage and Shi'i Islam within the Muslim tradition.

Few in the Western world understand the many fascinating linkages between Catholicism and Shi'ism. For example, in the Qur'an, Jesus is mentioned in over ninety verses. There are more references to Mary in the Qur'an than in the Bible; in fact, Mary is mentioned far more than any other woman. There are twelve Imams (charismatic leaders) according to Shi'i beliefs and twelve disciples in Christianity. The first eleven Imams are believed to have died as martyrs; with the exception of Judas Iscariot and St. John, the apostles were also reportedly martyred. Interestingly, the number 72 appears repeatedly in both traditions. When Imam Husayn undertook his ill-fated expedition to Karbala in 680, he was accompanied by 72 close friends and family members. According to John 10:1, Jesus sent a group of 72 disciples out to preach. One *hadith* (narrative tradition) attributed to the Prophet Muhammad asserts that the Muslim community will be split into 72 sects. Also, in Numbers 31:38, it is written that 72 oxen were part of the booty after Moses defeated the Midianites. According to Shi'i legend, 72 camels were slain at Fatima's wedding. In *Bahr al-Fawa'id*, a twelfth-century Persian treatise on politics, the author writes that if a king champions justice in his realm, 72 persons will intercede for him on the Day of Judgment.

A detailed comparative examination of these two influential religious movements offers four advantages for the promotion of better understanding and communication. First, by focusing on Roman Catholicism and Twelver Shi'ism, we are able to address a more manageable universe of analysis. The subject matter is more easily confronted. Second, because the Catholic-Shi'i comparison is particularly stimulating, it is more likely to foster discussion and debate. Third, a comparison of this type in all of its dimensions and ramifications has not yet been attempted. Renowned scholars such as Louis Massignon and Seyyed Hossein Nasr have called attention to notable similarities between Catholicism and Shi'ism from time to time, but attempts at systematic comparison have been lacking. Fourth, the issues that challenged both Catholicism and Shi'ism in the beginning remain relevant and important at the dawn of the twenty-first century. By analyzing the structures and histories of these two religious systems, we should be better equipped intellectually to understand civilizations that differ from our own.

In this book, we seek to wrestle with issues such as the relationship between God and humanity; the continuum between life and death; the dialectic between war and peace; the gap between rich and poor; the significance of religious ceremony and drama; the place of saints, martyrs, and confessors; the role of the inner (*batin*) as opposed to the outer (*zahir*) reality of humankind; the role of redemptive suffering; the relationship between religion and politics; and the similarities and differences in legal systems. By addressing these issues, we may learn more about ourselves. It is often far more difficult to know ourselves than it is to know our neighbors.

The overlapping of Catholicism and Islam is seen in a study of their doctrines and in the lives of key figures in both systems. A dramatic case in point is the life and thought of an eminent judge who served on the Pakistani Supreme Court from 1951 to 1968. A practicing Roman Catholic, A. R. Cornelius held the position of chief justice from 1960 to 1968 in one of the world's largest and most important Islamic states. Thoroughly conversant with Islamic law, Cornelius played a central role in the development of the Pakistani constitutional system. Esteemed by Christians and Muslims alike, Cornelius synthesized Islamic and Christian values. His intellectual scaffolding for this synthesis was the philosophy of Thomas Aquinas in general and the concept of natural law in particular. To Cornelius, the Catholic and Islamic legal traditions contained no major contradictions. He embodied the ability to live within two traditions. Despite his personal commitment to Catholicism, Cornelius was referred to by a Muslim colleague on the bench as "more Muslim than the Muslims."[5]

An estimated 140 million Twelver Shi'is live in the world today. Table 1 shows that the highest percentages of Shi'is live in countries clustered around the Persian Gulf and in Azerbaijan, Lebanon, and Afghanistan. Although their percentage of the overall population in each country is small, Twelver Shi'is also inhabit Pakistan, India, and Turkey in sizable numbers. Shi'ism is the state religion of the Islamic Republic of Iran, where nearly 95

Table 1. World Twelver Shi'i Populations, 2000

Country	Citizen Population	Number of Shi'is	% Shi'is
Iran	68,000,000	64,600,000	95
Pakistan	125,000,000	31,250,000	25
Iraq	19,000,000	11,400,000	60
Turkey	66,000,000	11,200,000	17
India	1,000,850,000	5,000,000	5
Azerbaijan	7,400,000	4,810,000	65
Afghanistan	16,500,000	4,125,000	25
Lebanon	3,200,000	1,170,000	35
Saudi Araba	13,000,000	1,120,000	9
Bahrain	605,000	423,000	70
Kuwait	750,000	225,000	30
U.A.E.	400,000	72,000	18
Qatar	220,000	35,000	16
Oman	1,400,000	28,000	2
Miscellaneous	N/A	5,000,000	N/A
Total		140,458,000	

Sources: Data provided to authors by governments of Shi'i countries, personal interviews during research trips to relevant Shi'i countries, and consultations with country specialists.

percent of the inhabitants are Twelvers. Shi'is make up 60 percent of Iraq's population and 70 percent of Bahrain's. Iran and Iraq together account for approximately 75 million Twelver Shi'is. Over a million Shi'is live in the eastern province of Saudi Arabia, and 1.1 million reside in Lebanon, where they account for 35 percent of the population. Another 47 million inhabit Pakistan (31 million), Turkey (11 million), and India (5 million). The miscellaneous category in Table 1 includes countries such as Syria and Kenya, which have small concentrations of Twelvers.[6]

The Shi'is assume geostrategic importance far beyond their numbers because they live in countries with the world's largest deposits of oil. This geographic congruence of Shi'is and petroleum is seen most dramatically in the eastern province of Saudi Arabia, where in the oil-rich regions of Dhahran, Dammam, and Qatif the populations are over 98 percent Shi'i.

Politically, the Shi'is came to the attention of the world because of the central role Shi'ism played in the Iranian revolution and the fall of the shah in 1978–79. The charismatic leader who inspired and directed the revolutionary forces was a Shiʿi cleric, Ayatollah Ruhollah Khomeini. With the collapse of the Pahlavi regime, Khomeini and his colleagues among the ʿulama (Muslim clerics) established the Islamic Republic. Historically, beginning with the rise of the Safavid dynasty in 1501, Shiʿi Islam had been the state religion of Iran. Shiʿi leaders played important roles in the politics of the day and often served as close advisers to the shahs. It was not until the revolution, however, that the clerics in fact took on the role of directly conducting the affairs of state. In postrevolutionary Iran, members of the Shiʿi ʿulama have served as cabinet ministers, parliamentary deputies, and government officials of all kinds. Clerics such as Ali Akbar Hashemi-Rafsanjani and Muhammad Khatami have held the elected post of president of the Islamic Republic.

Just as the Shiʿis are congregated in the Middle East and Central Asia, the 1 billion Roman Catholics are concentrated largely in North and South America and Europe. As the largest Christian denomination, however, Roman Catholicism is in fact present across the globe. Both Catholicism and Shiʿism are transnational, universalistic faith systems. Although the Shiʿis have a concentrated form of power due to their proximity to oil, the Catholics have a broader presence and outnumber the Shiʿis by a ratio of 10 to 1.

In chapter 1 of this book, we introduce the reader to Christianity and Islam in general terms. We then sort out Roman Catholicism and Twelver Shiʿism from their Christian and Muslim roots. Because of the confusion and misunderstanding concerning Shiʿi Islam, we focus chapter 2 on the history and beliefs of Twelver Shiʿism. In brief, we tell the story of the Shiʿis. In chapter 3, we compare four preeminent sacred actors: Jesus, Husayn, Mary, and Fatima. We also discuss the Imams and saints, focusing primarily on their roles as mediators and intercessors. The role of redemptive suffering and martyrdom is the subject of chapter 4, and in chapter 5, we analyze the place of mysticism in both faith systems. In chapter 6, we compare the role and substance of law and its relation to the state in the two systems. In chapter 7, we examine Twelver Shiʿism and Roman Catholicism in the context of politics and justice. Finally, we conclude with a series of propositions concerning the comparative politics of religion.

This is a story of two civilizations in which the extraordinary is often the ordinary. Compassion and forgiveness triumph over cruelty and vindictiveness when human beings with divine qualities make sacrifices in order to redeem their fellow men and women. Jesus the Messiah and 'Ali and Husayn, the first and third Imams, faced suffering and death. In so doing, they became powerful role models for other men and women who have tasted the salt of their tears and have worn masks of happiness in the darkest of times.

1

ROMAN CATHOLICISM AND TWELVER SHIʿISM

In this study, we seek to compare one tradition of Christianity with one tradition of Islam. We begin in this chapter by "mapping" or locating each of these traditions in relation to the other branches of its faith. Within the larger Christian tradition, we sketch what it means to be "Catholic" and within Catholicism what it means to be Roman Catholic. Within the larger Muslim community of faith, we indicate what it means to be "Shiʿi" and within Shiʿism what it means to be Twelver Shiʿi.

THE EARLY CHRISTIAN CHURCH

Less than 400 years after the life of Jesus Christ, the Christian faith had spread around the Mediterranean and beyond it. Christianity had achieved a regional organization of dioceses, each under the leadership of a bishop (from Greek *episcopos,* "supervisor"). Particularly respected were the bishops of important cities of the Roman Empire: Rome, in the Latin-speaking West; Alexandria and Antioch, important Greek-speaking centers; and Jerusalem, holy to both Jews and Christians. When Emperor Constantine shifted the state position from persecution to patronage early in the fourth century, he made Byzantium, renamed Constantinople, the "New Rome." This added a fifth city to the major episcopal jurisdictions. The result was the Pentarchy, "the five senses of the Empire," as Emperor Justinian the Great called the jurisdictions in the mid-sixth century.

Outside the empire, the king of Armenia had been baptized a Christian in 301, well before Constantine's first pro-Christian gestures. Roman or otherwise, after three centuries as the faith of a minority, Christianity was a state religion and the church a well-defined institution. Membership in it was marked by baptism (a ritual bath going back to Jewish religious ablution) and anointing, followed by participation in communion with the local Christians. This followed a course of instruction, or *catechesis* (hence catechism), and profession of faith. Christians were defining the content of their faith in doctrinal terms, developing propositions of faith that required assent.[1]

The Nicene-Constantinopolitan Creed is a Christian creedal formulation dating from the fourth century. Among other articles, one article states: "We believe in One, Holy, Catholic and Apostolic Church," a unique, sanctifying, universal assembly founded by Jesus and faithful to the teachings of his apostles and their successors to this day.

Christians, like Muslims and Jews, worship the God of Abraham, who is transcendent, beyond normal knowing, except insofar as He has chosen to reveal Himself. For Christians, the perfect revelation of God's holy and inaccessible mystery is in His Word or Logos. This doctrine emerges primarily from the Wisdom literature of the Bible. There Hokhmah (Sophia in the Greek Septuagint) or Wisdom is represented as a distinct principle, firstborn of God, active with Him in the creation, proceeding from the mouth of God, with Him in the highest heaven and then sent to Israel, the image of His perfection.[2] The Fourth Gospel states that the divine Logos/Word/Sophia became incarnated in Jesus and that "all that came to be had life in him, life that was the light of Humankind . . . which enlightens all people."[3] It is then entirely comprehensible for Christians that Jesus said, "No-one comes to the Father except through me,"[4] because all have life itself through the Logos and can only return to God by His agency. In short, Jesus discloses the heart of God to Christians.

The Western branch of the Catholic communion recognizes the bishop of Rome as the successor of St. Peter, chief of the apostles of Jesus,[5] and acknowledges this chief bishop's direct control as *patriarch*, or "father governor." It is the largest church of Christendom and by far the largest of the sister churches of the Catholic communion. A number of the Catholic churches of the Eastern world have historically separate patriarchs[6] who govern their own churches but acknowledge the pope's jurisdiction in matters of faith and morals. A Catholic follows a bishop who is in communion with the pope and who accepts the Petrine supremacy. The histories and traditions, liturgical usages and languages of other Catholic communities may lead to the formation of separate ecclesial cultures from that of the Latin Western Church of Rome.

The Catholic Church is a "sacrament" (Latin) or "mystery" (Greek), in which God is united with the assembly and conveys divine assistance through visible signs (also called sacraments): baptism, communion, confirmation, penance, holy orders, matrimony, and unction (anointing of the sick). In this book, "Roman Catholic" will refer to the church directly governed by the patriarch of the West, the pope,[7] rather than the Catholic Church of the creed, which, as its name states, is neither Latin nor Roman but universal. In Catholic social thought, society is a set of relationships ideally governed by love. It is therefore redeemable, indeed already redeemed (in the church). Catholics agree that the church is infallible and that the majority of its bishops in council together will be protected from error in matters of faith and morals. This is especially the position of the Eastern "Orthodox" Churches, for example, Greek, Russian, Bulgarian, Romanian, Serbian, and Georgian. For over a millennium, these churches were in communion with the Church of Rome. In the eleventh century, they came to believe that Rome had separated itself from the universal church of the creed by accepting words inserted in the creed by a pope acting without a council.[8] They felt this represented a monarchical universal jurisdiction never contemplated in the original church. There was a widening breach between the Western and the Eastern patriarchates. Roman Catholics on their side have come to hold that in the absence of a council, the pope of Rome may authentically speak for the entire church.

THE CATHOLIC CHURCH IN THE WEST

In the fifth century, the West was faced with the invasions of Germanic tribes, who came as pagans or heretics and had no friendship with the universal church of the empire. Outside peoples continued to migrate to the West for 600 years. The Roman state in the West collapsed and was replaced by barbarian rulers who over time came to accept the faith of their Catholic subjects. Conversion offered political advantages for such rulers: the cooperation of the bishops and their literate clerics, the sacralizing of royal authority through "anointing," and the powerful blessing of the Christian God.

Gregory I (pope, 590–604) was the first missionary pope of Rome and the first monk to become pope. At the time, Western society was torn by violence, anarchy, and incoherence. Gregory himself described the Church of Rome as "an old ship woefully shattered; for the waters are entering on all sides, and the joints, buffeted by the daily stress of the storm, are growing rotten and herald shipwreck."[9]

Gregory's admiration for St. Benedict of Nursia insured that the Benedictine form of monasticism would become dominant in the West. Unable to obtain help from the faraway emperor in Constantinople, Gregory used funds from the estates of the papacy in Italy, Sicily, and North Africa to feed the hungry people of Rome and to aid monks in Egypt. He also sent forty monks from his own monastery in Rome to convert the remote Anglo-Saxons of Britain. As Pius X wrote, Gregory "liberally succored the impoverished people, Christian society, and individual churches according to the necessities of each . . . and stood up in public as the defender of social justice."[10]

When Gregory died in 604, the future still looked bleak for Christians in northwest Europe, but the results of his initiatives were impressive. By 700, all of the Anglo-Saxon kingdoms had adopted Roman Christianity. The Christian Celts of Wales, Ireland, and North Britain, long cut off from the Continent, were now accepting Roman leadership, and Anglo-Saxon monks and nuns loyal to Rome were creating disciplined religious houses in Germany. Roman Christianity came to be the established church of a Frankish empire with a ruler anointed as emperor of the Romans by the successor of Peter.

The Carolingian emperors[11] furthered the Roman form of Christianity, made the popes independent rulers of central Italy, actively converted the peoples on their eastern borders, and used Catholic bishops as administrators. The Germanic emperors also expected to appoint their bishops and to intervene in church affairs. Importantly, the Carolingians and their Ottonian successors in their own domains used the *filioque*[12] in the creed, but the popes resisted the formula until 1014. The laity's instruction in Christianity was meager: men, women, and children were taught the Our Father and the Apostle's Creed.[13]

The Frankish state was a far cry from the opulent empire of Byzantium and was built on a fragile economic and political base. By 900, it had collapsed due to internal strife and external invasions. North African Muslims conquered Sicily, Sardinia, and Corsica, and in 846 they looted the Basilica of St. Peter in Rome. Much more destructive were the invasions of the Norsemen. Western Christianity in England, Ireland, and Western Frankish lands was intellectually decapitated. Although Irish monks had once studied Greek, increasingly the Latin West could not read the language in which the New Testament had been written and first preached.

In the Eastern Frankish empire of Germany, Switzerland, and north Italy, the passing of the Carolingians led to the election in 919 of a strong man to lead the war against invading Magyars from Hungary. A victory against the "Huns" in 955 resulted in the crowning of a German emperor, Otto I. The Hungarians, led by King Stephen (d. 1038), finally accepted Roman Catholicism. Nonetheless, the tenth century was a miserable, disordered period in the West and the low point of the papacy as brawling noble families made and unmade popes of their relatives in the ruins of Rome and emperors intervened as it suited them.

Change in the state of the church began in the monasteries north of the Alps, particularly through the reform of the rule of St. Benedict in the monastery of Cluny in Burgundy. By the end of the eleventh century, some 600 monasteries cultivated a dignified, liturgical, and well-ordered monastic life, with an estimated 10,000 monks answerable to the abbot of Cluny.[14] The monks also favored a celibate clergy and the revival of lapsed canon law. The monasteries fostered Latin learning, and increasingly the cathedral schools where some nonmonastic clergy received training did so as well. Pope Urban II, who preached the first crusade in 1095, was a monk of Cluny. By 1076, a pope, Gregory VII, had ended the struggle for control of the Latin church by excommunicating an emperor, Henry IV. This punishment did not prevent the emperor from later besieging Rome for three years and forcing the pope to flee.

THE PROTESTANT MOVEMENT

Protestant Christians recite the same creed as Catholics but historically have rebelled against Rome's interpretations. They tend to see church unity as guaranteed by faithfulness to the Christian scriptures written by the apostles of Jesus and their immediate successors, certainly not by the successor of Peter. Protestants insist on their right to interpret these scriptures in the light of conscience, not by tradition. They see the sacred character of their churches as provisional on faith in the sanctifying work of Jesus, and they generally limit the sacraments to baptism and communion. Society is commonly seen as an oppressive order, forsaken by God, in constant need of re-formation.

Western Christians, Protestant and Catholic, have been profoundly influenced by the thought of St. Augustine of Hippo (d. 430), a doctor of the early church who wrote in Latin and was little read among Eastern Catholics. Augustine's view of the sin of Adam was radical by Eastern terms: humankind was fatally damaged by the fall of its first parents and unable to attain the good it desired, except by divine grace.[15] After Augustine, this doctrine became part of the religious culture of all Western Christianity. A total dependence on grace in turn led many Protestants, followers of early reformers such as Martin Luther, Huldrych Zwingli, and John Calvin, as well as supporters of the Jansenist movement among Roman Catholics,[16] to a belief that one's eternal happiness depends on divine predestination. Although Jansenism attracted many Roman Catholics, its characteristic doctrines were eventually condemned by the church, whereas many of the leading Protestant bodies are still heavily Calvinistic in theology.

Right doctrine, orthodoxy, for Catholics is to believe what the church teaches. Protestants have insisted that the leadership of the majority does not guarantee freedom from error: the majority has in fact often been wrong, and the minority has been the "saving remnant."

Indeed, sectarian Protestantism of the sort that has flourished in North America has tended to see acceptance of Jesus Christ as personal lord and savior as almost the whole of religion. In such a persuasion, any "church" can easily be dispensed with, for one can always found another church closer to one's preferences or one can do without a church altogether. The individual human conscience alone is sacred in matters of faith, and one may well be right if one feels that one is right. *Haeresis*, believing as one chooses, is right doctrine. Such a view necessarily fosters individualism and the conviction that one is entitled to whatever worldly goods one can obtain.[17]

ISLAM AND ITS BEGINNINGS

Muslims hold that God reveals Himself in His Word, given to prophets ever since Adam. After many revelations, this Word, as complete as it would ever be, was given to the last of the prophets, Muhammad, and is the divine Recitation, the Arabic Qur'an. If you want to know what God is like and hear His authentic speech, Muslims say, look to that book. Jesus was the promised Messiah, the "Word of God and Spirit from Him," son of the sinless Virgin Mary, but his true message was distorted by his followers, and Muhammad was sent not only to bring the eternal message in its definitive form but also to create a community that would protect it from misconstruction. To do this, the Prophet performed a great miracle with God's aid: he united the Arab tribes, the most quarrelsome and divided people in Muhammad's seventh-century world. This community, or *umma*, now embracing many peoples, is not permitted to "turn the other cheek" when it is threatened; it is commanded to deter assailants if it can. Such a struggle has the same name as the struggle to overcome one's own selfishness: *jihad*.

The Muslim calendar begins numbering its years at the beginning of the community, when the Prophet Muhammad, with some early followers, moved in 622 from the trading city of Mecca to the agricultural oasis later renamed Madina. There he became the arbiter of interclan conflicts and inaugurated the governance of the society according to revealed principles. To become a Muslim, one "bears witness" in an affirmation that is repeated in the call to prayer and is more universal than the creeds of Christianity since all Muslim groups affirm it and there is no difference of opinion about it. One affirms that there is no god but the God of Abraham and that Muhammad is His messenger, implying that his position is the culmination or "seal" of the prophets the world has known and that his words and acts are spiritual and institutional norms.

During the ten years he lived after being driven from his home city, only the last two of which were after he brought it to his side, Muhammad ruled the community of Muslims as lawgiver, teacher, exemplar, magistrate, and religious and political head. He continued to recite new revelations given to him, Muslims believe, by the Archangel Gabriel. His sudden death from an illness after leading a pilgrimage from Madina to Mecca in March 632 came as a great shock to his followers. What happened next resulted in the division of the community into Sunnis and Shi'is. Muhammad made no provision for a successor. It is tenaciously held by all Shi'is and conceded by many Sunni scholars that on his way home from the pilgrimage, Muhammad had halted the caravan before it began to split up to go to different towns[18] and made a somewhat ambiguous public announcement about his young first cousin 'Ali, who was also the husband of his only surviving child, his daughter Fatima. 'Ali was also the father of the Prophet's only living grandsons, Hasan and Husayn. Muhammad reportedly said, "If I was any-one's *mawla*, then ʿAli is his *mawla*."[19] The ambiguity is in the word *mawla*, which can mean either "master" or "friend." Sunnis who take notice of the incident have held that he was commending a none-too-popular son-in-law to his followers' affections. Shiʿis insist that there was no ambiguity: Muhammad was telling the Muslims that ʿAli was to be their next master.

Two and a half months later, Muhammad was dead. While ʿAli and his relatives washed and shrouded the body for burial, three of the Prophet's nearest associates from Mecca met with chiefs of the people of Madina. They agreed to swear allegiance to one of the leading companions, Abu Bakr, as Muhammad's successor in every function but prophecy. Abu Bakr's young daughter ʿAʾisha was also Muhammad's favorite wife and had nursed him in his last illness.[20] The next morning, their choice was announced in the mosque as an accomplished fact, and the majority of the residents of the town also swore allegiance. ʿAli and his close relatives and partisans held back, but they were won over one by one. ʿAli himself, after Fatima (who was bitterly critical of the arrangement) died a few months later, agreed to recognize Abu Bakr so as not to divide the community. "Sunni" means "fol-lowing the tradition of the majority" (not of the Prophet), whereas "Shiʿi" means "partisan of the Prophet's family."[21] It is characteristic of Islam that what appears to be a political dispute about the authentic succession has far-reaching doctrinal ramifications.[22]

SUNNIS, SHIʿIS, AND THE IMAMATE

All Muslim groups hold that there should be an Imam,[23] or religious leader, for the followers of Muhammad. Sunnis state that the Imam may be any righteous Muslim male descendant of the Prophet's tribe of Quraysh above the age of puberty who is elected by the authorities or designated by his predecessor. He is not impeccable and may under some circumstances be deposed. He need not be a religious scholar or a man of war. All legal authority in the community derives from him because he is the successor of the Prophet (*khalifa*, or caliph), the Commander of the Faithful. Sunnis have differed over whether two or more Imams can exist at the same time. The king of Morocco has been recognized as Commander of the Faithful in his jurisdiction, but elsewhere Sunnis have not agreed on a caliph since the end of the Ottoman Empire in 1924.[24] The lack of a caliph is regarded by many Sunnis as intolerable. They insist that reinstitution of the caliphate should be the first order of business for today's resurgent Muslim community.

To be a Shi'i is to believe that God intended the leadership of the community to be held by a descendant of the Prophet. Many Shi'i sects have emerged as the claims of different members of the family were put forward. Three major divisions remain today: Zaydi, Isma'ili, and Twelver.

The Zaydis are found chiefly in the Yemeni highlands. They teach that the leader of the community after Muhammad may be any adult male descendant of Fatima's two sons ('Ali's sons by other women are not eligible) who is a learned interpreter of the law of Islam, mature, capable, and a warrior who rises to defend the just claims of his family. He is called the Imam, but he must also rule as Commander of the Faithful in his area and be acclaimed by the community leaders. There can be more than one Imam at a time in widely separated regions. The Imam is not regarded as infallible or impeccable and may be deposed if he goes astray and commits a major sin (for example, murder, adultery, sodomy, false witness, or wine drinking). There may also be times when it is not feasible to have an Imam, as is currently the case in Yemen. Religious leadership is then vested in the Zaydi scholars until they agree to recognize a new Imam.

In the other major branches of Shi'ism, the Imam may be a child, but he is appointed by God, not by man, and he must be clearly designated as the appointee by an infallible and impeccable source: that is, the Prophet or the previous Imam. Hasan was recognized as an Imam, but after him, all the Imams have been of the line of Husayn. The Imam is sinless and unerring, since Muslims have a need for an impeccable authority; hence he cannot be deposed. He need not rule and is rarely able to do so, but he is the religious leader and cannot lead his followers astray. There must always be an Imam, and there can never be more than one Imam in the world at the same time.

In the eighth century, conflicting claims were put forth about which son the sixth Imam, Ja'far al-Sadiq, had designated as his successor. The Twelvers followed the line of Imam Ja'far's younger son, Musa al-Kazim. Another group, the Isma'ilis, followed the line of his older son, Isma'il. Isma'ilis themselves divided over the claims of two sons of an Imam in the eleventh century. One group supported the claim of the elder son, Nizar, and its members see the Aga Khan as his descendant and their infallible Imam. The other group backed the claim of the younger son; its members have experienced subsequent divisions but are generally known today as the Buhura (Bohra) Isma'ilis. They teach that their line of Imams has never become extinct but that the identity and whereabouts of the current Imam is a closely guarded secret. Visible authority is exercised on his behalf by one of a line of scholars, called the "Absolute Herald" (Da'i Mutlaq).

TWELVER SHI'IS

The Shi'is that we are concerned with in this book are the Twelver or Ithna'ashari Shi'is. After several almost self-destructive attempts to gain power from the Sunni majority, they were ordered by their sixth Imam to hide their true sympathies and even deny them to persecutors if necessary. Meanwhile, they were to remain faithful to the Imam in their hearts. This practice, which is called *taqiyya* (warding off evil), is an essential part of the Shi'i doctrine.[25] The Twelvers' subsequent Imams were kept under house arrest and close surveillance, though they offered no resistance, by the 'Abbasid Sunni caliphs. It is believed that the sixth to the eleventh Imams were poisoned.

Furthermore, doctrine asserts, when it was finally clear to all that the Imams would not be allowed to exercise their God-given function, the young boy who was twelfth Imam disappeared from view in the 'Abbasid capital of Samarra in 874. Like Jesus, who the Qur'an says was neither crucified nor slain but taken to God to return in God's time, the twelfth Imam will return at the end of history to establish the kingdom of God on earth as the expected Mahdi.[26] In the meantime, he is alive and is the legitimate Imam, though in *ghayba,* meaning absence or occultation. Legitimate political authority is his and can be exercised only provisionally in his absence; religious authority is his and is exercised on his behalf by the *mujtahids,* or interpreters of the law, though unlike him they are not impeccable and their status is conceded to them by other *mujtahids.* Those of the highest rank today are called *ayatullah,* "sign of God," and one (or more) of them is recognized by the others as a *marja' al-taqlid,* or "source of imitation" for other scholars.

Theology exists in Sunni Islam, but it always takes second place to the law, *shari'a.* Many Sunnis argue that there is no need for the explication of doctrine. A Muslim is required to believe only the two propositions of the testimony of faith: "There is no God but God, and Muhammad is the messenger of God." A Shi'i will add, "And 'Ali is the *wali* [empowered friend] of God." Faith in Islam is a matter of acting rather than believing, a matter of ethics and law rather than theology. Generally, this is a useful characterization in all of Islam, which is much less theological than Christianity.

Twelver Shiʿism, however, is considerably more "theological" than Sunnism. Twelver Shiʿis must believe many things, and they do so not on their own authority. Like a Catholic, who believes "all truth that the church teaches," a Shiʿi believes what the Imams and the *mujtahids* have taught, which is carefully worked out as doctrine. Reason may be trusted, when adequately guided, and it is for just such guidance that the Imams are necessary. In the absence of the Imam, reason is the best guide.

Greek philosophy and science were translated into Arabic and entered into the mainstream of Islamic culture between the eighth and tenth centuries. They were commented on and elaborated by Muslim scholars like al-Farabi (d. 950), Ibn Sina (Avicenna, d. 1037), and Ibn Rushd (Averroës, d. 1139). By the twelfth century, however, the study of philosophy came under heavy attack among Sunnis because of the opposition of the scholars of the East to Neoplatonism and especially the study of metaphysics. Such studies, they felt, challenged revelation and were not necessary in any case because the Muslim majority was divinely protected from error.

Shiʿis continued to use philosophy and to study it because it helped them understand a world that did not seem to proceed at all according to God's plan. They felt they had sufficient demonstration that the majority of the Muslim community had been in error since the night the Prophet died, and both the Qurʾan and the Imams ordered them to observe the world and use their minds. The early Shiʿi theologians had close ties with the Muʿtazili rationalist theologians,[27] who sought wisdom in the study of philosophy. In particular, the Muʿtazila did not accept the doctrine held by the majority of Sunnis that the Qurʾan is the uncreated and eternal Word of God. However authoritative the Qurʾan might be, they argued, reason indicated that nothing is uncreated and eternal but God Himself. Hence He had formed His Speech when He had need of it. The implications here are interesting: perhaps the final Word has not yet been spoken; God could create Speech again. All of the Shiʿi theologians, Zaydi to Twelver, seem to have shared this doctrine with the Muʿtazila.

The other doctrine of the Muʿtazila that was deeply congenial to the Shiʿis was that God does not predestine souls to eternal bliss or damnation and does not predestine human actions, despite the existence of *hadith* attributed to Muhammad that might indicate otherwise. Twelvers hold that God gives people the choice of their actions, or *ikhtiyar*. It is His will that human beings freely choose their actions. From human beings' wrong choices arises all of the suffering in the world. There is no "fallen world" here but only human willfulness and weakness. Muhammad's earliest revelation states, "Recite! Your Lord is the most Generous, who taught by the Pen; taught Man what he knew not. And yet Man is rebellious, for he thinks him self-sufficient. Surely your return is unto your Lord."[28] Revelation begins by warning against human rebellious self-will and promising judgment.

It is a Twelver principle of law that "all that is ordered by reason is also ordered by religion."[29] Thus religious rules may be deduced by pure reason, even without resort to a tradition related by the Prophet or the Imams, though, of course, such deductions may never contradict these sources. This confidence in reason in Shi'i jurisprudence differs markedly from the beliefs of most Sunni authorities. According to most Twelvers, human beings need reason and philosophy to help them understand what appear to be bewildering triumphs of evil over good, particularly now that there is no Imam present to act as an impeccable guide.

From the Twelver point of view, the history of Islam has been almost unrelieved tragedy, in which the will of God and His messenger was violated by willful men as soon as the Prophet died. 'Ali's rights were despoiled, and his son Husayn, the third Imam, was martyred while trying to reassert the rights of the Prophet's family. Their innocent successors, chosen to rule, were set aside, persecuted, and murdered by hypocrites pretending to be good Muslims. Humanity is still largely made up of the arrogant (*mustakbarin*) and the oppressed (*mustaza'fin*), even after the revelation of God's guidance. God has permitted this, and the Imams have willingly offered Him their sufferings as an expiation for the sins of the Prophet's people. Yet God is not mocked: according to Twelver thought, the wicked and the virtuous will each be requited according to their acts, and before the end of history, the twelfth Imam will return as the Mahdi to bring the world at last to the perfect Islam that God has always willed for it. Jesus will return with him to refute both the Jews who rejected him and the Christians who made an idol of him and convert them to true faith.

In the meantime, although Shi'is are enjoined to throw their enemies off the scent as long as they can through *taqiyya*, there may come a time when they must embrace martyrdom by dying for God's cause. This is considered a blessing and an honor, the same honor that was given to the Imams, and Shi'is are taught to be fearless and resolute in the face of martyrdom, realizing that their reward will be great with God. Shi'ism has always been a protest movement against the perceived inequity of the Muslim majority, and it has often been a revolutionary movement, driven by a sense of injustice.

For most of its formative years, from the seventh to the eleventh centuries, Twelver Shi'ism was a quietist religion of dissent, often on the defensive. Shi'i scholars gathered its traditions and systematized them, laying the basis for its religious laws and theology. In this period, it stood in sharp contrast to Roman Catholicism, the established orthodoxy of the Western world. Early Christianity no doubt had much of the character of a protest movement among underprivileged subjects of the Roman Empire. Nonetheless, after the conversion of the empire in the fifth century, it had become the empire's official religion and a source of ideological strength and unity. From the sixth to the eleventh centuries, the Church of Rome was heavily involved in converting barbarian invaders. Shi'ism during this period existed as a challenge to a Muslim majority, and no Twelver would ever maintain that Shi'ism is not a part of a larger whole. Hence some of the characteristics of Sunni intellectual history are paralleled in the characteristics of Twelverism.

THE DEVELOPMENT OF LEGAL SCHOOLS
AMONG SUNNIS AND SHI'IS

There is a well-known division in Sunni jurisprudence between "People of the Traditions [*hadith*]" and "People of Opinion [*ra'y*]." The four *madhhabs,* or schools, of Sunni law fall along these lines, with the Malikis and Hanbalis in the first division and the Hanafis and Shafi'is in the second. The first two achieve insight into the laws of God, the *shari'a,* by referring only to the Qur'an and the practice of Madina or the Prophet, without resort to "weak human reason." The second two were given their patronizing name by their opponents. They argue that the reasoned opinions of qualified scholars are themselves a source of guidance and that statements attributed to Muhammad must be handled with discrimination.

Foremost among those who embrace reason is the Hanafi school. The Hanafis prefer legal reasoning to often shaky statements attributed to the

Prophet and support a variety of legal opinions. The Shafiʿis agree, but they have played a greater role in sifting through the *hadith* to find those that are most reliable. The Shafiʿis also believe that there should be a consensus among the opinions of the learned.

The Sunni Maliki school based itself on the practices of Madina, arguing that the people of that city knew better than anyone the example of the Prophet and his closest companions. Preserving tradition without discussion was correct legal procedure. The Hanbali school went far beyond the practices of Madina and used *hadith* of the Prophet preserved in any of the early Muslim centers of culture to the exclusion of tradition. Hanbalism was often soft in its standards of criticism of these *hadith,* preferring even a precarious *hadith* to a well-reasoned human opinion. Whereas the approach of the Malikis was traditionalist, that of the Hanbalis was fundamentalist, based literally and exclusively on the text of the Qurʾan and *hadith.*

The main lines of these divergent Sunni schools had been laid by the middle of the ninth century. We find a similar division in Twelver scholarship between those who base their thinking only on the traditions of the Prophet and the Imams and those who use these traditions as a base from which to draw rational conclusions. Still, the situation of the Twelvers was somewhat different. During the period before 874, while the Imams were present, though under house arrest and close surveillance most of the time, they encouraged their followers to use their minds for details and contented themselves with laying down general principles. It appears that some of their companions were quite capable theologians with significant opinions.[30]

The Twelver school of law is called the Jaʿfari school after the sixth Imam, Jaʿfar al-Sadiq. As the Jaʿfari school has evolved, it is most similar to the Hanafi and Shafiʿi schools and allows for a greater role for analogical reasoning. Sunni authorities have greatest difficulty in accepting the Twelver practice of giving equal weight to *hadith* of the Imams and those of the Prophet since the words of the Imams are also infallible in the eyes of their followers. Moreover, *hadith* of the Prophet related on the authority of enemies of the Imams such as ʿUmar, ʿAʾisha, and ʿUthman are rejected in Twelver law. Still, the practical differences between Jaʿfari law and the law of the four Sunni schools are not much greater than the differences among the Sunni schools. Notable exceptions are the *khums* or one-fifth to be paid to the Imam or his representatives and the permissibility of temporary marriage, or *mut'a*, which was practiced in early Islam and discontinued among the Sunnis. In some circumstances, Twelver inheritance law gives more to the female line than does Sunni law. Also, Shi'is add the phrase "hasten to the best of works" to the call to prayer. Since the eighteenth century, there have been calls for recognizing the Ja'faris as a "fifth school" of normative Islam. There has been no overwhelming support for the idea among either Twelvers or Sunnis.

During the period from the disappearance of their last Imam in 874 to 941, called the "lesser occultation," Twelvers believed that they continued to be in close contact with the hidden Imam. This was still generally a conservative time of gathering and systematizing the traditions of the Prophet and the Imams and seeking guidance from them. This school, centered at Qum in Iran, tended to dominate all Twelver scholarship, and the leading Twelver scholars of the tenth century[31] were deeply imbued with this restrained tendency.

Despite this conservative bent, the years 945–1055 were a great period for the Twelvers because the 'Abbasid caliphate at the time was controlled by a dynasty of Shi'i dictators, the Buyid princes from the Caspian Mountains. Shi'i scholars were able to teach openly, challenge Sunni scholars, and attract students from Baghdad with official patronage. Also, they maintained cordial contacts with Mu'tazili scholars.

The leading Shi'i doctor of this time was Muhammad b. Muhammad al-'Ukbari, known as Shaykh al-Mufid (d. 1022), who is regarded as a father of rationalist Twelver law and theology. He was a voluminous writer (he authored over 200 works, though many are lost) and was involved in the internecine quarrels of the Mu'tazila, as well as in polemics with Sunnis. In general, he sided with "the Baghdad group" against "the Basra group," although he rejected a basic principle of the Mu'tazila that the truths of religion must be based on reason alone. He maintained that what is transmitted from the Imams is essential for reason to function correctly.[32]

Through al-Mufid's pupils, the position of the rationalists among the Twelvers was solidified. They included Sharif[33] al-Murtada (d. 1044), a descendant of the seventh Imam and a theologian-litterateur in high esteem at the Buyid court. His career was paralleled by that of his brother, Sharif al-Radi (d. 1016), a renowned poet. Al-Radi's greatest contribution to Shi'ism was his compilation of addresses, homilies, and letters attributed to Imam 'Ali, *Nahj al-Balagha* (The peak of eloquence).

Muhammad b. Hasan al-Tusi (d. 1067), known simply as The Shaykh or Shaykh al-Ta'ifa (Shaykh of the Shi'i People), was one of the greatest Twelver doctors of law and theology. He essentially achieved a synthesis of the views of the traditionists and those of the rationalists and borrowed ideas that he judged useful from Sunni legal scholars. His magisterial collections of the Shi'i traditions and his treatment of their contradictions in two works, *Tahdhib al-Ahkam* (Rectifying the rules) and *Al-Istibsar* (Attentive observance), have deeply influenced Shi'i law,[34] as have his efforts to preserve the analytical and rational method. After 1055, the rule of the Turkish Saljuq sultans brought Sunni ascendancy in Baghdad, and al-Tusi moved his academy to the Shi'i holy city of Najaf, near the tomb of 'Ali. For at least a century, Twelver scholarship was content to simply comment on Shaykh al-Tusi's works.

In philosophy and mysticism, the Ishraqiyya, or Illuminationist, philosophy of Yahya al-Suhrawardi, suspected of Shi'ism and executed by Saladin in Aleppo in 1191, was to be one of Islamic philosophy's greatest achievements: a non-Aristotelian system that attempted to harmonize intuitive and deductive knowledge, mysticism and science. The Sufi mystical theosophy of Ibn 'Arabi of Spain (d. Damascus, 1240) and his disciples was harmonized with Shi'i esoteric doctrines by a succession of Shi'i teachers. The result was the important strand of Twelver thought called *hikma ilahiyya*, "divine wisdom" or theosophy.

The collapse of Sunni political power in the regions east of the Euphrates brought about by the Mongol invasions of 1220 and 1258 allowed latitude for Twelver theology and metaphysics to develop in relative freedom. The Mongols' Shi'i adviser Nasir al-Din Tusi (d. 1273) was a philosopher who, with his student 'Allama al-Hilli (d. 1326), laid the basis for an ordered system of Shi'i theology.[35]

Philosophy still holds a place of honor in Twelver Shi'i thought. Ayatullah Khomeini, who led the Iranian Revolution of 1978–79, was famous for his lectures on philosophy at the Center for Theological Studies in Qum, where he occupied the chair of mystical philosophy until the early 1950s. He was succeeded by 'Allama Muhammad Husayn Tabataba'i, who trained a whole generation of philosopher-*'ulama* (religious scholars) before his death in 1982. Sunni Islam has scarcely any parallel to this, even though in modern times there has been some movement to revive the interest of Sunni *'ulama* in Muslim philosophy, for example, at Al-Azhar University in Cairo.

SCHOOLS OF THE TWELVERS

We have thus far been describing chiefly the dominant school of Twelvers, the Usulis (those who study the "principles," or "the reasoners").[36] Their position is that the absence of the twelfth Imam has created a situation in which the community now consists of *muqallids*, those in need of living, active religious guidance, and *mujtahids*, interpreters or high-ranking *'ulama* who can collect the religious taxes, lead the Friday prayers, and give binding legal verdicts based on independent scholarship in every age. One cannot be guided by a dead *mujtahid*, only by one who is alive, dealing with the problems of one's own time in the light of reason and the transmitted wisdom of the past. Every believer who is not a *mujtahid* is obliged to have a *mujtahid* for religious guidance.[37]

This well-marked rationalist tendency of Twelver Shi'ism is not shared by all scholars. There is another, more fundamentalist denomination of thought based on the conservative traditional school that was prevalent until the tenth century, to which we have alluded. These scholars, known as the Akhbaris or traditionists, base their teachings only on the traditions of the infallible Prophet and Imams. Neither consensus nor the exercise of analogical reasoning can change a jot of this precious corpus of sayings, which provides the only sure guidance apart from the Qur'an. All of the community are *muqallids*, or followers, of the Imams; there are no *mujtahids* in the Usuli sense. A living, breathing *mujtahid* carries no special credibility in their eyes. There are few Akhbaris left today, except in the Shi'i Arab communities around the Persian Gulf, particularly in Bahrain.[38] We may see them as the survivors of a party of Twelvers who have been present since the occultation of the twelfth Imam.

In addition to the Usulis and Akhbaris, there is a third school of Twelverism known as the Shaykhis, an offshoot of Usuli Shi'ism that developed in the early nineteenth century. They were soon condemned for their mystical theology, and they emphasize *taqiyya* as a cardinal principle in their practice of the faith. The Shaykhis place special emphasis on the "fourteen inerrant ones"—that is, the Prophet, Fatima, and the twelve Imams—

and on great *shaykhs* who are "perfect Shi'is" and can be the mouthpiece of these infallible figures. Shaykhis continue to survive quietly in regions of Iran such as Kirman, Tabriz, and Shiraz. Not surprisingly, they were soon attacked by the Usulis for "exaggeration" or near-deification of the Imams. The new religion of Babism, whose leader was executed in 1850 for claiming to be the Bab or "Door" of the Imam, developed, along with its off-shoot Baha'ism, among the Shaykhis, though not all Shaykhis followed the Bab. In the 1980s and 1990s, the leading *mujtahid* in the Gulf states, Mirza Hasan, was widely considered to be a Shaykhi. With his headquarters in Kuwait, Mirza Hasan estimated that his following consisted of 10 million Shi'is from as far away as India, Pakistan, and Australia.[39]

Twelverism, while remaining a minority religion, occasionally found favor with some rulers. It became the established form of Islam in the Iranian Safavid Empire at the beginning of the sixteenth century. The Twelver learned men, now seen as a source of strength and unity to the state, were installed as virtual coregents with the monarchy. This partnership with the rulers continued even after the last Safavid shah was deposed in 1736. In Iran, Twelverism was the established faith. Those who did not choose to practice it were advised to leave the empire and usually did. Thus Iran is about 95 percent Shi'i. Bahrain is some 70 percent Twelver, and Iraq is an estimated 55 percent Twelver. Yet even during the Safavid Empire, with few exceptions, the sizable Twelver enclaves elsewhere in the Islamic world continued to be viewed with suspicion and were often embattled.[40]

Roman Catholicism, cut off from contact with its Eastern roots, had to live in a Western Europe where what remained of Roman civilization was ravaged by barbaric invaders. It coped admirably with this challenge, converting and helping to civilize these peoples, but the Dark Ages of destructive barbarian invasions endured until the eleventh century, when the Vikings and the Huns were both finally brought into the Catholic fold. The conversion of the barbarians was an extraordinary accomplishment. By the end of the eleventh century, with the blessing of the papacy, a reviving Western Europe was seeking to reestablish relations with the East through the misadventure of "crusades," ostensibly fought in the name of the cross. The result was military defeat and a nearly fatal wreck of relations with both Eastern Christendom and Islam.

Yet Western Europe was unquestionably fructified by these new contacts with Islam and the East. New trade routes brought new prosperity, new ideas, and old wisdom. Guilds of scholars in Paris, Oxford, and Bologna became the first universities, where clerics debated Greek philosophical ideas translated from Arabic into Latin. Roman Catholicism was now established as the faith of wealthy, vital, and powerful kingdoms, though it would never forget its days as a persecuted, struggling, and embattled religion. The Roman church remained the approved faith of Christians in the West until the sixteenth century, when much of Northern Europe joined the Protestant revolt. At that point, Roman Catholicism was forced to defend itself intellectually against its critics and often against the persecution of princes.

Twelverism and Roman Catholicism, then, both have had triumphant days and both have endured periods of hardship and persecution that have fostered the development of apologetics and intellectual defenses. Both Roman Catholicism and Twelverism have concluded that the justice and benevolence of God demand an infallible leadership for the religious community, though the impeccability of a Twelver Imam goes far beyond the infallibility in matters of faith and morals claimed for a Roman pope. Both Catholicism and Shi'ism have buttressed faith with the study of philosophy.

Beyond these similarities, there are many other fascinating parallels between these two faith systems. In order to understand them better, it is advisable to take a closer look at the Twelver phenomenon because it remains poorly understood in most of the world. In the next chapter, therefore, we will endeavor to tell the story of the Shi'is. In so doing, we will seek to present the perspective of the Shi'is themselves.

2

THE STORY OF THE PEOPLE OF THE HOUSE

Names such as ʿAli, Fatima, Hasan, Husayn, Muʿawiya, and Yazid may not be immediately recognizable to most Western readers, even those who have some basic knowledge of Islam. Yet these names summon up deep feelings from the inner soul of Shiʿis. In this chapter, we deal with early Islamic history as perceived by Shiʿis. Since we cannot understand Shiʿis if we do not familiarize ourselves with their point of view, we present their perspective. The story is that of five remarkable individuals and nine of their descendants.

THE PROPHET MUHAMMAD

This extraordinary human leader is recognized and revered for his central role in transmitting the revelation of the Qurʾan and for establishing the Islamic community, which was to defend and propagate this message. Wherever there are Muslims, his name is coupled with that of the God of Abraham in the call to prayer and the prelude to liturgical prayer known as the *iqama* (convoking). Wherever Shiʿis of any sect are praying, they add to the words "I testify that there is no god but God, I testify that Muhammad is the messenger of God" the statement "I testify that ʿAli is the empowered friend [*wali*] of God." Muslims see Muhammad as a perfect exemplar, a man who did all things well; as merchant, husband, father, teacher, strategist, friend, man of prayer, and man of action, he was faithful, kind, generous, and strong. In his own time, he achieved a degree of success unparalleled by that of the founder of any other world religion.

SAYYIDA FATIMA

Fatima was the youngest of the four daughters of the Prophet, and she was particularly dear to him. He later said of her, "Fatima is a part of me, and whatever offends her, offends me."[1] She is often referred to by another name, al-Zahra (the Radiant). She is remembered for her attempts to comfort her father after his uncle and her mother died and he was exposed to the coarse insults of the people of Mecca; hence she was called "a mother to her father." In 624, she married 'Ali, the Prophet's first cousin. At the time of their marriage, 'Ali may have been twenty-five and Fatima eighteen. 'Ali killed a sheep for the marriage feast and built a house not far from that of the Prophet. During the ceremony, Gabriel shouted, "Allahu akbar" (God is great). Muhammad heard and repeated this, and the companions followed suit, setting the precedent for what became an established practice. The groom's wedding gifts to the bride consisted of perfumes and a modest store of articles for the household. Before the couple retired, the Prophet visited them and gave them a special blessing, sprinkling them with water he had hallowed.

Like many of the emigrants from Mecca, Fatima and 'Ali were extremely poor and had to work hard. Fatima ground grain for bread, and 'Ali hired himself out to water lands on the oasis. When Fatima begged the Prophet to provide a servant to help her, Muhammad visited the couple and said he could not do this because others were more needy but he would teach them something much more useful. He taught them to say thirty-four times "God is greater [*Allahu akbar*]," thirty-three times "Glory be to God [*subhan Allah*]," and thirty-three times "Praise be to God [*al-hamdu lillah*]."[2] Recited while holding prayer beads, this later became the Muslim rosary. Only after the rich Jewish oasis of Khaybar agreed to pay tribute of dates and grain to the Prophet in 628 did the couple's circumstances ease.

'Ali exchanged their house for one abutting an outer wall of the Prophet's dwelling because Fatima wanted to be closer to her father. According to one account, 'Ali was given his famous nickname, Abu Turab (Father of Dust), by the Prophet because when Fatima scolded 'Ali, rather than answer the Prophet's daughter unkindly, he would go outside and throw dust over his head, a sign of mourning and humility. In 625, their first son, Hasan, was born, and a year later his brother, Husayn, was born. Of the children who lived, there were also two girls, Umm Kulthum and Zaynab, each named for one of Fatima's sisters. As long as Fatima lived, 'Ali married no other women, though after she died, he had several wives.

With their two sons, 'Ali and Fatima took part in the celebrated incident called "the Mubahala," or the Ordeal. Certain Christians from the oasis of Najran argued with the Prophet about christology and the function of prophecy. At last, Muhammad covered Fatima, 'Ali, Hasan, and Husayn with his cloak (kisa') and proposed that they and the leading Christians pray together that God's curse would fall on the side that was in error. The Christians, evidently filled with misgivings about what would befall them if they set themselves against the powerful Muslim community, preferred to withdraw and pay tribute in return for a written guarantee of protection.

Verse 61 of Sura 3 in the Qur'an is generally believed by Muslim scholars to be related to this incident: "Tell those who dispute with you about the Messiah after the knowledge that has come to you, 'Come now, let us gather our sons and your sons, our women and your women, ourselves and yourselves; then let us humbly pray and call down God's curse on the ones who speak falsely.'" The five Muslims involved are referred to later as "the People of the Cloak," and Shi'is argue that the rights of this family thus had been established from eternity and Imam 'Ali ranked alongside Muhammad as one of "ourselves." They commemorate the incident as "the Day of the Mubahala," generally the twenty-first of the Month of Pilgrimage in the Muslim calendar. Verse 33 of Sura 33 is also said to be related to the family: "God only desires to put away from you the uncleanness, People of the House; to cleanse you and purify you." Shi'is relate that after these words were revealed, when rising for the dawn prayer, Muhammad would knock on Fatima and 'Ali's door to remind them with these words of their duty to rise and perform ablution and prayer.

Fatima grieved profoundly at her father's illness, but on his deathbed, he comforted her by telling her that she would soon follow him. In fact, she died some six months later, deeply pained by the way the Prophet's family was slighted after his death.

IMAM I: 'ALI IBN ABI TALIB

'Ali was the Prophet's first cousin and was raised in his household. He was in fact a foster son and perhaps the first male convert to Islam. His father, Abu Talib, was head of the Hashimite clan of the Quraysh, and although he did not profess Islam openly, most Shi'is believe that he hid his belief in order to better protect the Prophet from his enemies. It is believed that Abu Talib secretly accepted Islam sometime before his death in 619. There has never been any question that 'Ali was a very early convert. Often-repeated stories assert that 'Ali served as a decoy at peril to his life by staying in Muhammad's house when Muhammad had to slip out of Mecca in 622 to elude his enemies.

During the time the community was struggling for its existence in Arabia, 'Ali was entrusted with leading a number of important military expeditions. He stood unwaveringly beside the Prophet, frequently as standard-bearer, in the military struggles of early Islam. He often took the field to fight a champion of the other side before the armies clashed en masse. As "Haydar," the Lion of Islam, he never lost such a confrontation. At the Battle of Badr in 624, the first great victory, when some 310 Muslims faced over 950 Meccans, he slew the Meccan champion, al-Walid b. 'Utba, and in the ensuing battle killed a great number of enemy soldiers (some reports name thirty-six, half the total number of enemy dead).[3] At the Battle of Uhud a year later, the Muslims were losing the day, but 'Ali defeated the enemy standard-bearers and again and again dispersed the enemy, consoling the heart of the Prophet, who said, "Surely he is of me, and I am of him!" It was at this battle that people first said (referring to Dhu al-Faqar, the Prophet's sword, which he gave to 'Ali): "There is no sword but Dhu al-Faqar, and no brave young man but 'Ali."[4]

At the Battle of the Trench the next year, 'Ali killed the champion of the Meccans, 'Amr b. 'Abd Wudd, reputed to have the strength of many men and to be splendidly armed. He issued a challenge to the Muslims that none but 'Ali was ready to accept. The Prophet was afraid to risk 'Ali's life and twice ordered him not to fight. At the third challenge, 'Ali begged to be allowed to go and won the combat, "like David against Goliath," the Muslims said.[5] At the siege of the Jewish oasis of Khaybar in 628, according to some accounts, it was 'Ali who killed the champion Marhab at the chief castle of the Jews.[6] In battle after battle, 'Ali distinguished himself as a young warrior, yet Shi'is stress that he was neither fierce nor vindictive.

Imam 'Ali and his second son, Imam Husayn, occupy exceptionally important places in the hearts and minds of Shi'is everywhere. As we have seen, Abu Bakr, 'Umar, and another companion of the Prophet, Abu

'Ubayda b. al-Jarrah, forestalled any claim 'Ali might have put forward to the leadership by having Abu Bakr acclaimed as Muhammad's successor on the night of the Prophet's death. Fatima did not long survive her father, whose death she mourned deeply. 'Ali was again deprived of leadership when Abu Bakr appointed 'Umar as his successor before his death in 634. Again, 'Ali hesitated to give him his allegiance, but he eventually recognized 'Umar as leader in order to preserve the unity of Muhammad's community.

During 'Umar's reign (634–44), the Arabs conquered an empire, building on conquests that Abu Bakr had initiated. The Fertile Crescent and Egypt were defeated, and new garrison settlements were established there: Basra and Kufa in Iraq and Fustat in Egypt. In Syria, the Arabs lived in cantonments outside existing cities such as Damascus, Hims, and Qinnisrin. 'Umar used much of the new wealth that came in to subsidize the Muslim tribes and pay stipends to those who emigrated to the new settlements. There they became a military caste and were forbidden to mingle with the local people (though many of them had slaves as concubines) or to engage in agriculture or artisanry. 'Umar adopted the new title Commander of the Faithful and ruled with a strong hand. The leading companions of Muhammad were given opportunities to enrich themselves greatly as governors of new territories. Out of the *ashara*, the ten leading companions, only 'Ali, who was critical of many of 'Umar's arrangements and whom 'Umar did not allow to move from Madina, remained in modest circumstances. 'Ali was especially revered by the southern tribes of Arabs, the Yemenis,[7] who had old traditions of agriculture and knew that 'Ali backed them in this and other matters. Kufa in Iraq, virtually a Yemeni city, was known to idealize him, and there were also many Yemenis in Fustat in Egypt. Many Arabs felt that 'Ali must at last become the ruler, and they regarded him as the man who would bring welcome changes.

When 'Umar was dying of knife wounds inflicted by a Persian slave, he was urged to appoint a successor, as Abu Bakr had done. Among those who reportedly made this request was 'A'isha, the daughter of Abu Bakr, who had been on bad terms with both Fatima and 'Ali. Instead, 'Umar ordered that the surviving six of the ten leading companions choose one of themselves as his successor and that if one or two held back from agreeing with the majority, the dissidents should be put to death. If three opposed three, 'Umar's son was to break the tie. Five of the six were Zubayr, a cousin of the Prophet and brother-in-law of 'A'isha; Talha, a younger relative of Abu Bakr who had become immensely wealthy; Saʿd b. Abi Waqqas, another early convert and heroic commander; ʿAbd al-Rahman b. ʿAwf, an ally of Abu Bakr and ʿAʾisha; and the very wealthy, aristocratic, and ineffectual ʿUthman, who had married Fatima's two sisters, Ruqayya and then after her death Umm Kulthum, though he had no surviving offspring from them. These five men had become rich under ʿUmar and thus were heavily invested in preserving the status quo. ʿAli was the sixth and the sole critic. It was clear from the beginning that the other electors would not allow ʿAli to come to power, and after much discussion and jockeying, they proclaimed ʿUthman the successor.

There was much dissatisfaction with ʿUthman's rule, even among many of the people who had backed him at first, including ʿAʾisha. The general prosperity and new wars of expansion kept criticism within bounds for some years, despite his nepotism and toleration of open corruption. At last, a mutiny broke out in the armies of Egypt and Iraq, and in preparation for the pilgrimage of the year 35 (June 656), troops of the dissidents made their way to Madina to press their demands on the caliph. He humbly agreed to do as they wished, and the men from Egypt started for home. On their journey, they apprehended a messenger coming from Madina and found on him a letter sealed by ʿUthman ordering his foster brother, the governor of Egypt, to kill or mutilate their leaders when they returned. Furious, they retraced their steps to Madina and called ʿUthman to account. He denied having authorized the letter but could not deny his seal. They demanded that he abdicate, but he refused. At this, they besieged his new mansion, blocking the delivery of supplies. None of the leading companions lifted a finger to assist ʿUthman except ʿAli. When the mutineers would not agree to end the siege, ʿAli sent the two grandsons of the Prophet with mules loaded with supplies, but the rebels would not allow them to pass. At last, word was received that Muʿawiya, ʿUthman's capable cousin—a brother-in-law of the Prophet who governed Syria—was coming in haste with troops from the north to quell the mutiny. At this point, a group of men led by a son of Abu Bakr burst into ʿUthman's mansion and killed him.

In this crisis, everyone realized that only ʿAli, long barred from any effective power, had the credibility and prestige to preserve the Muslims from civil war. He refused to accept the leadership unless the companions of the Prophet in Madina agreed that he should, and they did. With misgivings, ʿAli allowed himself to be installed as Commander of the Faithful. ʿAʾisha, an outspoken critic of ʿUthman, had left the city for a visit to the sanctuary of Mecca when the siege began. Talha and Zubayr, who did not trust each other but were both jealous of 'Ali, now joined her in Mecca, where she had been making public speeches denouncing the assassination and the "one who had benefited from it." Talha and Zubayr now asserted that they had pledged allegiance only because they were afraid they would be murdered like 'Uthman if they did not, and with 'A'isha, they moved to Basra in Iraq, where they seized the city and began gathering an army. They are said to have put to death over 600 men accused of having taken part in the siege of 'Uthman's house. 'A'isha issued a call to all Muslims for *islah*, the establishment of peace and order.

'Ali was forced to move near Kufa, where he had strong support and gathered an army of his own. All of the fighting men were now in the provinces; Madina could never have supported a large army and its transport, and no one could have imagined that it would be necessary to raise an army in the Prophet's own city. It was a measure of the decline in morale and spirit under the first three caliphs that it now became necessary to move the caliphate to a secure military base. The governor of the city, Abu Musa al-Ash'ari, a pious companion who had refused to obey 'Uthman, now refused to turn the city over to 'Ali. Some 6,000 to 12,000 men (accounts differ) came out to 'Ali's camp to join him.

Unhappily for 'Ali, some in this army had worked hard to undermine 'Uthman, and some were even implicated in his death. These people were fearful that they might have to answer for their activities and dreaded the possibility that 'Ali might agree to an inquiry into the events leading to 'Uthman's murder.

When 'Ali moved in early December of the year 35 (656) to the outskirts of Basra to negotiate with the rebels, it appeared to all that agreement was near, when fighting broke out between the two armies.[8] The result was the infamous Day of the Camel, when 'A'isha rode in an armored camel litter among the combatants shouting encouragement to her troops, and Talha and Zubayr, along with many others, were slain. It was the first time in Islam's history that Muslims confronted Muslims with swords in hand, an action the Prophet had repeatedly warned against. Despite 'A'isha's role in this tragedy, 'Ali treated her with magnanimity and saw to it that she was honorably escorted back to sanctuary in Mecca, where she praised his conduct.

Mu'awiya, the kinsman of 'Uthman, was still governor of Syria and had stayed out of the quarrel. He now raised the cry of vengeance for the murder of 'Uthman, exhibiting the bloodstained shirt of 'Uthman "the Martyr" and the fingers severed from the hand of his wife, Na'ila of Kalb (a Syrian tribe), who had tried to shield 'Uthman from his assassins. When Mu'awiya's hostile intentions were obvious, 'Ali moved in late 36 (657) with his army up the Euphrates from Kufa, now his capital, to a site called Siffin near Raqqa in Syrian Mesopotamia, where he confronted Mu'awiya's forces for over two months. 'Ali reportedly gave the following orders to his warriors:

(1) Do not begin the fight until they attack you first. Praise be to God, you have the better cause, and if you let them alone until they attack, you strengthen it. (2) If you fight them and put them to flight, do not kill the fugitives, do not finish off the wounded, do not uncover their nakedness, and do not mutilate the dead. (3) If you get to their dwellings, do not offend the modesty of their women; do not enter a dwelling without permission. (4) Do not take any of their possessions, except what you find in their camp. (5) Do not hurt a woman, even if she attacks your honor and utters abuse of your leaders and righteous men, for women are weak of body and soul.[9]

In early 37 (July 26, 657), a celebrated series of battles and skirmishes began, rich in conflicting reports and counterclaims. 'Ali's forces included many of the Prophet's veterans and companions; Mu'awiya was backed by many of the old Arab elite who had opposed the Prophet until it was clear that he was going to win his struggle with Mecca. Despite this, brothers and clansmen fought on both sides of the Battle of Siffin, and most accounts agree that the armies were large for the day (over 100,000 on each side) and the carnage was great. Although Mu'awiya's forces were larger and better equipped, 'Ali was winning the day. In danger of sustaining a terrible defeat, Mu'awiya's partisans suddenly proposed that the Book of God, the Qur'an, be used to "arbitrate" between Muslims to avoid further bloodshed. It was a plea calculated to win over the pietists on 'Ali's side, and he agreed to a truce, after which Mu'awiya's differences with him were to be submitted to judgment.

At this, some of the same people who had attacked Talha and Zubayr at the Battle of the Camel for much the same reasons now raised the cry "No judgment but God's." 'Uthman had deserved to die, they maintained, and they reproached 'Ali for "compromising with rebels," adducing the Qur'an verse: "If one party of you rebels against the other, fight the rebellious group until it returns to God's command" (49:9). God had spoken, and 'Ali had rejected His Word, they said, and now he was no longer a Muslim, much less a caliph. They went out (*kharaju*) from his camp and from Kufa to a place called Harura', thus earning the names Khariji and Haruri. There they attracted to their party many non-Arabs and began committing atrocities against those who accepted 'Ali's rule. 'Ali was forced to take up arms against them the next year, there was bloodshed, and the Kharijis swore vengeance. Mu'awiya had succeeded in dividing 'Ali's supporters. With the help of 'Amr b. al-'As, the crafty Meccan general who had conquered Egypt years earlier but who had not been trusted by either 'Umar or 'Uthman to rule there, Mu'awiya was also able to take over that rich province and put to death Abu Bakr's son, who was governor for 'Ali there. The Kharijis went on to become the third major division of Islam, after the Sunnis and Shi'is. They were to play an often weighty role in Islamic history, particularly in North Africa and Oman, where some of their descendants can still be found.

Mu'awiya was a shrewd political manipulator, whereas 'Ali was a man motivated by an ideal. 'Ali was perceived by some of his contemporaries as impractical and overly strict, but he inspired tremendous devotion in others. His impartiality, eloquence and insight, physical courage, and sheer vitality became the stuff of legends. For the Twelvers, he will always be the Commander of the Faithful.

The "arbitration" was a farce. The Kufans demanded that 'Ali choose their old governor, Abu Musa al-Ash'ari, as his representative. He had already been disobliging to 'Ali, and his piety was considerably greater than his common sense. He was outmaneuvered by Mu'awiya's representative, the devious 'Amr ibn al-'As, to agree that 'Uthman had done nothing to merit death, that 'Ali had been compromised by the allegiance of the murderers, and that the caliphate should be considered vacant and a new caliph chosen. At this, 'Ali and his followers retired in disgust, Abu Musa fled to Mecca, and Mu'awiya's followers went back to Syria and "elected" him their caliph in Jerusalem. Now three Muslim leaders—'Ali, Mu'awiya, and the leader chosen by the Kharijis—claimed to be the lawful successor of the Prophet.

'Ali, deeply hurt by the vacillating behavior of many of his followers and the division among them, now bided his time in Kufa, preparing for a new war against Mu'awiya. It was not to be. In 660, a Khariji struck him with a poisoned sword as he entered the mosque in Kufa to lead the dawn prayer. He died two days later.

IMAM II: AL-HASAN IBN 'ALI

Al-Hasan ibn 'Ali was designated by 'Ali and acclaimed as caliph in Kufa after his father's death. The Prophet had delighted in him and his brother Husayn and called them his "two sweet-smelling herbs." Hasan is judged to have closely resembled his grandfather in appearance. Shi'i *hadith* report variants of statements by Muhammad that the two boys would be "leaders in this world and in paradise." Hasan is said to have spent much of his childhood in his grandfather's house and later could report what he had seen the Prophet do or heard him say. Soon after Hasan's installation as caliph, Mu'awiya invaded Iraq. It seems likely that Imam Hasan, well aware of his weaker position, decided to try to come to terms with Mu'awiya to spare the Shi'i party, but some of his followers feared this would expose them to reprisals for events such as the murder of 'Uthman. As Hasan prepared to confront Mu'awiya, one of his soldiers reportedly cut Hasan deeply in the thigh with a dagger or an axe, crying, "You have become an infidel like your father!" Mu'awiya used the recuperation period to offer amnesty to Hasan's followers if they would forsake him.

The terms of Hasan's abdication agreement are fiercely debated, with many contradictory claims. What seems generally conceded is that in return for amnesty and security, Hasan was to live in retirement in Madina for at least as long as Mu'awiya lived, receiving a princely stipend. The matters in dispute include how much the stipend amounted to; whether more than a small part of it was ever actually paid; whether Mu'awiya promised to be guided by the Book, the *sunna* of the Prophet, and the conduct of "the righteous caliphs"; whether there was an understanding that at Mu'awiya's death, Hasan's claim to the succession would be revived; and whether the actual decision would be made by a new *shura* (council). In any event, Imam Hasan appeared with Mu'awiya in the mosque of Kufa and declared that he renounced his claim to the government. For those who had followed him, this did not impair in any way his position of religious leadership, which Mu'awiya was not fit to exercise. Sunnis have claimed that he had "sold the caliphate" and had no further right to allegiance.

It is also agreed that in Madina Hasan lived a pious and generous life under close surveillance, making pilgrimages to Mecca on foot and being visited by people who wanted his help or counsel. He also married and divorced perhaps as many as sixty noble women. His detractors have characterized this as simply sensual indulgence, whereas the Shi'is argue that he was making alliances with prominent clans and families. In any case, it awakened little criticism at the time. Imam Hasan died of a prolonged illness; the date is contested, ranging from 670 to 680. Shi'is claim that he was poisoned by his wife, Ja'da, daughter of the Yemeni chief al-Ash'ath, and that Mu'awiya had told her that she could then marry his son Yazid, whom Mu'awiya was grooming to be his successor. Instead, he married her off to a son of Talha. Imam Hasan had designated his brother Husayn as his successor.

IMAM III: AL-HUSAYN IBN 'ALI

When Mu'awiya died in 60 (680), Husayn and 'Abdallah ibn Zubayr were summoned to the governor's palace in Madina by night. Realizing that they would probably be asked to swear their allegiance to Yazid b. Mu'awiya, they put the governor off and fled to Mecca for sanctuary. At the same time, the Shi'is of Kufa, who had been warned to do nothing as long as Mu'awiya remained alive, contacted Husayn offering to oppose Yazid if he would lead them. He did not rebuff them but sent his cousin, Muslim b. 'Aqil (brother of 'Ali), to investigate the situation and prepare the way for Husayn. Muslim reportedly gathered thousands of pledges of support and sent a very optimistic report, but he also awakened the suspicion of Yazid's agents, who put him to death. Meanwhile, Imam Husayn slipped out of Mecca on the road to Kufa with his household on the eighth of the month of Hajj (September 10, 680), when the whole town and its governor were busy with the rites of the pilgrimage. Besides the women and children, Husayn's group included about fifty men able to bear arms. As they rode across Arabia, others joined them.

Knowing that Husayn and his party were on the way, the governor of Iraq, 'Ubaydallah b. Ziyad, had stationed patrols on all of the roads that led out of the desert to the Euphrates, where they would be obliged to go for water after their desert journey. It is said that Imam Husayn was warned of this and told the men with him that they were free to leave. Only a few who had joined him on the way chose to do so, and the original band stayed with him. On 2 Muharram 61 (October 2, 680), he made his camp at Karbala, not far from the Euphrates. Shi'is have memorialized the journey to Karbala and all that happened there in poetry, mourning pieces, passion plays, and legend. These stories are of central importance to the Twelvers and will be discussed in detail in chapter 4.

Husayn and his companions were surrounded by an immensely superior force, some 4,000 men under the leadership of 'Umar b. Sa'd b. Abi Waqqas, son of the prominent companion. He had tried to escape from this assignment and was not so much evil as weak and under the orders of the governor of Iraq, 'Ubaydallah.[10] A sinister role as adviser to them both was played by a former follower of 'Ali named Shamir, who had gone over to Mu'awiya. Ibn Sa'd was ordered to cut the insurgents off from water and force them to give homage to Yazid as Commander of the Faithful, although it was certain that Husayn would never agree to such terms. Husayn is represented as knowing and accepting his own doleful fate from the first. He and his companions were tormented with thirst, and valiant attempts by his half-brother, 'Abbas b. 'Ali, to break through to the river brought back only a few skins of water.

On 9 Muharram (October 9, 680), Ibn Sa'd advanced and presented the demand for surrender and homage. Husayn asked if he could reply the next morning, and when this request was granted, he absolved his relatives and followers of allegiance to him, urging them to leave under cover of the night, but they refused. They spent the night in prayer and preparation for death.[11] The next day, Imam Husayn and his followers, seventy-two in all, died in battle against overwhelming odds. Husayn's body was deliberately trampled by horses as a mark of disrespect, and even some of the women and children in his party met death, including an infant son. The victors cut off Husayn's head and sent it to the governor, 'Ubaydallah. Only the courageous behavior of Zaynab, the daughter of Fatima, prevented the governor from killing Husayn's only surviving son, 'Ali, in cold blood. She enfolded him in her arms and demanded bravely that she be slain with him until 'Ubaydallah relented and let them both go. After displaying Husayn's head in Kufa, the governor ordered that it and the survivors be sent to Yazid in Syria. It is told that when the head was brought to 'Ubaydallah, he began to poke it with a cane. A companion of the Prophet who was present, Zayd b. Arqam, cried out weeping: "Raise that cane, by God! I have seen the lips of the messenger of God kiss those very lips!"[12]

The unequal Battle of Karbala had taken place on 'Ashura', 10 Muharram

61 (October 10, 681), and the symbolism was striking. In the early days of Islam, before the Jewish and Muslim calendars diverged, this day had concurred with 10 Tishri, or 'Asor, the Jewish Day of Atonement. It was a day of fasting by Muslims to atone for sins. Although replaced as an obligatory day of fasting in the year 2 by the month of Ramadan, it is still a voluntary day of expiatory fasting and almsgiving for Muslims. It thus seemed clear to many Muslims that Imam Husayn had poured out his life on this day and resisted iniquity until death as an atonement for the grave sins his grandfather's people had committed by disregarding the will of their Prophet.

The martyrdom of Imam Husayn and his small band left a deep imprint on the minds and souls of Shi'is. Twelvers have built thousands of mourning houses, known as *ma'tams* and *Husayniyyas*, where they gather to mourn communally and meditate on the events at Karbala. Highly dramatic passion plays and/or emotionally charged religious processions, including flagellants, commemorating the battle may be seen in almost any country where Twelvers are gathered.

IMAM IV: 'ALI B. HUSAYN, ZAYN AL-'ABIDIN

Some of the earliest accounts suggest that 'Ali b. Husayn had just attained puberty by the time of the Battle of Karbala and survived only because he was sick and being nursed by his aunt. Shi'i accounts make him older and already the father of a son of his own by Fatima, the daughter of Hasan. He was Husayn's only surviving son, ancestor of all of the later Husaynis. His mother is said to have been a daughter of Yazdegird III, the last Sasanian Shah of Iran, captured and given to Husayn by Imam 'Ali. He was allowed to live under close surveillance in Madina and was so noted for his resemblance to Imam 'Ali and for his piety and forbearance that he was called Zayn al-'Abidin, the Ornament of Devotees. It is recalled that when he performed the ritual ablutions, his skin would turn yellow (that is, pale). Asked what was afflicting him, he said, "Do you not know Whom you are preparing to stand before?"[13] He is reported to be the author of a collection of prayers that are so beautiful they are sometimes called the *Psalms of the Family of the Prophet*, the *Sahifa Sajjadiyya*.[14] The fourth Imam was a noted jurist in Madina and died there in 95 (713). Some Shi'i authorities state that he was poisoned by Caliph Walid b. 'Abd al-Malik (ruled 705–15), of the Umayyad dynasty founded by Mu'awiya,[15] even though he refused to support any revolts against the dynasty. Imam ʿAli Zayn al-ʿAbidin was buried near his uncle Hasan and his grandmother Fatima in the Madinan cemetery of al-Baqiʿ.

IMAM V: MUHAMMAD AL-BAQIR B. ʿALI ZAYN AL-ʿABIDIN

Although Muhammad al-Baqir, grandson of both Husayn and Hasan, pursued quietist policies, his learning and revered reputation made him suspect to the Umayyads, and he is said to have been summoned to Damascus to answer for himself more than once. He began publicly to lay the foundations of Shiʿi law and recite traditions on the basis of what he had learned from his father. His title "al-Baqir" means "one who splits open knowledge," that is, revealing its heart. He sometimes differed significantly from Sunni jurists, though Abu Hanifa, for whom the Hanafi school of Sunni jurisprudence is named, described himself as al-Baqir's student.[16] He taught his followers that *taqiyya,* or prudent dissimulation of Shiʿism, was mandatory if life or limb was in danger. Sunni authorities generally regard him as a reliable traditionist, and he was also noted for his asceticism and generosity. Imam Baqir is said to have warned his half-brother Zayd, son of his father's concubine[17] and an early claimant to Mahdi-hood, from whom the Zaydis take their name, not to incite an uprising in Kufa against the Umayyads, but Zayd did not heed him and was slain there.[18] There is a wide discrepancy in the years given for his death, ranging from 733 to 744. Many Shiʿi authorities believe he was poisoned by the Umayyads.[19]

IMAM VI: JAʿFAR AL-SADIQ

Jaʿfar al-Sadiq was the eldest son of Imam Baqir, who had been groomed to be the successor of his father. He lived quietly in Madina through the turbulent period of the revolution of the House of ʿAbbas against the Umayyad caliphs and the movement of the capital to Baghdad. He refused to be associated with several uprisings and is quoted as saying, "I have the weapons of the Apostle of God, may God bless him and his family, but I will never fight with them."[20] Instead, he ordered his supporters to observe *taqiyya* and spent his time teaching law and *hadith.* His followers regarded him as the only authoritative teacher of the age. Twelvers therefore call their school of Islamic law the Jaʿfari school. Despite his great authority, the Imami Shiʿis split in the last days of Jaʿfar's Imamate. He had discreetly said that the oldest of his sons would be his successor. Many believed that this would be

Isma'il, son of a granddaughter of Zayn al-'Abidin. When Isma'il died in his father's lifetime, a group of more revolutionary Shi'is asserted that Isma'il had passed the Imamate to his own son, Muhammad, with whom they went into hiding to plan a revolution against the 'Abbasid caliphs. These are the Isma'ili Shi'is.[21] Others expected that Isma'il's brother, 'Abdallah, now the eldest, would be the next Imam, but he also died a few weeks later, leaving no sons. The eldest was now Musa, the son of a concubine of Ja'far al-Sadiq, and he became the next Imam. Imam Ja'far was buried in Madina at al-Baqi'; his tomb was destroyed by the Wahhabi sect in recent times to prevent its veneration. According to Twelver tradition, Ja'far al-Sadiq was poisoned by the 'Abbasid caliph Mansur.

IMAM VII: MUSA AL-KAZIM

The word *kazim* means one who restrains himself or keeps silent. Musa al-Kazim's mother was a concubine from the Western Islamic world who was identified as a "Berber" in some sources and an "Andalusian" in others. Musa al-Kazim lived under the tyrannical Caliph Mansur, who dreaded 'Alid uprisings above all things and put many of the family of 'Ali to death.[22] Like his father before him, al-Kazim focused on prayer, withdrawal, and teaching his disciples. His refusal to risk the lives of Muslims in a civil war, even if the Shi'is had the better cause, characterizes the teaching of his family. This is in marked contrast to the doctrine of the Zaydis, who believe that it is precisely the pursuit of power by armed means that makes an able descendant of Hasan or Husayn an Imam.

Al-Kazim also taught that it was permissible to cooperate with a tyrannical government in matters of mutual concern if it furthered the just cause of the Shi'is.[23] This view did not spare him from the suspicions of Mansur or his son and successor, Mahdi, who had him brought to Baghdad and imprisoned. However, Mahdi so trusted the Imam's probity that he released him in 785 in exchange for his word that he would not rebel against Mahdi or his sons.[24]

The Imam's ordeal was to come in the time of Mahdi's son, Harun al-Rashid, who ruled in 786–809. While on a pilgrimage to Mecca in early 796, al-Kazim was seized and taken to Basra, where the caliph ordered his cousin the governor to execute al-Kazim. Impressed by the Imam's piety and goodness, the cousin preferred to send him to Baghdad, where he was kept under house arrest under the supervision of the *wazir* (prime minister), Fadl al-Barmaki, who was similarly impressed and treated the Imam with courtesy and respect. When Harun got word of this, he continued to press for al-Kazim's death. The *wazir* then handed al-Kazim over to the police prefect, Sindi b. Shahak, under whose care he died. Sunni authorities report his death without comment, but Shiʿi accounts state that he was poisoned.[25]

Some Shiʿi sources add that the Imam voluntarily offered his life as a ransom for the sins of the Shiʿis, whom he believed God would soon punish for their lack of *taqiyya* and loyalty to the Imam in this time of trial. Because of the heightened expectations of Shiʿis, word had been circulating that he was the expected Mahdi, the twelfth Imam. To combat this, religious scholars were recruited to testify that he had died of natural causes, and the public was allowed to visit his bier. The best authorities state that he died in 799. He was buried in Baghdad, and his tomb, with that of his grandson, the ninth Imam, is one of the most important Twelver shrines today. This quarter of the city is called Kazimain, "the two Kazims."

IMAM VIII: ʿALI AL-RIDA

The most reliable sources state that ʿAli al-Rida was born in 768 or 770 in Madina. His mother was a Nubian concubine. Many witnesses testified that his father had designated him as his successor before he died. He seems to have lived quietly in Madina, teaching and relating *hadith* from his family, until 816, when the reigning ʿAbbasid, Maʾmun, the son of Harun, summoned him to his residence at Marw in Khurasan in northeastern Iran. There he appointed him as his heir and gave him the title al-Rida, the Well Pleasing. It was a name full of meaning: the revolution of the ʿAbbasids against the Umayyads had been conducted in the name of "al-Rida, of the People of the [Prophet's] House." Followers of the ʿAlids and the ʿAbbasids had joined together, and when the fighting was over, an ʿAbbasid had been installed suddenly in Kufa. Now Maʾmun appeared to be trying to unify all Muslims and restore unquestioned legitimacy to the caliphate. ʿAli b. Musa was reluctant to accept the nomination, but the caliph insisted, and all of the dignitaries, now dressed in green, not black, the official color of the ʿAbbasid house, gave him homage as the heir.

There was widespread rejoicing, even though the question of the succession after al-Rida was not addressed. But in Iraq, the Baghdadis, who were already in disorder because they feared the removal of the capital to Marw, were enraged, especially against Fadl b. Sahl, the head of Ma'mun's military and civil administration. They elected a half-brother of Harun al-Rashid as their caliph, declared that Ma'mun was deposed, and attacked his garrison. This grave situation was concealed from Ma'mun in Marw by his *wazir*, Fadl b. Sahl, but the Imam was informed and told Ma'mun. Before July 818, Ma'mun married one of his daughters to al-Rida, and another was betrothed to the Imam's young son Muhammad. Ma'mun also decided to return to Baghdad with the army. In the city of Sarakhs en route, the *wazir* was murdered in a bath under suspicious circumstances.

When Ma'mun traveled to Tus, he visited the tomb of Harun outside the city, where Harun had died and been buried on his way to visit Ma'mun in 809. Here al-Rida also died, apparently in early September 818. Shi'i accounts state that he was given poisoned fruit because Ma'mun now perceived him as a liability.[26] The caliph manifested great grief for him and had him buried beside Harun. Since then, this site of Mashhad, the Martyr's Shrine, has become the nucleus of the holiest city of Iran.

IMAM IX: MUHAMMAD AL-JAWAD (OR AL-TAQI)

Al-Taqi was the only son of his father and a Nubian concubine named Sabika but called Khayzuran. He was only seven when his father died, but his father had foretold his birth, had designated him as successor, and had left him the family documents. He was reared in Madina among his father's relatives and disciples. He already had a son, his future successor, by a concubine, when Ma'mun summoned him to Iraq in 830 to marry him to the princess Umm al-Fadl, to whom he had been betrothed. They were given a mansion on the Tigris, but the next year, the Imam returned to Madina with all of his dependents. Umm al-Fadl gave him no descendants, and on August 9, 833, Ma'mun died during a campaign in Cilicia and was succeeded by his brother Mu'tasim. The following year, Mu'tasim summoned al-Taqi to Baghdad, and after about ten months there, he died in November 835 at the age of twenty-five. He was buried, as we have seen, near his grandfather, al-Kazim, on the west bank of the Tigris in Baghdad. Some Shi'i sources state that Mu'tasim poisoned him,[27] but Shaykh Mufid says this allegation is unfounded.[28] The Imam left two sons and two daughters.

IMAM X: ʿALI B. MUHAMMAD AL-HADI (OR AL-NAQI)

Al-Hadi's mother was a concubine named Sumana, and he was born in Madina in 828 and designated by his father as the next Imam. In 857, Muʿtasim's son, Caliph Mutawakkil, ordered al-Hadi to come to the new capital of Samarra on the Tigris, apparently because he had been slandered by the ʿAbbasid governor of the city. He was furnished with a residence and given honor, but he was closely watched. After about ten years in Samarra, he died in 868 at the age of forty-one. Ibn Babuyi, for whom it was an article of Shiʿi faith that the prophets and the Imams were all murdered, states that Mutawakkil poisoned him. Like the Prophet, he was buried in his house.

IMAM XI: HASAN B. MUHAMMAD AL-ʿASKARI

The name ʿAskari derives from al-ʿAskar, the Camp, another name for Samarra, but the eleventh Imam was born in Madina, most likely in 844. His mother was a concubine named Hudayth. He is also known as al-Samit, the Silent. Even in his life of strict retirement, he was under close surveillance. His brother Jaʿfar was induced to intrigue against him, and he was imprisoned for a period by Caliph Muʿtamid. His brother Muhammad was apparently designated before him, but after Muhammad's untimely death, their father announced that Hasan was his choice a few months before his own death. Despite his circumscribed existence, many miracles are reported of this Imam. It was a fractured time for the Shiʿis. Many did not know who their leader should be, and many claimed leadership of the partisans of ʿAli. Various sects are reported to have formed in this period. There is even disagreement on whether Hasan left a son, but the accepted view among the Twelvers is that he concealed the birth of his son due to the watchfulness of the authorities (a *hadith* stated that the Prophet had said he would have only twelve successors); in the unsettled times in Samarra, knowing that the Shiʿis were expecting the rise of a deliverer, the Sunni authorities were closely watching the Imam.

The eleventh Imam fell ill on December 25, 873, and died a week later, attended by the caliph's physicians. The later Twelver sources say that Muʿtamid poisoned him. The Imam was buried next to his father in their house in Samarra. After his death, his profligate brother Jaʿfar seized his property (with the consent of the authorities), laid claim to his title, and mistreated his womenfolk. Had his attempt at gaining power been successful, it would have been a profitable affair because Shi'is gave the *khums*, the freewill tax of one-fifth of the year's profits, to the Imam to use for charity. However, Ja'far found few followers.[29]

IMAM XII: MUHAMMAD B. AL-HASAN AL-MAHDI, AL-QA'IM, AL-HUJJA

Twelvers hold that the twelfth Imam was five when his father died at the age of twenty-eight and that his mother was a slavegirl named Narjis, said to have been a daughter of the Byzantine emperor. His existence was so secret that for a long time, pious Twelvers would only refer to him by a circumlocution, such as al-Gharim, the Creditor. Soon after his father's death, he went into *ghayba*, or "occultation," and thereafter was known only through his spokesmen, *safirs* (emissaries), *babs* (doors), or *na'ibs* (deputies), of whom there were four in succession, but many people testified that they had seen him or had dealings with him. This period, called "the lesser occultation," came to an end in 940. Since that time, it is said that the hidden Imam will be seen only in visions until he comes to restore true Islam, convert the world with the help of Jesus, and fill the earth with justice and abundance instead of iniquity and need. He will rule for a period of seven, or some say nineteen, years. Human history will have achieved its apogee and its purpose, and the Day of Judgment will be ushered in.

The lives of the Imams were all shaped by their relations with the rulers of the Sunni majority. Imam 'Ali was kept in the background by the first three caliphs, Imam Hasan felt he had no choice but to abdicate under Mu'awiya, and Imam Husayn was martyred under Mu'awiya's son. According to tradition, Hasan and Husayn are the "Peacocks of the Garden of Paradise," but the later Imams lived like caged birds. Zayn al-'Abidin lived reclusively in Madina as an ascetic devotee and teacher. Under the powerful police state of the early 'Abbasids, the Imams counseled patience and dissimulation in order to prevent bloodshed. Al-Rida was a pawn in the dynastic intrigues of the 'Abbasids, and his descendants lived closely observed under house arrest in the 'Abbasid capitals. The Shi'i Imams had to be content with carrying out their mission of guidance as religious teachers under severe restrictions. There was no question of their exercising political power, except in the illusory appointment of Imam Rida as heir to the imperial throne. After Imam 'Ali, they were all men of peace, including Imam Husayn, who died with sword in hand.

The sufferings of the Imams were all permitted by God, Shi'i scholars teach, in order to maintain humanity's freedom to choose its acts. By generously offering their suffering to God as an expiation for the sins of the Muslims, the Imams interceded for God's mercy. It is related that on the long Day of Resurrection, when people are waiting for judgment and tortured with thirst, the martyred Imam Husayn will dispense the sweet waters of the Pool of Kawthar to the faithful, and none who taste it will ever suffer from thirst again.

In the meantime, the Shi'i "Partisans of the House" are not deprived of guidance, for the twelfth Imam still lives and inspires the *mujtahids* to guide them to the truth. In life and in death, the Imams and the saints intercede for their partisans before God.

3

SACRED ACTORS AND INTERCESSORS

Shi'i Islam and Roman Catholicism have several striking structural similarities. Some of the most significant concern the holy personalities at the origin and center of the two religions. Shi'ism and Catholicism have at the core of their faith systems a transcendent martyr who is part of a holy family that includes a powerful mother figure. Jesus Christ and Imam Husayn and the Virgin Mary and Sayyida Fatima are paired personalities that manifest many notable parallels.

JESUS CHRIST AND IMAM HUSAYN

Muslims consider Jesus ('Isa) to be one of the greatest prophets. In the Muslim mind, he ranks with Noah, Abraham, Moses, and Muhammad himself. The Qur'an states that Jesus was the "Word of God and Spirit from Him," born of a virgin mother, and that he was the promised Messiah who performed miracles from birth. In Sura 19, Jesus is quoted as saying: "I am a servant of God; He has given me the Book, and appointed me a prophet. Blessed has He made me, wherever I may be, and enjoined on me prayer and to give alms so long as I live."[1]

Although the Imams, who disclose the true understanding of the revelation brought by Muhammad, may be compared with Jesus as he is understood by Christians, individually it is the figure of Husayn that best parallels that of Jesus. The fact that Christians believe that Jesus is a *persona* of God is of course a fundamental difference that will always separate Muslims and Christians. Muslims simply do not accept the doctrine of the Incarnation and the mystery of the Trinity, which they believe contradicts God's Oneness.[2] Despite the great praise heaped upon Jesus in the Qur'an, it is nonetheless sternly written in Sura 4 that "the Messiah Jesus, the Son of Mary, is only a messenger of God and His Word that He conveyed unto Mary, and a Spirit from Him. So believe in God and His messengers and do not say 'Three.' Desist: It is better for you. God is only one God."[3] When one looks beyond this crucial difference, however, a number of arresting similarities in the lives, personalities, and missions of Jesus and Husayn become sharply evident.

According to their respective faith systems, Jesus and Husayn were sinless. Jesus, viewed as the son of God, is described by the Epistle to the Hebrews as "one tempted in every way that we are, but without sin."[4] Shi'is since the time of Shaykh Mufid have held that the prophets and Imams, after their vocation, were immune to sin. Thus Husayn, as one of the Imams or fourteen "pure ones" of Islam, is considered impeccable by Twelvers. Most Muslims affirm that Jesus as a prophet was impeccable, that he was the promised Christ, and that he could perform miracles from infancy. Shi'is also believe that the twelve Imams had supernatural powers. As members of special holy families, Jesus and Husayn shared a number of experiences and characteristics. They both led simple lives and suffered poverty and hardship. Born in a stable, the child of a carpenter, a companion to shepherds and fishermen, Jesus lived with the common people of his time. Husayn endured great hardship in a family that suffered from lack of food and adequate clothing and shelter. Shi'i sources stress the fact that Husayn's parents, Imam 'Ali and Sayyida Fatima, witnessed great deprivations. The following extraordinary statement attributed to Imam 'Ali speaks directly to this culture of poverty:

If you desire I will tell you about 'Isa [Jesus] son of Maryam [Mary]. He used a stone for his pillow, put on coarse clothes and ate rough food. His condiment was hunger. His lamp at night was the moon. His shade during the winter was just the expanse of earth Eastward and Westward. His fruits and flowers were only what grows from the earth for cattle. He had no wife to allure him, nor any son to give grief, nor wealth to deviate his attention, nor greed to disgrace him. His two feet were his conveyance and his two hands his servant.[5]

Jesus and Husayn each can be described as the "martyr of martyrs" in their respective religions. It is in this sense that Husayn, not the Prophet Muhammad or Imam 'Ali, is best compared to Jesus Christ. As martyrs par excellence, Jesus and Husayn offered themselves for the redemption of sinners. Each hero foresaw his fate as martyr. Each had the choice of passing up this painful role. Each feared the suffering that such a role entailed. And each chose death, apparently for similar reasons. Each understood that this kind of gesture, the ultimate sacrifice, would leave a lasting legacy while serving to atone for humanity, which had lost its way.

The crucifixion of Jesus for Christians and the massacre and beheading of Imam Husayn for Muslims were certainly incidents of vast importance. Catholics and Twelvers see them as cosmic events, and they commemorate the passion and death of their heroes in massive ceremonies of grief every year. In this sense, Jesus the Christ and Husayn the impeccable Imam succeeded in their missions of martyrdom.

It is sometimes argued that there is a fundamental difference between the martyrdom of Jesus and that of Husayn. On one hand, Jesus is portrayed as a gentle, pacific figure who eschewed the use of force. According to this position, he could in no way be considered a military warrior. Imam Husayn's death, on the other hand, occurred during a military campaign and involved violence and warfare. Those who hold this perspective sometimes point to it as evidence of basic differences between Islam and Christianity, alleging that Islam is a more aggressive belief system. According to this argument, Islam is in essence a militant religion, one that spreads its message through violence. The story of Husayn's death is used as a prime example of this Islamic militancy.

A closer examination of Imam Husayn's martyrdom reveals a different interpretation. Unlike his father 'Ali, Husayn was not known for his battle exploits. Badly outnumbered on the plains of Karbala, he realized the futility of fighting there. He was well aware that his small band of family and friends was marching directly into the jaws of death, and he tried to negotiate his way out of an impossible situation. When he failed, he accepted the inevitable slaughter that ensued. This behavior is best described by the term *mazlum*, which means wronged or unjustly oppressed. In everyday Persian, however, *mazlum* refers to "a person who is unwilling to act against others, even when he is oppressed, not out of cowardice or diffidence but because of generosity and forbearance."[6] Both Jesus and Husayn stand as central suffering figures whose violent deaths at the hands of ruthless temporal adversaries have been interpreted by their followers as universal redemptive acts. Both deaths represented the climax of a terrible period of passion and suffering that helped cleanse the world of injustice, tyranny, and corruption and set a great example for their followers. In their physical deaths and temporal defeats, both Jesus and Husayn achieved major spiritual triumphs and everlasting victory. In addition, their acts of ultimate sacrifice initiated a long history of similar acts of martyrdom by Christians and Muslims alike. Each is a powerful intercessor: Jesus, "seated at the right hand of the Father, receive[s] our prayers,"[7] and Husayn dispenses the waters of the Pool of Kawthar and is granted the keys of the treasury of intercession.[8]

THE VIRGIN MARY AND SAYYIDA FATIMA

Mary, the mother of Jesus, is a central figure and symbol in Catholic Christianity. Especially blessed and immaculately conceived, she was privileged to be the virginal mother of the Logos, through whom the world was created—hence, she was truly Theotokos, or Mother of God. In the words of Jaroslav Pelikan: "The Virgin Mary has been more of an inspiration to more people than any other woman who ever lived."[9] In the first chapter of Luke, one reads, "And in the sixth month the angel Gabriel was sent from God unto a city in Galilee, named Nazareth, to a virgin espoused to a man named Joseph, of the house of David; and the virgin's name was Mary."[10]

Two sections of the Qur'an are devoted to Mary (Maryam). The Qur'anic passages that refer to Mary are powerful and poetic. In Sura 3, the Qur'an says:

> Behold! The angels said: "O Mary! God has chosen you and purified you—chosen you above all the women of creation. O Mary! be obedient to your Lord: prostrate yourself, and bow down with those who bow in worship." . . . Remember when the angels said: "O Mary! God gives you glad tidings of a Word from Him: his name is the Messiah, Jesus Son of Mary, held in honor in this world and the Hereafter, and one of those brought near to God. He shall speak unto mankind in his cradle and in his manhood, and he is of the righteous."[11]

As mother of the promised Messiah, Mary is recognized in the Qur'an as purified and "chosen . . . above all the women of creation" by God, who

Himself ordained the virginal birth. The Virgin Mary is thus a sacred historical and theological link binding Christians and Muslims. Catholics and Orthodox Christians view her as mother of Christ, the divine Logos. Muslims consider her mother of the Messiah, purified by God for her special role and responsibility.

An elaborate Catholic theology has developed around the immaculate state of Mary beginning with her conception by her mother Ann, the annunciation, the virginal birth, and the assumption of Mary into heaven. Roman Catholic teachings have sometimes even portrayed Mary as an integral part of the universal cause of human redemption and as coredemptrix of the human race. Although she is subordinate to Christ, she is sometimes called "second redeemer" in this sense and a second Eve, mother of a new race.

Protestant theologians have often criticized what they consider the unseemly glorification of Mary in Catholicism. The Catholic emphasis on Mary's holiness and special grace and her "motherhood of God" has been compared to pagan goddess worship. The Catholic doctrine that Mary was taken into heaven body and soul is also seriously questioned. The fact that Catholics direct many prayers to Mary is thought to detract from the worship of God Himself, and many Protestants criticize the intermediary and intercessionary roles that Catholics have assigned to Mary.

The differences in the Catholic and Protestant views of Mary are reflected in actual religious practices. The everyday devotional importance of Mary is deeply evident in Catholicism. Catholics emphasize Mary in numerous feast days, litanies, prayers, songs, devotions, and pilgrimages, as well as in such common prayer practices as the Angelus and the rosary. The short but powerful Ave Maria is, with the Lord's Prayer, the most popular prayer recited by Catholics. For them, the Virgin Mary, by virtue of her holiness and divine maternity, is a special intermediary and channel to God given to the disciples by Jesus on the cross. Furthermore, because Mary gave birth to Christ and is contained herself in God, she is sometimes viewed as an extension of the will and being of God. It is through Mary, who is herself immaculate, that many Catholics attempt to merge with the divine. In the Western Middle Ages, it was only after the time of St. Francis of Assisi (1180–1226) that Catholics stressed the humanity of Jesus as a baby in a manger and a faithful companion. Catholics in earlier centuries tended to see Jesus as an awesome teacher and stern judge. Christians came to him as a child in the arms of a loving mother, through whom he was made man. Mary has never ceased to be a connection point for Catholics, humanity's gift to God and His gift to it.

There is a fascinating parallel between the Virgin Mary and Sayyida Fatima, the daughter of the Prophet Muhammad, the wife of Imam 'Ali, and the mother of Imams Hasan and Husayn. Fatima, as we have seen, was the youngest daughter of the Prophet and enjoyed a special relationship with her father. Her entire being became linked with him. In words attributed to the Prophet himself: "The contentment of Fatima is my contentment, her anger is my anger. Whosoever loves my daughter Fatima loves me. Whosoever makes Fatima content makes me content. Whosoever makes Fatima unhappy makes me unhappy. Fatima is a part of my body. Whosoever hurts her, has hurt me, and whosoever hurts me has hurt God."[12]

Fatima is enormously important because she represents the crucial link in the family chain that binds the Prophet to the twelve Imams. In the words of a leading biographer of Fatima: "The final link in this chain of Divine Justice, the rightful chain of truth is Fatima, the last daughter of a family who had anticipated a son."[13]

Although she was historically viewed by some as a weak, sad, suffering, and self-pitying woman, her image has changed significantly over the years. As a young girl, she suffered physically because of the poverty of her family in the early years. Later, she suffered psychologically because of a number of painful ordeals. First, her mother, Khadija, died; then her beloved father, the Prophet Muhammad, passed away; and shortly thereafter she saw her spouse, 'Ali, lose the mantle of Muslim leadership that her father had ordained for him to Abu Bakr, who then deprived her of her inheritance. Although she showed great courage by speaking out bitterly against this decision, she spent her last days incessantly weeping. Fatima died approximately six months after her father died. She did not live to witness the calamitous death of her son Husayn but is associated with it in popular piety.

The life and role of Sayyida Fatima have been reinterpreted in recent years by Western scholars such as the Catholic Louis Massignon and Muslim analysts such as Ali Shariati. In this view, Fatima was far more than a passive, weeping figure. She served as an active and inspiring companion to her father, a staunch defender of her family, the conscience of the earliest community of Muslims, and a model for women and men who suffer through extraordinary trials and tribulations.

Both Fatima and the Virgin Mary stand as female members of a central holy family; both are considered immaculate and impeccable; both are extensions of their fathers and sons; both are mothers of sorrows. Whereas Mary links her son Jesus with the human race, Fatima is linked in the minds of Shiʿi believers with her father Muhammad, her husband ʿAli, and her sons Hasan and Husayn. In Shiʿi legend, the figures of Mary and Fatima and Jesus and Husayn become curiously intertwined. Fatima is sometimes referred to by Shiʿis as al-Maryam al-Kubra (the Greater Mary), and Jesus is thought of as "in some sense, the brother of Husayn."[14]

Fatima and Mary lived lives of virginal purity, according to popular Shiʿi piety. In medieval Shiʿi sources, Fatima is referred to as al-Batul, the Maiden, and al-Tahira, the Pure. Although she is not believed to have virginally conceived her children, Fatima is thought to have been free from the polluting effects of menstruation and parturition, as defined in Islamic laws of purity.[15]

Like Mary, Fatima was believed to have been visited by angels and therefore is often called al-Muhaddatha (the One Spoken to by Angels) "because angels spoke to her as to Mary, and she to them: they told her 'God has chosen you and purified you; He has chosen you from among the women of the world.'"[16] Shiʿi piety teaches that the angel Gabriel arranged the marriage of Fatima to ʿAli.

Suffering is a central element in the comparative study of Mary and Fatima. Whereas Mary suffered at the foot of the cross upon which her son was crucified, Fatima's image is bracketed by the traumatic deaths of her father, her husband, and her son. In Roman Catholicism, many prayers begin with the phrase "O Mary Most Sorrowful," and the quintessential poem of sorrow, the "Stabat Mater," begins: "At the Cross her station keeping, / Stood the mournful mother weeping." One of the feasts historically commemorated by Catholics is the feast of Mary's seven dolors (sorrows). The first of these is Simeon's grim prophecy to Mary that "thy own soul a sword shall pierce."[17] In Shiʿi beliefs, Fatima is considered to be "one of the most tragic characters in all of human history . . . who dwelt all her short life in the House of Sorrows."[18]

In the cases of Mary and Fatima, their severe sorrow carried special intercessionary meaning. Their sorrow demonstrates the difficulties the faithful must face while at the same time holding out the hope of everlasting happiness. This drama of intercession is especially powerful in the case of Fatima, who Shi'is believe will have a major voice in determining who will enter paradise on the Day of Resurrection. Louis Massignon cites a Shi'i text that provides a powerful vision of Fatima that reportedly appeared to the ancestors of all humanity in the Garden of Paradise: "He showed them a Being, adorned with a myriad of glittering lights of various colors, who sat on a throne, a crown on her head, rings in her ears, a drawn sword by her side. The radiance streaming forth from her illumined the whole garden. When the first humans asked, 'Who is this?' the following answer was given to them: 'This is the form of Fatima, as she appears in Paradise. Her crown is Muhammad; her earrings are Hasan and Husayn; her sword is 'Ali.'" [19]

As supreme intercessors who witnessed great pain and sorrow, Mary and Fatima reflect compassion and mercy, especially toward the poor and the deprived. Fatima lived a life of poverty and privation, particularly during the early years of her marriage to 'Ali. Shi'i legend teaches that despite this poverty, however, Fatima gave away what little she had to those who were even poorer. On such occasions, she is reported to have tasted only water during the day and to have slept hungry at night. Her possessions at the time of her marriage to 'Ali are reported to have been only a goatskin bottle, a cup, a hand mill, and a cotton rug. Mary also led a simple life as a carpenter's wife who gave birth in a stable. In the Magnificat, Mary states, "My soul magnifies the Lord," and exults that God has humbled the proud, the mighty, and the rich while exalting the lowly, the hungry, and the poor.[20]

Both the Virgin Mary and Sayyida Fatima have exerted enormous influence long after their deaths. Both have become cult figures, and millions of believers have made pilgrimages to their shrines and holy places. The Roman Catholic Church has recognized places and incidents in which the "Blessed Mother" appeared to ordinary people throughout the world. These reported appearances have numbered over 200 since the 1930s. The sites of three apparitions that have been recognized by the church include Guadalupe in Mexico in 1531, Lourdes in France in 1858, and Fatima in Portugal in 1917. More recently, the site of the Virgin's reported appearance in Medjugorje in Croatia was visited by over 20 million people during the 1980s and 1990s.[21]

Feast days are dedicated to Fatima, and Shi'is commemorate the anniversaries of her birth and her death. Shi'i pilgrims visit her reputed tomb in the Baqi' al-Gharqad cemetery of Madina and a site in the Great Mosque of Madina known as Fatima's Garden. Every year, hundreds of thousands of Muslims weep for Fatima in religious gatherings, prayer meetings, sacred festivals, and mourning ceremonies.

Shi'i sources include the Virgin Mary and Sayyida Fatima among the four most respected women in religious history, alongside the pharaoh's wife, 'Asiya, who reared Moses, and Khadija, the first wife of the Prophet Muhammad.[22] Elaborate stories and interpretations have grown up around Mary and Fatima, two revered women who have inspired entire systems of popular devotion. They have the following similarities, according to the beliefs of their followers (whether Roman Catholic or Shi'i Muslim):

1. Both Mary and Fatima are the central female members of their respective holy families.
2. Both are considered to be immaculate and impeccable.
3. Both stand as models of extraordinary purity.
4. Both are critical links in a divine chain that connects the human and the divine. Both are major intercessionary figures to whom their followers direct their prayers and requests.
5. Mary's role emanates from that of her son, Jesus, and Fatima is an extension of the personality of her father, the Prophet Muhammad.
6. Both lived lives of extraordinary suffering, focused most dramatically on the martyrdom of their sons.
7. Both empathized particularly with the poor and the deprived. They themselves endured great poverty and deprivation in their lives.
8. Both holy women, often portrayed as passive and debile, were in fact thoroughly engaged in the events of their day.
9. Both continue to be strong role models and sources of consolation and inspiration for the faithful in their respective faith systems.

THE IMAMS AS INTERCESSORS

In Twelver Shi'ism, the Imamate consists of a glittering chain of holy Imams that links the Prophet through 'Ali and Fatima with the other eleven Imams. According to Shi'i piety, this linking through space and time in turn enables believers to attain access to the divine. The Imam, "the one before you," is best defined as a special sacred leader.[23] The Twelve Imam is not selected by the community but comes to his exalted position by virtue of divine appointment, which is then made known through an infallible source. This appointment is called the *nass*. The Imam is the vicegerent of God, and the line of Imams consists of a divinely fashioned chain of emanation that is an unquestioned reality in the minds of faithful Shiʿis. Although the Sunni caliph is also called "the Imam" in Sunni legal texts, he is an ordinary erring mortal. The Twelve Shiʿi Imams, however, are thought to exist in a state of permanent grace and divine guidance that renders them infallible and impeccable (*maʿsum*). This greatly enhances their station in the Shiʿi universe of faith. Protected from all error, like the prophets, they enjoy this gift from the time they become aware of the difference between good and evil until their deaths. Without this special immunity, revelation itself would be in jeopardy, thus obviating God's purpose in speaking through His prophets. Sunnis argue that prophets are immune only to grave sin and error, but the Twelver view is that they are preserved even from minor sin and error.

Shiʿis also teach that God's gracious kindness (*lutf*) is intrinsic; it is not simply a quality He may choose to manifest at times, which implies the possibility of His being less than kind. He is at all times the Lord of gracious kindness. It follows that because no one ordinary mortal understands all of revelation, even when it is plainly written in scripture, and because human beings are all too prone to error and sin, even to the point of perverting scripture, God would not have provided the definitive scripture, the Qurʾan, without also furnishing an infallible and impeccable guide to it. This guide is the Imam.

Shiʿis draw a conscious parallel between ʿAli, the chosen vicegerent and successor of Muhammad, and Peter the Rock, whom they see as the designated vicegerent and earthly successor of Jesus. Each major prophet, they claim, had a chosen successor and interpreter of his message.

The Imam is, moreover, ruler by the will of God and in the name of God. He is the successor of the Prophet on earth, and his office is to interpret correctly what the Prophet brought. All political authority that derives from God and His messenger belongs to him. The Imams are known as the "Signs of God," "the Lights of God," and "the Cords of God." These references to signs, lights, and cords signify the special role played by the Imams in Shiʿism. They are divinely inspired, guiding connectors.

The Imams are intercessors par excellence. According to a leading scholar of Shi'ism, they are "the intermediaries between man and God. To ask for their succor is to appeal to the channel God placed before man so as to enable man to return to Him."[24] As intermediaries, they are by definition guides and guardians of humankind's interior religious life and actions, as well as the external visible dimensions of life. This important point is elegantly summarized by a learned Shi'i *mujtahid:* "In the same way that the Imam is the guide and leader of men in their external actions so does he possess the function of inward and esoteric leadership and guidance. He is the guide of the caravan of humanity which is moving inwardly and esoterically toward God."[25]

As guides and intermediaries in both the external and the internal dimensions of human religious life, the Imams shape the behavior of the faithful in three ways. First, members of the Shi'i community look to the lives and teachings of the original twelve Imams for guidance. The most obvious example of this practice is seen in the continuing attention and devotion to Imam 'Ali. 'Ali's sayings and teachings are constantly quoted by Shi'i leaders in the contemporary world. Examples include leaders in the Islamic Republic of Iran such as the late Ayatollah Khomeini and his successors. In Saudi Arabia, Shaykh Hasan al-Saffar has regularly drawn on 'Ali's life and statements in his campaign of political dissent. In the absence of the Imams, the learned *mujtahids* (interpreters of religion) provide the advice and explanations required by the faithful. This is the function of interpretation (*ijtihad*). Every Twelver is required to select a *mujtahid* "to pray behind." According to strict Shi'i doctrine, as representatives of the Imams, the *mujtahids* are the major sources of interpretation in all social, political, and religious affairs. Unlike the Imams, however, the *mujtahids* are neither infallible nor impeccable. Because of his credibility and charisma at the time of the Iranian Revolution, Ayatollah Khomeini was often called Imam Khomeini. Khomeini, of course, was not an Imam, and he explicitly rejected any notion that he might be considered the Imam. He was an *imam* in the general "prayer leader" sense of the term, but not an Imam in the chain of twelve begun by 'Ali.

Finally, practicing Shi'is are acutely aware of the existence everywhere of the twelfth Imam, who disappeared in 874. Shi'i piety teaches that the hidden Imam will return with Jesus Christ to set up the messianic kingdom before the final Judgment Day, when all humanity will stand before God.

The Imams and Fatima will have a direct impact on the judgments rendered on that day. This will represent the ultimate intercession. Faithful Twelvers meanwhile lead their lives with the full conviction that the twelfth Imam, Muhammad the Mahdi, observes them and is generally aware of their actions.

On the Iranian calendar, twenty-three days are officially set aside for the commemoration of the births and deaths of the twelve Imams.[26] The strong belief in the Imams as mediators and intercessors is seen in the massive pilgrimages (*ziyarat*) of Shi'is to the tombs of the Imams. Indeed, far more Shi'is visit these more accessible shrines than make the Hajj, the grand pilgrimage to Mecca.[27]

IMAMZADAS AND SAINTS

In addition to the shrines of the Imams, there exist, especially in Iran, many hundreds of *imamzadas*. These are the tombs of lesser-known saintly figures who are considered to be the lineal or spiritual "seed" of the Imams. An example is the splendid shrine of Shah 'Abd al-'Azim at Rayy, just south of Tehran, which commemorates Husayn, the martyred son of Imam Rida. It is a major site of religious visitation in the Iranian capital. Hundreds of thousands of Shi'is visit these *imamzadas* in search of assistance in their everyday lives. At many of these shrines, miracles and healings are regularly reported.

The belief in the intercessionary power of the Imams and their descendants is seen in the moving and emotional behavior of Shi'i pilgrims of all social classes and socioeconomic backgrounds at the various shrines and tombs. The psychological release and the weeping reveal the perceived power of these intercessors. In 1974, one of the authors spent an afternoon in the inner sanctum of the shrine of Imam Rida in Mashhad. On that occasion, a group of wealthy, worldly, Westernized women close to the shah's royal family desperately gripped the silver bars surrounding the tomb and one by one disintegrated into tears. From the seeming depths of their souls, they cried out for help, begging the eighth Imam to intercede for them. Similar scenes may be found at the shrine of Imam Husayn's sister Zaynab in Damascus.

Shi'is view 'Ali as the *wali* of God par excellence. Here, the word *wali* means protector or friend, but it also has the connotation of one who acts on behalf of someone else. Islam has an elaborate doctrine of saints, or *awliya'*. "The principle and foundation of Sufism and knowledge of God rests on saintship," wrote a prominent theorist in 1057; "the visible proof of this religion is to be found among the saints and the elect of God."[28]

Sufi (Islamic mystic) doctrine seeks to go beyond the relation of "slave of God" taught by the *'ulama* to one of living intimacy or friendship (*walaya*) with Him, and this is done by following the path of the *walis*, His friends. The concept of intercessory Imams is paralleled by the belief in "the friends of God," a word generally if somewhat inadequately translated as "saints." The translation is inadequate because it does not convey the emotional freight of the word for Muslims in general and Shi'is in particular. The *wali* is one who *loves* God.

Among the shrines of the great saints and intercessors in Sunnism are Mulayy Idris's (a descendant of Imam Hasan) in Fez, Shaykh Muhyi al-Din ibn 'Arabi's in Damascus, and Shaykh 'Abd al-Qadir al-Jilani's in Baghdad. In North Africa, there is a rich heritage of saints (often referred to as *marabouts*) who act as intermediaries. Shi'is share many saints with Sunnis, and most Sunni Sufis consider the twelve Imams to be great saints whose intercession is highly valued. One of the most irenic areas of Shi'i-Sunni relations is the doctrine of sainthood and intercession. In Shi'ism, friendship with God necessarily involves friendship with the Imams and saints. Because the saints are seen as the mystical family of the Imams, their intercession, like that of the Imams, is eagerly sought. Sunnis would not agree with Shi'is that it is by virtue of their mystical relation with the Imams that the saints are saints, however; they see sainthood as the result of the saints' direct relationship with God. Yet in practical popular piety, the two categories, Imams and saints, merge into each other. The same scathing criticism of saint veneration found among some Protestants has been launched among some Sunnis since the time of Ibn Taymiyya of Damascus (d. 1328), the Muslim Martin Luther.

Shi'is often visit the tombs of the great Sufi saints who lived as Sunnis, and Sunnis pay homage at the tombs of the Imams and their descendants. Although the Imams possess the extraordinary characteristics of infallibility and impeccability, the saints have the capacity to perform miracles (*karamat*, gifts or charisms from God) and to intercede in this life and even on Judgment Day. According to one source, "As in the Roman Catholic worship, saints are patrons of towns, villages, trades and corporations."[29]

The intertwined nature of Imams, saints, Shi'is, and Sunnis can be seen in the case of a popular mosque in Cairo. Originally created by Isma'ili Shi'i rulers but now known as a Sunni establishment, the al-Husayn Mosque is still in many ways a Shi'i shrine. Pilgrims from all social classes across Egypt and the Middle East go there to seek the assistance of Imam Husayn, whose head is believed by many to be buried in this holy place. Isma'ili Shi'is and Egyptian Sunnis alike believe fervently that the relic is present. In visiting this mosque, the authors have noted that the atmosphere and the piety of the pilgrims present are much like those at the mosques in Mashhad, Qum, Najaf, and Karbala.[30]

We have noted that the *wali* is one who loves God, and the Imams and those who are in communion with them and, through them, with God are all seen as participating in a rich emotional religion of love. In fact, this very love is the *batin*, the esoteric aspect of the Qur'anic revelation.[31]

Unlike Catholicism, however, there is no final authority in Islam that can attest to the existence or nonexistence of a saint. The formal process of canonization is alien to Islam. When Muslims decide that the tomb of a holy person is a locus of *baraka* (divine blessing) and make visits there, that holy figure is recognized as a *wali*. As a result, there are huge numbers of saints in the Muslim world, who, as spiritual mediators and intercessors, buttress for the Twelvers the roles of the Imams.[32]

SAINTS IN CATHOLICISM

The existence of both the Catholic cult of saints and the cult of the Imams and their attendant constellation of saints in Shi'i Islam is one fundamental similarity between the two religious traditions. Both accept a mediator between man and God, "one whose essential being and place in human history plays a determining role in the divine plan for creation, revelation, and salvation."[33]

In the Catholic tradition, the "communion of saints" is a creedal principle. The *Catechism of the Catholic Church* describes the intercession of the saints as follows: "Being more closely united to Christ, those who dwell in heaven fix the whole Church more firmly in holiness. . . . They do not cease to intercede with the Father for us, as they proffer the merits which they acquired on earth through the one mediator between God and men, Christ Jesus. . . . So by their fraternal concern is our weakness greatly helped."[34]

The saint is a holy personage who has pursued a life of special fidelity to God. In the general New Testament sense, all Christians are saints (holy, set apart) for none but the holy may stand before God. All of those "with God" are saints. However, saints in the canon of the Catholic tradition are "those Christians . . . who, by loving God and their neighbor, have lived their Christian faith in an extraordinary and exemplary manner and have been given the title of saint *by the official church.*"[35]

Since the thirteenth century, the Roman Catholic Church has developed a formal process of beatification and canonization. This policy effectively places some limitations on popular claims to sainthood. The Protestant reformers criticized what they considered to be saint "worship" at the expense of the true worship of God. Martin Luther sardonically wrote: "If someone has a toothache, he fasts and prays to St. Apollonia; if he fears danger from fire, he makes St. Lawrence his helper in distress; if he is afraid of the plague, he makes his vows to St. Sebastian or St. Ottila; Rochus is invoked for eye disease, Blaise for sore throats, while St. Anthony of Padua returns lost objects."[36] Erasmus voiced a similar criticism but approved the veneration of saints as holy models. In his view, their greatest legacy was their lives.[37]

The Catholic Church historically has been sensitive to the charge that it "deifies" saints and invests them with specific supernatural powers, but it has not retreated from its recognition of the significance of the saint. At Vatican II (1962–65), for example, the council fathers warned against the adoration of saints, but in the end, they reinforced the role of the saints as a path to worship God. According to the Vatican documents, "Our companionship with the saints joins us to Christ," and "for our own greater good and that of the Church, we seek from the saints example in their way of life, fellowship in their communion, and aid by their intercession."[38]

The major role of the saints is their intercession, which "is their most exalted service to God's plan. We can and should ask them to intercede for us and for the whole world."[39] In the Christian tradition, the first saints whose intercession was sought were the martyrs—those who had literally laid down their lives for Christ. The first wave of saints were inevitably those martyred by the Roman authorities, and their lives became an essential part of the foundation of the church.

Catholic doctrine teaches that saints have a special relationship with Christ and, through Christ, with God the Father. According to one source, "Prompted by this disinterested love, the saint offers in Christ and with Christ his merits and prayers for wayfarers, becoming their advocate and protector: that is to say, he intercedes for them with Christ and through Him with the Father."[40]

Roman Catholicism also teaches that God would not have left the saving community, the church, without a guide who is infallible in matters of faith and morals; that this legatee was St. Peter; and that St. Peter's successor is the bishop of Rome. Catholics believe that only Jesus and his mother were preserved from sin, so only they may be termed impeccable. It follows then that the bishop of Rome is not free from the possibility of grave sin and error in conducting his personal life or even in governing the church. Infallibility is said to be operative only "when the Roman pontiff, in discharge of his office as shepherd and teacher of all Christians, in accord with his supreme apostolic authority, defines a doctrine concerning faith or morals to be held by the whole Church."[41] The more sweeping Twelver Shi'i view of the preservation from all error of the Prophets and Imams appears to Twelvers as a logical consequence of the Logos-nature of the Qur'an, the willfulness of human nature, and human freedom.

Both Catholicism and Shi'ism emphasize the place of intermediaries and intercessors in their faith systems. These figures act as sacred connectors who help bind the human and the divine and as special channels to God through whom the faithful can send their prayers and petitions. Finally, these intercessors act as guides and guardians, and their lives serve as powerful role models.

Many of the greatest saints in both traditions were also martyrs. The first eleven Imams are believed to have died as martyrs, ten of the twelve disciples of Christ were martyred, and the first thirty-three Roman popes died as martyrs. Martyrdom seals sainthood in religious systems. Who better to intercede for one than someone who has "borne witness" to God by making the ultimate sacrifice? Roman Catholics and Twelver Shi'is would agree that God is accessible to individual prayer and that there is still much virtue and profit to the faithful in seeking the assistance of these great friends of God.

4

REDEMPTIVE
SUFFERING
AND
MARTYRDOM

A leading Shiʻi intellectual and cleric has explained the essence of martyrdom in the following words: "The *shahid* [martyr] can be compared to a candle whose job it is to burn out and get extinguished in order to shed light for the benefit of others. The *shuhada* [martyrs] are the candles of society. They burn themselves out and illuminate society. If they do not shed their light, no organization can shine. . . . Had they not shed their light on the darkness of despotism and suppression, humanity would have made no progress."[1] English Catholicism's best-known martyr, Thomas Becket, has been described as a "bright candle on God's candlestick."[2] An important element in the analogy of martyr as candle is that the candle must burn itself out in a public and political setting. In order to give "witness" (the meaning of Greek *martyr*), after all, one must have others to whom to bear witness. Martyrdom is the "most dramatic symbol of defiance and condemnation that a man or woman can achieve, a display of individuality sealed and sanctified by death. It strikes at the legitimacy of the dominant group."[3] In the Catholic tradition, the establishment that the Christian believers challenged was the Roman Empire. In Shiʻi Islam, the "dominant group of the day" consisted of the Meccan elite and the various Sunni religious regimes that harshly opposed "the People of the House of the Prophet" (*Ahl al-Bayt*). In martyrdom, "death is swallowed up in victory" (I Corinthians 15:54).

Suffering and martyrdom are central themes in both Islam and Christianity. The theme of *redemptive* suffering is especially emphasized in Roman Catholicism and Twelver Shiʿism. The early Christian church witnessed the growth of a cult of martyrs whose commitment was no less genuine than that of Shiʿi martyrs. St. Ignatius, the second-century bishop of Antioch, for example, eagerly sought martyrdom. On his way to the arena in Rome after his arrest for failure to worship the emperor's gods, where he was to face savage lions, he wrote to the Christians in Rome:

> Oh, may the beasts prepared for me be my joy! And I pray that they may be found ready for me. I will even coax them to make short work of me. And should they be unwilling to attack me, I will myself compel them. Pardon me—I know very well where my advantage lies. At last I am well on the way to being a disciple. Fire, cross, struggles with wild beasts, wrenching of bones, mangling of limbs, crunching of the whole body, cruel tortures of the devil—let these come upon me, provided only that I make my way to Jesus Christ.[4]

Over the years, the church developed a system of recognition of those who suffered persecution for their beliefs. Those who were put to death were called martyrs. Those who were persecuted for their faith but not killed were termed confessors. After the wave of Roman persecution, many saints who led exemplary and holy lives received the not insignificant title of "confessor." The Catholic Church has preserved these distinctions and continues to emphasize the significance of martyrs and confessors.

Redemption, in the sense of deliverance from sin, is a necessary part of both Catholic and Twelver teaching. Catholic theology emphasizes the deep offense of the first humans and the inherited sin of their offspring. Jesus is quoted as saying, "The Son of Man did not come to be served but to serve, and to give his life as a ransom for many" (Mark 10:45). The death of Jesus is thus a ransom, but in the past, some theologians explained the death of Jesus as the *substitution* of a sinless victim for a guilty humanity. Protestant theology still often accepts this interpretation. The offensiveness of this notion to the idea of God's justice is obvious. Rather, Roman Catholic theology has come to hold that Jesus suffered *on behalf* of humanity, in a free act of moral solidarity that is still part of his legacy to the church. The historic event of his death is seen as the instrument of God for producing the grace that will deliver humanity from sin.[5] This deliverance from sin is still in progress. Thus martyrs, those who "put on Christ" and follow him to "bear witness," may associate or be one with the redemptive suffering of Christ.

Moreover, this work of redemption is accomplished through the Spirit of God, which the death and resurrection of Jesus breathed into his followers. St. Paul says clearly, "This Good News is about Jesus Christ our Lord, who in the order of the spirit, the spirit of holiness that was in him, was proclaimed Son of God in all his power through his resurrection from the dead and through him we received grace and our apostolic mission to preach the obedience of faith to all nations in his name" (Romans 4–6). Thus, "the Risen Christ becomes the redemptive source of social reform and the cause of personal conversion."[6]

Finally, in Christian history, the martyrs are seen as blessed intercessors. The "souls of the martyrs" in the Book of Revelation (6:9–11) plead with God for justice but also for mercy. Martyrs, as we have seen, were the first to be revered as saints. With the passing of time, monks and nuns were thought to "offer themselves as a living sacrifice to God, dedicated to His service and pleasing to Him" (Romans 12:1), and to serve as "witnesses," hence martyrs.

Islam does not accept the idea of "original sin" or of the crucifixion of Jesus and his resurrection on the third day. Martyrdom "in the way of God," death in His service, is highly commended in the Qur'an; the souls of the martyrs are "alive" and are thought to go directly to paradise without waiting for the resurrection. Sunni Islam sees no need for any doctrine of redemption. God delivers the faithful who "believe and do good works" from sin. But Shi'i Islam is deeply conscious of the sin of the Muslim community after the death of the Prophet.

According to the Shi'is, the Muslims had not "believed and done good works"; they had rejected Muhammad's chosen successor and shed each other's blood. Their works were not good, and they were led astray by leaders who were not the Imams that God had chosen for them. All of the Imams, but Imam Husayn in particular, saw clearly that the Muslims were going astray, and all suffered on behalf of their followers, the followers of truth. Husayn and the other Imams freely offered their lives in acts of moral solidarity with their coreligionists, with compassion for the sins of the Muslims. Thus they "opened wide the gates of intercession," and their suffering had redemptive power. According to Mahmoud Ayoub, "This intercession is the direct reward of the sufferings of the entire family of the Prophet, and of Husayn especially, as his status could be attained only through martyrdom. Redemption in Shiʻi piety must be understood within the context of intercession."[7] Those who suffered in support of the Imams participate in this redemptive power and in the intercession of the Imams and the saints. This helps explain the great power of the idea of martyrdom in Shiʻi Islam.

In Catholic teaching, Christ's life, death, and resurrection are deeply redemptive events. Death and resurrection were necessary for humankind's redemption. As stated in the Gospel of John, "Unless the grain of wheat falls into the ground and dies, it remains just a grain of wheat. But if it dies, it brings forth much fruit" (12:24–25).

According to Shiʻi beliefs, the resurrection of the Imams lies ahead, with the resurrection of all of the dead. But on the day of resurrection and judgment, the Imams will intercede for the Muslims. Their death too is seen as "bring[ing] forth much fruit."

The continuing force of martyrdom remains relevant both in Shiʻi Islam and in Roman Catholicism. In Shiʻism, the reality of suffering and martyrdom results from the intertwined nature of religion, society, and politics. In Roman Catholicism, the division of church and state and the lessening of persecution have deemphasized the importance of the experience of martyrdom. Despite this difference in emphasis, the drama of suffering and the legends of martyrdom remain institutionalized, living, integral parts of the respective faith systems.

MARTYRDOM AND POLITICS

Martyrdom is more than a religious act; it is a political statement. According to one scholar, "Martyrdom is a political act affecting the allocation of power between two societies, or between a subgroup and the larger society."[8] During the first three centuries of Christianity, the Roman authorities increasingly considered the movement a direct threat to their authority and acted accordingly. Imam Husayn's march to Karbala represented a political challenge to the caliphate. Husayn's campaign, in the context of the time, can be described as a revolutionary act. Ayatollah Motahhari argued that a *shahid* "is one who, by his courage and death, infuses new blood into an otherwise anaemic society."[9]

The political ramifications of martyrdom are evident throughout history. The Christian martyrs died in challenging some kind of establishment. The story of Joan of Arc, who resisted the unjust English occupation of France, is a case in point. In the contemporary world, large numbers of Shiʿi believers have died in Lebanon and Iran. In Lebanon, young Shiʿis have challenged Israeli authority by turning themselves into human bombs. From the perspective of the Shiʿi population, these young men and women are *shahids*, or martyred heroes. From the point of view of the Israelis, however, they are terrorists whose actions kill and maim innocent people. The same scenario existed in the Iran-Iraq War, when Saddam Hussein invaded Iran in September 1980. Badly outgunned and overmatched technologically, Iran became a nation of martyrs as hundreds of thousands of young people died in support of their country, their leader Ayatollah Khomeini, and their religion.

Politically, martyrdom in Shiʿism can be a potent force. For example, on October 16, 1983, Lebanese Shiʿis were commemorating ʿAshura in the south Lebanese town of Nabatiyya when an Israeli military convoy, in a blatant display of insensitivity, tried to force its way through an emotional passion procession attended by 50,000 people. The Shiʿis, angered by the intrusion, mobbed the convoy, and the panicky Israeli troops opened fire, killing at least two Shiʿis and wounding many others. The Shiʿis considered the Israeli action a brutal intrusion and began an anti-Israeli campaign in south Lebanon. Those who were killed became instant martyrs, and the Israelis found themselves identified with the hated troops of Yazid, who had killed Imam Husayn and his small band of followers in 680. Shiʿi clerics condemned Israel and urged their followers to combat the invaders. Thus, the Nabatiyya incident sparked a long and costly struggle in which the Shiʿis sought martyrdom against Israeli forces. In so doing, they proved that they were willing to do more than fight and, if necessary, kill. They were willing to die.

The Israelis had been warned many times about Shiʿi power and commitment. One Israeli scholar, for example, had been told by a Lebanese Shiʿi: "Do not join those who murdered Husayn, because if you bring the Shiʿis to identify with the history of their suffering, the enmity that will be directed at you will have no bounds and no limits. You will have created for yourselves a foe whose hostility will have a mystical nature and a momentum which you will be unable to arrest."[10]

An examination of the historical and political record could lead to the conclusion that Christian martyrdom is quite different from Shi'i Islamic martyrdom. There is an element of pacifism in Catholic teachings. Jesus may have said that he came to bring "not peace, but a sword," but when Peter took up a sword against the High Priest's servant, Jesus admonished him. The apostles were neither soldiers nor warriors. Christian martyrs are remembered as walking quietly and serenely to their deaths. As we know, many early Christians were forced to apostatize by the Roman authorities. Only a very small minority of Christians were martyrs, yet their equanimity in the face of cruel death gave force to the Christian message.

But although Imam 'Ali is remembered as "the lion of Islam" who despatched hundreds of enemy soldiers to their eternal recompense and the Prophet was a noted strategist who led campaigns, the later Imams were not known for their martial skills and scarcely participated in military campaigns. Imam Husayn and his companions carried arms only for self-defense when they marched to Karbala and used them in a hopeless struggle.

One authority on martyrdom has developed a typology that compares politically "growth-producing" martyrdom to actively belligerent expansive martyrdom. In his view, "Christian communities within the Roman Empire were a politically crescive minority. The martyrs of this minority suffered passively, inviting violence but inflicting only moral or psychological pressure on the adversary. An expansive Islam in its early centuries exemplifies the self-determining society. Its martyrs were active and belligerent."[11] This distinction is useful but should be applied very carefully. Some saints and martyrs in Christianity were military figures and are invoked as protectors, including George, Theodore, Sergius, Martin, Maurice, Demetrius, and Louis. The militant side of Western Christianity is also visible in the Crusades, military orders, and the Inquisition as it grew out of the crusade against the Albigensians. One might argue that Islam, with its strong ethical impulse to combat evil and tyranny, produced martyrs of an active nature, whereas Christianity produced more pacifistic martyrs.

In Shi'ism and Catholicism alike, the passion and death of Christ and Imam Husayn are commemorated every day of every year. In Catholicism, this daily commemoration is the Mass. In addition, yearly during the Lenten season (especially during Holy Week and on Good Friday), Christ's crucifixion and death represent profound spiritual re-creations in the life of the practicing Roman Catholic. Likewise, in Shi'ism, the death of Imam Husayn at Karbala is vividly recalled throughout the year in Shi'i mosques, prayer sessions, and devotional readings. Every year, during the month of Muharram, Shi'is mourn collectively. The first ten days of Muharram are days of sorrow. The actual death of Imam Husayn is recalled on the tenth of Muharram ('Ashura), and the month is marked by ceremonies, fasting, and prayer recitations.

MOURNING CEREMONIES AND PASSION PLAYS

With the exception of the final, triumphant resurrection of Christ, Holy Week in Roman Catholic practice is not unlike the ten days of Muharram as commemorated by the Shi'is. Catholics begin Holy Week by contemplating and meditating on the passion of Jesus. The lamenting believers practice a wide variety of enactments of the passion, including recitations of the stations of the cross, in which they revisit each of fourteen stops along Christ's final route. The first station is entitled "Jesus Condemned to Death," and the inscription at the final stop reads "Jesus Is Laid in the Tomb." Each of the fourteen recitations begins with the prayer: "We adore you O Christ, and we bless you, because by your holy cross you have redeemed the world."

The Catholic tradition of fasting and abstaining from eating meat on Wednesday (the day Jesus was betrayed) and Friday (the day he was put to death) during Lent and the long vigil on Good Friday are constant remembrances of Jesus' passion. Special ceremonies are conducted during what is known as the Forty Hours Devotion, commemorating the time that passed from the moment of Jesus' death to the morning of his resurrection. Prayer rituals dwell on the five wounds suffered by Jesus and the seven words that he uttered while hanging on the cross. Often, Catholics fast during this time. Other special ceremonies include the adoration of the cross, the symbol and instrument of Christ's sacrifice. This involves prostration and kissing the foot of the cross, which in Germany is known as "creeping to the cross" (*zum Kreuz kriechen*). At the same time, the clergy, dressed in black vestments, emphasize the suffering and death of Jesus in their sermons and homilies.

Good Friday has been a time for mourning processions. In many European countries, especially in Spain, penitent laypeople, wearing hoods, carrying lighted candles, and often barefoot, walk for miles in such processions. The practice spread to Spain's colonies, and in Venezuela, for example, the Good Friday processions can last 4–5 hours. In order to extend the time, the pilgrims take three steps forward and two steps backward. In India, Catholics perform the "purana," a service of weeping and wailing during the Good Friday mourning period that is reminiscent of Shi'i passion ceremonies. Finally, the suffering of Christ is stressed repeatedly in prayers such as the following: "Hail, Precious Blood flowing from the wounds of our crucified Lord Jesus Christ, and washing away the sins of the whole world."[12]

Shi'i Muslims have an equally elaborate and intense mourning season, primarily during the month of Muharram. The institutionalization of Imam Husayn's act of martyrdom is evidenced by such sites as *Husayniyyas* (or *ma'tams*) and such ceremonies as *rawzas*. *Husayniyyas* or *ma'tams* are structures (usually separate from mosques) where Twelver Shi'is gather during Muharram to commemorate the martyrdom of Imam Husayn and his companions. *Rawzas* are meetings that take place in private settings in which members of the *'ulama* read emotional narrations of the tragedy at Karbala.

Catholics and Shi'is have long histories of mourning processions and passion plays. In Shi'ism, the passion plays are called *ta'ziyyas*, dramatic religious rituals that reenact onstage the Karbala tragedy. Although their roots can be traced to the Safavid period (1501–1722), Islamic passion plays achieved their full form in Iran in the middle of the nineteenth century. The productions were first held in town squares and courtyards but later were conducted in special theaters called *takiyyas* that represented the plain of Karbala. The action of the *ta'ziyya* revolves around the central figure of Husayn. The spectators in these passion plays are in many ways active participants; the audience grieves and weeps along with the actors onstage. Often this grieving process is connected as much to an individual's personal problems as to the sorrowful events unfolding onstage. Many Iranologists view the mourning process in Shi'i religious rituals as a kind of psychological catharsis for citizens who suffer economic deprivation and political oppression. In the words of one Iranian philosopher: "The people mourning are not grieving for Husayn; they are grieving for themselves."[13]

Besides reenacting the bloody events as they transpired at Karbala, the *ta'ziyya* confronts directly the issues of martyrdom, intercession, and forgiveness. In some scripts, for example, the Prophet Muhammad appears to the suffering Husayn: "O Husayn . . . Martyrdom is indeed the crown; trials bring thee near to God and establish a close union between Him and thee. Think not about thy former trials. Let the tree of intercession bear fruit, and bestir thyself now on behalf of the sinners amongst my people."[14]

In this script, after enduring terrible suffering, the third Imam forgives the sinners: "O my friends, be ye relieved from grief, and come along with me to the mansions of the blest. Sorrow has passed away; it is now time for joy and rest." According to many observers, "As a Passion play, it [the ta'ziyya] is strongly reminiscent of the death of Christ."[15]

In Europe during the Middle Ages, religious drama that focused on the life, passion, and death of Christ was extremely popular. Passion plays have their origin as early as the tenth century and were first performed by monks and clergy in churches. They flourished in the fourteenth and fifteenth centuries and persisted into the eighteenth century. Like the ta'ziyya, these plays became one of the chief ways in which common people could manifest their faith. They were also staged in town squares and fields and later in theaters built especially for the purpose. Hence, there has always been a strong element of folk religion in these observances. Many of these plays reenacted major moments of salvation history, from the creation to the resurrection. Although the Christian passion plays have lost some of their color and appeal in the Western world, they are still produced and attended by large numbers of Christians. Two of the better-known examples of contemporary passion plays are those staged at Oberammergau in Bavaria in Germany and in the Black Hills of South Dakota in the United States.

The Oberammergau Passionsspiel has been presented with few interruptions every ten years since 1634. More than half a million pilgrims attend this spectacular performance each season. Held in a modern open-air theater during the summer, the play lasts for over seven hours and utilizes the services of approximately 500 actors. Like Shi'is, who see their own lives and suffering in the ta'ziyya, the pilgrims who attend the Oberammergau play come "not only to see a theater, but rather to find answers to questions which perplex them, questions of isolation, questions of frustration. They seek answers and they find them by identifying themselves with the events of the Passion."[16]

Also part of the venerable history of reenacting Christ's last days is the passion play of the Norbertine monks of Kappenberg at Luenen in Rhineland Germany, which was brought to the United States in 1932. Since that time, the passion play has been performed in Spearfish, South Dakota, in the Black Hills, where a total of some 3 million people have traveled to participate in the event. Another 6 million have attended annual performances of the play on tour or at the troupe's theater in Lake Wales, Florida. Attending the Black Hills passion play has thus become a kind of pilgrimage in which millions of Christians can witness a powerful and professional reenactment of the passion and death of Christ.

The passion plays developed out of holy processions and pilgrimages that can still be seen in both the Shi'i and the Catholic worlds. Shi'i processions consist of black-clad young men beating their breasts in eerie unison while shouting slogans of praise in memory of the Imams. Wheeled platforms carrying actors who depict memorable scenes from Karbala rumble along the parade route. While shouting lamentations concerning the suffering of Husayn and his followers at Karbala, young men sometimes flagellate themselves with chains and slash their foreheads with swords. Such emotional events continue to take place in Iran, Iraq, Bahrain, and Pakistan.

In a poor Shi'i village in Bahrain in October 1983, one of the authors witnessed firsthand such a Muharram passion parade. For hours, the parade moved down the narrow dusty street of the village of Sannabis. Groups of younger men drew blood when they beat themselves with chains (*zanjirs*) and then used rags to wipe away the blood that spurted from their foreheads. They threw the bloody cloths to the crowd lining both sides of the narrow unpaved street. Two obsolete ambulances that carried the badly injured marchers to nearby medical facilities were an integral part of the parade. This particular passion procession carried deep social and political meaning. The Ma'tam Bin Saloum sponsored a riderless horse with replicas of Imam Husayn's green turban and sword attached to the saddle. Among the chanting marchers were individuals who carried placards and banners that presented political demands in Arabic. One huge banner carried by representatives from Ma'tam Bin Zabar, for example, included the words "equality," "unity," "God," "justice," "freedom," and "reform."

Passion parades, flagellations, and reenactments of the terrible suffering of martyrs and heroes can be seen throughout Western religious history as well. In Perugia in Italy in the thirteenth century, for example, "hundreds or even thousands, preceded by the cross and the clergy, made their way through the city, chanting and crying out for peace, scourging themselves to blood."[17] In rural areas of Spain, the Philippines, and Latin America, the passion parades often include actors who, playing the role of Christ, wear a crown of thorns and endure an actual crucifixion, though not to the death.

The Shiʿi tradition of memorializing suffering and martyrdom is more complex and emotional than the Catholic commemoration of the passion and death of Jesus. The Shiʿi commemoration is a profound ceremony of grief, punctuated throughout by cries of sadness and incessant weeping. The object is to move people to tears because those who weep for Husayn are believed to be pardoned for their sins. The Catholic ceremonies are somewhat more restrained, are less protracted, and do not permeate both the public and private spheres in the same way. Whereas the events at Calvary involved the death of a God-man who brought victory from defeat and joy from sorrow by rising from the dead, the tragedy at Karbala was marked by the martyrdom of a holy Imam and some seventy others who had no such happy ending. There is no Easter after the Shiʿi Good Friday.

Despite these differences, the similarities between Catholicism and Shiʿism concerning the martyrdoms and deaths of Jesus Christ and Imam Husayn are noteworthy. The redemptive deaths of Imam Husayn and Jesus Christ became the sources and symbols of martyrdom in Shiʿism and Catholicism, respectively. Husayn's martyrdom was only the most significant of a long series of Shiʿi martyrdoms.[18] Both Catholics and Shiʿis believe that the martyr courageously chose death when he could have chosen to forgo it; both see the deaths as ultimately victorious; both view these acts of supreme martyrdom as redemptive in nature; both hold these deaths to be at the very center of their faith systems; and both have constructed an elaborate system of ceremonies around these tragedies that are reenacted on a regular basis. In this way, these sacrifices remain vivid parts of the lives of the believers. The example of martyrdom radiates outward from the central martyr, whether Jesus or Husayn, to thousands of saints in each religion who are themselves martyrs and confessors. Catholics recite numerous prayers and lamentations in remembrance of a suffering and martyred Christ, and Shiʿis repeatedly voice supplications of great grief to the martyred Imam Husayn.

The reality of suffering and martyrdom has strengthened the faith systems of both Catholics and Shiʿis. An external adversary who is willing to resort to the most inhumane and terrible methods of compulsion becomes a force for unity and community among the persecuted group. At another level of analysis, the willingness to make the ultimate sacrifice stands as a living model that provides the path to redemption and salvation for all believers. It is the martyr who triumphs in the end. An eminent scholar of Shi'ism has explained this conclusion in the following words:

> The lamentations for Husayn enable the mourners not only to gain an assurance of divine forgiveness, but also contribute to the triumph of the Shi'i cause. Accordingly, Husayn's martyrdom makes sense on two levels: first, in terms of a soteriology not dissimilar from the one invoked in the case of Christ's crucifixion: just as Christ sacrificed himself on the altar of the cross to redeem humanity, so did Husayn allow himself to be killed on the plains of Karbala to purify the Muslim community of sins; and second, as an active factor vindicating the Shi'i cause, contributing to its ultimate triumph.[19]

5

CATHOLIC MYSTICS
AND ISLAMIC SUFIS:
THE CONFLUENCE
OF EXPERIENCE

We have created man, and We know what his soul
whispers within him, for We are closer to him than
his jugular vein.
    Qur'an 50:16
God is innermost in each and every thing, just as its own
being is innermost in the thing.
[Deus est unicuique intimus sicut esse proprium rei est
intimum ipsi.]
    St. Thomas Aquinas, quoted in Etienne Gilson,
    The Spirit of Thomism (1964)

Roman Catholicism and Shi'i Islam share a deep commit-
ment to the internal and experiential dimensions of faith. Both traditions
have long enjoyed closer relations in these dimensions than in the more
formal, external realm of life. In this chapter, we will compare the realm of
mysticism in the Catholic and Shi'i traditions. Because it is a distortion in
this context to cut Catholicism and Shi'ism out of their place in Christianity
and Islam, we will often compare the Christian and Muslim experiences in
our discussion of the mystical. In so doing, we will, of course, be analyzing
Catholicism and Shi'ism as integral parts of the greater religious whole.

Mysticism is a search for the experience of ultimate reality. In theistic
systems, it is a search for God. Mystics tend to place a low priority on the

material aspects of life. In both Christianity and Islam, mystics tend also to be ascetics or at least to have experienced an ascetic period.

THE *ZAHIR* AND THE *BATIN*

For the theologian al-Ghazali, the esoteric science (*'ilm al-batin*) is one of the six disciplines that make up the scholarly articulation of Islam, along with theology, principles of jurisprudence, the branches of jurisprudence, *hadith,* and *tafsir* (explication of the Qur'an).[1] Muslim mystics, Shi'i or Sunni, generally follow al-Ghazali in stressing the importance of both the *zahir* (exoteric) and the *batin* (esoteric), the external and the internal. The path to God is traversed on two complementary levels. The external route, the *zahir*, is open to everyone and consists of the laws, customs, practices, and doctrines of the religion. The *batin* is the internal consciousness whereby the believer "tastes God" (in the words of al-Ghazali). The mystics believe that in order to move to the deeper level of *batin*, one must first walk the path of *zahir*. Understanding the fundamental doctrine is essential in both Shi'ism and Catholicism. For Christians, "believing" precedes all else in religion. For Muslims, practicing the *shari'a*, or Muslim law, is paramount. Shi'is, for their part, must accept the existence of one God, His messengers, the Qur'an, the *shari'a*, and the *sunna* (traditions) while also acknowledging the special position of 'Ali and the Imams. Once Shi'is are good practicing believers on the *zahir* track, they are prepared to move to the interior dimensions of their belief system. Shi'ism carries an irreducible esoteric element. The same may be said, *mutatis mutandis*, of Catholicism.

In order to make room in their lives for the experience of God, Christian and Muslim mystics stress simplicity and self-denial and elevate the importance of values such as poverty, patience, generosity, and obedience. Early Christians and Muslims alike viewed Jesus as a model for mystical religion. Jesus' simple way of life appealed to Muslims as well as to Christians. In one of the *hadith*, the Prophet quotes Jesus as saying: "My seasoning is hunger, my undergarment is fear of Allah, my outergarment is wool, my fire in winter is the rays of the sun, my lamp is the moon, my riding beast is my feet, and my food and fruit are what the earth brings forth. At night I have nothing and in the morning I have nothing, yet there is no one on earth richer than I." Another *hadith* quotes Jesus as saying, "He who seeks after the world is one who drinks sea water; the more he drinks, the more his thirst increases until it kills him."[2] Similarly, according to Imam 'Ali,

"The Prophet used to eat on the ground, and sat like a slave. He repaired his shoe with his hand, and patched his clothes with his hand. He would ride an unsaddled ass and would seat someone behind him."[3]

The early Christian mystics institutionalized their existence through the establishment of monasteries, hermitages, *lauras*,[4] and secluded organizations of various kinds in which they dedicated their lives to the search for unity with God. Mystics represented a special threat to the status quo because they were largely immune to material incentives and completely committed to their cause. Because their priorities were not of this world, they did not respond predictably to social and political pressures. The greatest Christian mystics, in fact, often died as martyrs.

By the time of the appearance of the Prophet Muhammad in the seventh century, ascetics seeking experience of the divine were found widely throughout Christendom. Muhammad and his contemporaries were well aware of them, and they had an impact on the Muslims. Sufism found a responsive chord in the faith and practice of Christian mystics such as Ephraim the Syrian, Dionysius of Syria, and Isaac of Nineveh.[5] When Abu Bakr sent Muslim troops into Syria, he enjoined them to allow monks to continue their devotions.[6] Christian writers of the time attest to Muslim respect for monks and Christian holy places. Meaningful dialogue took place between Christian and Muslim devotees during the first century of Islamic history. As Islam developed and spread its message across the world, mysticism became an even more popular movement. Sufism sank deeply into the history and consciousness of both Sunnis and Shiʿis. The Sufis were especially gifted in winning over people from other religious traditions and thus became an important missionary force.

ORDERS AND BROTHERHOODS

In Islam, among the mystical orders and brotherhoods that have institutionalized the Sufi spirit are the Qadiris, the Bektashis, the Mawlawis, the Niʿmatullahis, and the Nurbakhshis. Mystical life does not take place in cloisters but in residential institutions called *khanqahs* or meetinghouses called *tekkes* or *zawiyas*. Political exigencies throughout history have influenced the strength of these brotherhoods. Today, many Sufi orders continue to exert social and political influence, including the Niʿmatullahis in Iran, the Qadiris and Nurbakhshis in Central Asia, the Rifaʿis in Iraq and Kuwait, and the Shadhilis, Ahmadis, and Burhanis in Egypt. In Catholicism, the closest counterparts to the Sufi brotherhoods are orders such as the Benedictines, the Franciscans, the Dominicans, which radiate out into lay society through their "third orders," and the Jesuits. Catholic Christianity envisions separate spheres for secular and spiritual powers and activities. Hence, the Catholic orders have often enjoined, but not always practiced, disengagement from political questions, not unlike the Sufi orders.

In Central Asia and the Caucasus, mystical movements such as the Naqshbandi and Qadiri orders kept Islam alive during the dark, oppressive days of Soviet communist rule. After the collapse of the Soviet Union, the efforts of the Chechen liberation movement, based on the Qadiri and Naqshbandi brotherhoods, brought the Russian army to a standstill. Over the years, the Sufi movement in Chechnya has provided coherence that enabled the Chechens to resist Russian oppression. The *dhikr* (the chanted "remembrance of God"), in particular, fostered a special esprit among the people of Chechnya. Between 1925 and 1960, the Soviet government destroyed every mosque or shrine in Chechnya. The Soviets, however, were unable to eradicate the Sufi tradition and failed to penetrate the Sufi societies in Chechnya.

In each tradition, the role of the spiritual director or guide is of vital importance. An independent quest for mystical experience is regarded with mistrust. Early Christian mystics rallied around a father figure, the Abba, who later evolved into the abbot. Seekers after the mystical life are urged to have a wise confessor, or a director, who can tell them if they are being led astray by subjective experience and can prescribe prayers, fasting, or discipline as needed. Islamic Sufism puts the matter succinctly: "One who has no *murshid* [guide] has the devil as a *murshid*."

Celibacy has been seen as a positive religious practice in Roman Catholicism, but although it is not unknown in the Islamic world, it is viewed with great suspicion there. Muhammad is quoted as condemning celibacy: "I marry women. Whosoever turns away from my practice is none of mine."[7] The Qur'an states that God created mankind male and female (46:13). This duality continues through all of creation: "Glory to Him who created pairs of all that earth produces, out of themselves, and of what they know not. . . . Neither can the sun overtake the moon, nor the night outpace the day" (36:36, 40). In the ideal Islamic society, men glory in masculinity and women in femininity, and each are rewarded for this. Each gender was created for immortal glory with God and must keep to its own role; the genders are expressions of God's attributes of power (*jalal*) and beauty (*jamal*). Transvestitism and "unisex" styles are viewed negatively. When man and woman unite appropriately, they approach perfection and become a symbol of union with the divine. This explains why Islamic marriage is seen as a civil contract—it regulates the terms so that this sacramental union may take place fittingly. This also helps explain the drive to keep the two sexes in separate spheres.[8]

Thus, what is seen as an esoteric truth in creation has far-reaching consequences in the external world and serves to illustrate the interplay of *zahir* and *batin*. In a similar way, the human and the divine are viewed as longing for a transcendent union: "God will produce a people He loves as they love Him" (Qur'an 5:54). Humankind is the eternal lover; God the eternal beloved. In the Catholic world, the erotic imagery of the Song of Songs has been read as celebrating the love between Christ and the church, of which marriage is a mystical reflection, according to St. Paul (Ephesians 5:32), but it has also been seen as glorifying the love of the soul for God.

There are a number of striking similarities in the external practices of Catholics and Shi'is. Such common practices include fasting and prayer, the use of rosaries and scapulars, and reliance on the role of nature and the environment in approaching the divine. The created world is full of divine signs for the Muslim; it was created through the Logos for the Catholic mystic, and may when properly contemplated reveal God. The practice of fasting during Ramadan is believed to have been patterned after the great fast of Christians during the time of Lent. Prayer five times a day was foreshadowed in Christianity by the prayers of the hours (prime, tierce, sext, none, and vespers) offered by monks and devout laity. In addition, in Sufi practice, as in the services in a monastic community, communal prayer involves repetition and chanting, which generates altered, sometimes ecstatic consciousness. *Dhikr* involves the invocation of God's names over an extended period of time. In Catholicism, the repetition of prayer occurs in observances such as the litanies and the rosary, in which the Ave Maria is repeated over fifty times.

Although the experience of mysticism is deeply revered in Sunni Islam, a number of influential Sufis have been Shi'is or have had Shi'i tendencies.[9] Imam 'Ali is, after all, an admired figure among Sunnis, a close associate of the Prophet, and one of the rightly guided first four successors of

Muhammad. 'Ali is also a major personality in the minds of Islamic mystics and has served as a model for them outwardly and inwardly. Many Sufi orders connect their origins to 'Ali and see him as a spiritual authority of great importance. The eleventh-century Sufi *shaykh* and saint 'Ali Hujwiri includes the first six Imams of the Twelvers among the great friends of God, or saints.[10] The distinction between Sunni and Shi'i Islam is of relatively little significance when assessing esoteric mysticism, or gnosis (*'irfan*). The correspondence is so clear that some Sunni scholars have viewed Sufism as a Trojan horse for the importation of Shi'ism to Sunni Islam, and some Shi'i scholars have looked askance at the Sufi brotherhoods because their adepts have threatened to trespass on the territory of the Imams. This is because Shi'ism is itself an esoteric tradition in its entirety, whereas Sunni Islam's esoteric aspect is largely found in Sufism.

From the very beginning, Shi'ism has contained elements conducive to the promotion of Sufism. These elements include devotion to the holy family of the Imams, an eschatological focus and preoccupation with the next world, a willingness to sacrifice self for other in martyrdom, and the nonestablishment nature of Shi'ism. In Sufism, the central guiding role of the *shaykh* or *pir* is generally similar to the position of the Imam or *mujtahid* in Shi'ism, and indeed in Shi'i orders, the *pir* or *murshid* is generally considered to be the mystical representative of the Imam. In the context of mysticism, the role of the "pole" (*qutb*) is easily understood by Shi'is. The chain that binds Sufis to their leaders, and through them to the Prophet, the *silsila*, is similar to the spiritual chain of Imams. The Imams are "the Friends of God," and the saints are called *imamzada*, or the "seed of the Imams." Shi'i believers seek the path to God through the Imams just as the Sufis seek union with God through following the path of the saints. The Shi'i, like the Sufi, is often an outsider, forced to challenge the ongoing formal power structure from the periphery and from a position of relative weakness. According to Henri Corbin, Shi'ism is the "sanctuary of Islamic esoterism."[11]

Throughout the history of Islam, there has been tension between the formal practitioners of the faith and the mystical movements of the Sufis. This tension exists in both Sunni and Twelver Islam. An excellent example of this conflict as it has waxed and waned over time can be seen in the case of Iran, the heartland of Twelver Shi'ism. In 1501, a thirteen-year-old leader named Shah Isma'il rode into Tabriz from the highlands of Anatolia and established the Safavid dynasty (1501–1722). In the process, he proclaimed Twelver Shi'ism as the official religion of the Safavid polity. Shah Isma'il himself was a mystic who traced his ancestry back to Shaykh Safi ad-Din of Ardebil (1252–1334). Shaykh Safi ad-Din was a Sufi saint and poet of considerable influence. Isma'il also penned mystical poems.

Shah Isma'il rode to power on the steed of mystical Shi'ism. His political movement was supported by numerous tribes (*oymaqs*) whose members believed fervently in esoteric causes. Once he became shah, however, Isma'il, though he remained the *murshid* or guide of his order, opened the state to Shi'i religious scholars who took a dim view of the enthusiasts of the mystical way. Twelver Shi'ism became the official religion of Iran. Scholars of other schools were persecuted and driven away, and Sufi brotherhoods other than that of the shah were proscribed. Under Shah Isma'il and his son Shah Tahmasb (1524–76), the Safavid *tariqa*, or mystical path, with the shah as its powerful *murshid*, was still a dominating Sufi force. At the same time, however, the early Safavid shahs imported Twelver Shi'i scholars known as *mujtahids*, who formed the religious scaffolding that buttressed the state. This launched 500 years of tension between the Shi'i *'ulama*, represented by these learned *mujtahids*, and the inherent tendencies of Sufism, which grew quietly just beneath the surface in Shi'i Iran. Although the *mujtahids* and the state dominated the scene in Iran, strong strains of Sufism have always been present in its culture. Sufism is omnipresent, for example, in the works of the great poets of Iran, where it can be shared by Sunnis and Shi'is, even by hedonists and the religious.

An excellent example is the work of Hafiz of Shiraz (d. 1389), a Sufi, apparently a Shi'i, and one of the greatest poets in any language, whose translated odes inspired even Goethe.[12] People from around the world make the pilgrimage to his tomb, some to ask for his intercession and some simply to pay homage to the author of magnificent poems. It is customary to seek guidance or tell one's fortune from the *ghazals* or "odes" of Hafiz by opening the book at random and putting one's finger on a verse. There is something there for everyone. Does he speak of earthly or divine loves? Is the distinction even valid for one who sees God in all things? He writes:

Love knows no difference between the cloister and the tavern;
   the radiance of the Friend's face illuminates all.

Where the business of the ascetic's cell is rightly done,
   is the sound of the Christians' gong, and the Cross.[13]

For many Iranians, a transcendent voice speaks through the ambiguous, haunting verses of this "memorizer of the Qur'an." One *ghazal*, "The House of Hope," serves as a useful example. In this *ghazal*, there is a unifying message: do not put your hope in this shaky world; you have a much higher destiny. Yet each two-line verse carries a separate thought:

The house of worldly hope is built on sand:
   bring wine; life's foundations are rooted in wind.
That man's will enslaves me who under this turquoise bowl
   burns bright for nothing that ties us down here.[14]
Shall I tell you what good news the angel of the Unseen
   brought me last night as I lay on the tavern floor?
"O keen-eyed royal falcon, whose perch is the Tree of Life,
   why is this corner of Affliction-town your nest?
"They whistle you home from the battlements of heaven;
   what will you do in this place of snares?"
Don't look to hold this tottering world to her promise,
   that old bride has deceived a thousand bridegrooms.
There is no permanence even in the smile of a rose;
   lament, enamored nightingale; you have ground for complaint.
And why should those who love poetry be jealous of Hafiz?
   To please with subtle words is the gift of God alone.[15]

In Iran, the Islamic mystics or Sufis strive for *'irfan* (gnosis, or esoteric knowledge), which Arab Sufis call *ma'rifa*. The continuing power and influence of *'irfan* in Iran are seen in the extraordinary personality of Ayatollah Ruhollah Khomeini. In the 1920s, Khomeini studied for six years with Mirza Muhammad 'Ali Shahabadi, a leading scholar of mysticism.[16] Like Shaykh Safi ad-Din of Ardebil and Shah Isma'il before him, Khomeini composed numerous mystical poems throughout his life. In the 1980s, he wrote dozens of mystical *ghazals*.[17] When he taught in Qum, Khomeini's courses on the philosophy of Islam emphasized the mystical. Indeed, as he led the movement that overthrew the shah and established the Islamic Republic, Khomeini was often condemned by the shah's policy elite for promoting *'irfan*. Other contemporary Iranian religious and political figures with special sensitivity to Islamic mysticism include Seyyed 'Ali Khamene'i, who replaced Khomeini as *faqih* (religious jurisconsult).

Politically, Sufis have often challenged the status quo and allied themselves with the forces aiming to topple the system. Once in power, however, the new leadership may turn on its Sufi allies and take on the nature of religious rigorism. The Safavid shahs discussed above are a case in point. Even the career of Ayatollah Khomeini reflects this pattern. Once he became involved in the struggle for political power, Khomeini adopted a position of unwavering support for the principles of Twelver Shi'ism while quietly contemplating his *'irfan* ideas.

As we noted in chapter 1, Shi'ism is divided into two schools of practice, the Usulis and the Akhbaris. The Usulis believe that every Shi'i should pray behind a *mujtahid*, who is ever available to help interpret the new and the different. The Usulis, therefore, profess the importance of living intermediaries who act as guides and guardians for the faithful. The Akhbaris, however, rely on the *hadith* and *akhbar* (reports) of earlier times and place the responsibility for interpretation on the individuals, who they believe are capable of making decisions for themselves through their own knowledge and through the teachings of learned past religious figures. The experience of mysticism cuts across this division, though the overwhelming majority of Shi'i Sufis belong to the Usuli school of thought.

In the Christian tradition, Protestants have generally viewed mysticism with distrust. Scholars have noted "the Protestant suspicion of mysticism."[18] One observer has written that "as a rule, Catholic cultures have always been more hospitable than Protestant cultures to the mystical, the miraculous, the supernatural."[19] Such statements may be oversimplified, but there is little doubt that Catholicism has a long history of mystical movements, reaching back to the desert fathers and beyond. Great mystics such as Paul, Augustine, Patrick, Bernard of Clairvaux, Francis of Assisi, Catherine of Siena, Teresa of Avila, and John of the Cross have shaped the development of Christianity and Catholicism.

CHRISTIAN MYSTICISM, TWELVER SHI'ISM, AND NATURE

Shi'i and Catholic mystics alike place heavy emphasis on nature and the environment. Deserts, gardens, fauna and flora, and water are central to mystical poetry and parables. The desert carries both real and symbolic meanings to Christian and Muslim believers. Outwardly terrifying, it is also a refuge where the soul may put aside worldly matters and be alone with the Creator. The early monks and many saints and mystics in Christianity lived in the desert, where they could avoid the snares of the sensual world. John the Baptist and Jesus often retreated to the desert to fast and pray. Holy hermits such as St. Paul of the Thebaid (d. ca. 347) and St. Antony of the Desert (d. 356) were extremely influential role models in early Christianity and in later Catholicism, and the first monasteries were established in the desert. Early Muslim mystics testified to their encounters with these desert monks.[20]

In Islamic piety, the desert also has special meaning. Sufi saints such as 'Abd al-Qadir al-Jilani (d. 1166) spent years in the desert in meditation and isolation. The massacre of Imam Husayn and his followers in 680 occurred in the desert near Karbala. Much of this saga of martyrdom focuses on the terrible thirst that consumed the men, women, and children after they were cut off from the water supply of the nearby Euphrates.

In Islam, the Qur'an promises the faithful "sublime gardens," and among peoples of the Middle East, the garden represents a special place of refuge, an oasis of relief and shelter in an otherwise harsh environment. The carpet, for example, represents a garden (hence, paradise), extended into the home. Flowers such as the rose are symbols of beauty and the beloved. The beloved is a figure for God, and the lover a figure for humanity. The nightingale is the lover of the rose. Animals, especially birds, are used to teach important exoteric and esoteric lessons. In both religious traditions, paradise is imagined as a luxuriant garden. The great thirteenth-century Persian mystic poet, Jalal ad-Din Rumi (d. 1273), emphasized the essence of physical nature in the following poem that compares the souls of mystics to fish in the sea of the divine:

> Earth and heaven are bucket and pitcher;
>   water is outside earth and heaven.
> Do you also speed forth from heaven and earth,
>   that you may behold water flowing from placelessness,
> That the fish of your soul may escape from this pool,
>   and sip water from the boundless sea.
> In that sea whose fishes are all Khidrs,[21] therein
>   the fish is immortal, immortal the water.
> From that vision came the light of the eye,

from that roof is the water in the spout;
From that garden are these roses of the cheeks,
     from that waterwheel the rosebower obtains water;
From that date-tree are the dates of Mary; that water[22]
     derives not from secondary causes and suchlike things.
Your soul and spirit will then become truly happy, when the
     water comes flowing towards you from hence.
Shake no more your rattle like a nightwatchman,
     for the water itself is the guardian of these fishes.[23]

In Catholic imagery, nature also plays an important role. The Spanish
Catholic mystic, St. John of the Cross, very likely influenced by Muslim
imagery,[24] makes many references to nature and the environment in his
poetry. In his haunting words:

My Beloved is the mountains,
And lovely wooded valleys,
Strange islands,
And resounding rivers,
The whistling of love-stirring breezes.
The tranquil night
At the time of the rising dawn,
Silent music,
Sounding solitude,
The supper that refreshes, and deepens love.[25]

A predecessor of John of the Cross in Spain was Ramon Lull, a Cata-
lan courtier, philosopher, and mystic born in Majorca around 1235. Lull
was conversant in Arabic, and his *Libre del contemplacio en deu* (Book of
the contemplation of God) was partly written in that language. This contemporary of Jalal ad-Din Rumi drew from some of the same sources as
the Spanish Muslim mystic Muhyi ad-Din Ibn al-ʿArabi (d. 1240), considered "the Greatest Shaykh" by many Sufis, who was active in Arabia and
Syria at this time. Lull believed that Christianity was the true faith, but he
praised Islam as closer to the truth than other religions because of its faith
in the unity of God, its practice of *dhikr,* and its belief in the virgin birth of
Jesus. His visions of Christ began around 1265, and in 1272, Lull had a great
vision of the entire universe reflecting the divine attributes, the *dignitates* or

"names" of God. His philosophical-romantic novel *Blaquerna*, about a wise and holy hermit who rises to become pope, closes with Blaquerna's "Book of the Lover and the Beloved."[26] At the Council of Vienne (1311–12), Lull was instrumental in having chairs of Hebrew, Arabic, and Syriac set up at universities in Paris, Oxford, Bologna, Salamanca, and Rome. Spiritually, he was a Franciscan, reflecting the Neoplatonism of Duns Scotus Erigena. Lull was certain that through the "Art" of the divine names, Muslims, Christians, and Jews would see divine matters similarly. In pursuit of this goal, Lull made several trips to Muslim lands. According to legend, he was martyred in Tunis around 1316 for seeking to convert Muslims to his faith. Lull was also charged with heresy in the West but was exonerated and beatified and is venerated in the Franciscan order and in Majorca, although he was never canonized. He had an undeniable influence on later Christian mystics, including the Renaissance mystical philosopher, Cardinal Nicholas of Cusa (d. 1464).[27]

In the Gospels, Jesus goes into the wilderness, finds refuge in the garden of olives, and dies an accursed death, hanged on a tree (the cross).[28] Born in a manger, accompanied by shepherds and animals, Jesus was the son of a carpenter, who worked wood with his hands. Jesus' closest disciples were fishermen, and many biblical stories relate incidents that took place on water or involved fish. In Western Christian monasteries, the monks are encouraged to create self-supporting communities, tilling the soil, raising fish and honey, and working with their hands close to nature. St. Francis of Assisi, the Christian *faqir* or poor man,[29] is remembered as a champion of nature and a friend of animals. In 1979, Pope John Paul II named St. Francis the *poverello* patron saint of ecologists.

The Sufis make an important comparison between the Prophet Muhammad and the Virgin Mary. Just as the Prophet was unlettered and symbolically ready to receive the Word of God, the Virgin was immaculate and ready to bear the Word of God. These human slates are seen as pure and free from intervening, intrusive elements. According to Frithjof Schuon, "This purity is the first condition for the reception of the Paracletic Gift, just as in the spiritual order chastity, poverty, humility, and other forms of simplicity or unity are indispensable for the reception of the Divine Light. . . . It may be added that the particular state in which the Prophet was immersed at the time of the Revelations is directly comparable to that of the Virgin when carrying or giving birth to the Child Jesus."[30]

The architecture of Roman Catholicism and that of Islam also have func-
tional similarities, despite the existence of wide-ranging differences in style
and ornament. Both traditions see the temple as a house of congregational
prayer, not simply a place of private devotion. God is believed to inhabit
the building through the acts that are done there in His name, and His presence is considered "real." Towers are prominent. In Islam, *manar* is the
Arabic and Farsi word for a beacon-tower (in Turkish, a minaret), a place
for the light of Islam to shine. These towers may or may not be used for
actually calling the faithful to prayer, but their existence marks the presence of Islam. In the case of Catholic church architecture, towers have been
used to house bells to call the faithful to Mass, pray for the deceased, and
mark devotions such as the Angelus morning, noon, and night. The chief
mosque or cathedral of a city traditionally dominates the surrounding area
and offers a place of peace in the bustling life of the community around it.

That Catholic mysticism and Sufi mysticism have much in common is
not surprising given the origins of these movements. Over the centuries,
a healthy cross-fertilization of ideas has occurred between these esoteric
systems. Shi'ism and Catholicism share twelve major characteristics at the
mystical level:

1. The search for the experience of transcendent reality, the essence
   of mysticism, is accepted by both religious systems.
2. Both emphasize asceticism and recognize the need to serve the
   poor, the oppressed, and the alienated.
3. They concur that the most important quest in life is to prepare for
   the next world.
4. They see a fundamental foundation of human existence in the
   esoteric experience and the core power of the *batin*.
5. Both foster the existence of mystical brotherhoods and the
   formation of living communities or orders.
6. Both envision a similar role for their holy figures.
7. Both recognize the significance of the charismatic leadership of
   the *pir* or *shaykh* or spiritual director.
8. They preach commitment to following the path to God even if it
   requires the ultimate act of martyrdom.
9. They stress the importance of unity with nature, community, and
   God Himself.

10. Both conduct elaborate ceremonies such as passion processions, prayer sessions, retreats, feast days, and periods of fasting.
11. They believe the mystical life may also be engaged with the world of politics and political issues.
12. Both find companionship and inspiration in the lives of conspicuous friends of God (saints), often through resort to their tombs and relics.

JESUS AND AL-HALLAJ

In the contemporary period, an interesting and meaningful link in the Catholic/Sufi/Shi'i connection was forged by the French Catholic scholar-priest Louis Massignon (1883–1962). Although he was not a Roman Catholic cleric but a married priest of the Melkite (Syro-Byzantine) Catholic Church, his great service was to persuade high circles in French and Roman Catholicism that Islam is a revealed religion. At the heart of the discussion were the life and ideas of an extraordinary tenth-century Sufi martyr known as Husayn ibn Mansur al-Hallaj.

Massignon was raised an agnostic and became a devoted Catholic after his contact with the faith of Muslims in the Arab world. He has been described by a leading exponent of Shi'i Islam as "perhaps the greatest academic scholar of Islam that the (Western) world has ever produced."[31] This greatness lay more in the *batin* realm than in the *zahir;* Massignon's scholarship may in places be faulted but not his profound empathy with the subject. He was a Catholic mystic in his own right, and his sensitive interpretation of Mansur al-Hallaj indicated his belief in the intertwined nature of Sufism and Catholic mysticism. As a French intellectual with access to the highest levels of the church, Massignon, in rediscovering and rehabilitating the ideas, life, and death of al-Hallaj, became a bridge between Catholic Christianity and Islam.[32]

Abu al-Mughith al-Husayn ibn Mansur al-Hallaj was born in the Fars province of Iran in 858. The son of a wool carder, he was a devout Muslim at an early age, memorizing the entire Qur'an and practicing the conventional religion. In his late teens, restless, bored, and unfulfilled spiritually, he began to search for deeper dimensions of his faith by studying with a number of Sufi masters, including the brilliant Abu al-Qasim al-Junayd of Baghdad. As he developed a strong mystical spirituality, al-Hallaj took his experience on the road, carrying messages of mystical religion far and wide.

Besides traveling to Mecca three times, he is said to have visited Turkey, India, and Central Asia. His blunt and intense proselytizing and his ecstatic utterances alienated both his Sufi masters and the Muslim scholars of the law. He also alienated the 'Abbasid political elite in Baghdad. The caliph at the time was al-Muqtadir (908–32).

The ninth and tenth centuries were a time of great ferment in the Middle East. The old system had broken down, and social and political incoherence shook society. On the one hand, the period witnessed enormous activity in the arts and sciences. On the other hand, personal corruption, injustice, social upheaval, political repression, and social inequity dominated the events of the day. The court basked in splendid luxury and ostentatious privilege, while the people were subjected to grinding poverty and near slavery. Shi'i activists of the Isma'ili sect challenged the Sunni establishment and took part in a number of powerful rebellions of the oppressed masses in the ninth century. A revolt of black slaves, known as the Zanj rebellion, threatened to bring down the 'Abbasid dynasty before the uprising was quelled in 883. Another serious challenge to the ruling elite followed in the so-called Qarmati (Carmathian) movement in the early tenth century.[33] These class rebellions shook the 'Abbasid system to the core. It was during this period of upheaval and instability that al-Hallaj traversed the region, calling for reform and personal and spiritual renewal.

In such a world of transition, rootless and alienated people turned against the traditional social, political, and religious systems and lost faith in the established religious leaders. Great numbers of people, all searching desperately for justice and meaning in their lives, flocked to new doctrines, philosophy, Shi'ism, and the Sufi message. In short, they sought new paths to ultimate meaning. In order to find this path and to traverse the internal world, they sought guides and guardians. Such a role was often played by the Sufi *shaykhs*. Because of the sociopolitical turmoil of the day and because of his personal charisma, direct approach, and increasingly intense mystical experiences, al-Hallaj found himself with a huge following. Meanwhile, he experienced powerful moments of ecstasy and became a man with a mission. This mission threatened the status quo, and al-Hallaj was arrested and imprisoned. The *'ulama* of Baghdad agreed that he should be put to death, and the caliph's *wazir*, Hamid, reportedly attended the execution of al-Hallaj and oversaw the death sentence.

A major scholar of Sufism concludes that "aside from the subtle problems of mystical love, political and social problems were at stake."[34] Refusing to compromise his faith or his ideals, al-Hallaj continued to spread his message of love and unity. He apparently often forcefully stated, "*Ana al-haqq:* I am Reality." Because "the Reality" is one of the ninety-nine "names" of God, this statement was interpreted by many Muslims to mean that al-Hallaj was claiming to be one with God, and it ultimately doomed him. Furthermore, it reminded Muslims of the Christian doctrine of the Incarnation. Partly because of his known admiration of Jesus, many of his contemporaries considered al-Hallaj to be an apostate, a crypto-Christian.

On March 26, 922, al-Hallaj was put to the death reserved in Islamic law for "those who war against God and His messenger, and hasten about the land to work corruption" (Qur'an 5:33). After he was scourged, his hands and feet were cut off, he was crucified, and his body was burned and the ashes thrown into the Tigris. While hanging on the gibbet, he forgave his enemies; indeed, he considered them instruments of God's plan that he die for his faith. Al-Hallaj reportedly prayed: "And these Your servants, gathered together to kill me . . . forgive them. For if you had revealed to them what You revealed to me, they would not have done this; had You withheld from me what You have withheld from them, I would never have been tried with this trial. To You be praise in all that you do; to You be praise in all that You will."[35]

Al-Hallaj's approach to life and death is sensitively portrayed in the account of the execution written by his son:

> On the morning of the execution
> He was taken from his prison,
> Put on one of the pack mules,
> Led away, jostled by grooms
> Who ran alongside him
>
> .   .   .   .
>
> To the esplanade, near the Khurasani
> Gate, on the West Bank of the Tigris
> Where the gibbet was set up.
> Everyone who lived in Baghdad
> And hundreds of foreign visitors
> To the City of Peace were there.
> Never had such a crowd formed

To witness an execution.
The guards lifted him from the mule
And he began dancing in his chains.
The guards were shocked, the people
Who could see burst into nervous laughter,
And then they led him to the gibbet.[36]

Dancing in his chains and then martyred: this image captures the essence of Mansur al-Hallaj. It also fits comfortably among the archetypes of Catholics and Shi'i Muslims.

Despite the pain and pressure, al-Hallaj had refused to modify his message. He propagated his ideas fearlessly; he practiced nonviolence; he welcomed the suffering and death that awaited him; he forgave his enemies and executioners; and he promoted his ministry to the poor and his message of peace, love, and unity to the very end. Muslims were divided in their assessment of the Persian mystic. Many considered him an evil and dangerous force, a charlatan, and even likened him to the devil incarnate; others viewed him as a hero and a saint who faced martyrdom with courage and conviction. In the words of Seyyed Hossein Nasr, "Hallaj represents within Sufism the special grace of Christ as it manifests itself in the Islamic universe. He is a Christic-Sufi. . . . He represents a Christic embodiment within the Muhammadan universe of spirituality."[37] Like Jesus and Imam Husayn, al-Hallaj became much more influential after his martyrdom than he had been during his lifetime.

Another twentieth-century Roman Catholic mystic was the Cistercian (Trappist) monk, Thomas Merton (1915–68), a complex and often troubled figure who carried on a voluminous correspondence with intellectuals of other religious traditions. The author of some sixty books, Merton was influenced both by Massignon, whom he knew personally, and by a Pakistani Muslim named 'Abdul 'Aziz, with whom he corresponded for eight years. Like Massignon, Merton was a convert to Catholicism. The two Catholic intellectuals built a friendship and exchanged ideas. In 1959, during a visit to Karachi, Massignon had given Merton's name and address to 'Abdul 'Aziz when he asked for the name of a practicing Christian mystic he could contact.

Merton is well known for his contributions to Buddhist-Christian dialogue, but Massignon led him to become knowledgeable about Islam as well. Merton gave lectures to the novices and conducted conferences on Sufism.[38] In his words, "There is much in common, on the level of experience, between Sufism and Christian mysticism." He declared, "I am always most interested in Islamic mysticism."[39] Although Merton was greatly impressed by the writings of Massignon, he was also inspired by the ideas of other leading authorities on Sufism. Among those whose work Merton particularly valued were Henri Corbin, Titus Burkhardt, Frithjof Schuon, and Seyyed Hossein Nasr. Merton's efforts to draw together various religious traditions were admirable. Thirty years after his death in 1968, there has been a renaissance of interest in Merton's books, journals, and poems.[40] Increasing numbers of people have visited his monastery, the Cistercian Abbey of Gethsemani in Kentucky. Merton's life was spent in an uneven but intense search for God, and he stressed the overwhelming importance of contemplative awareness.

When Massignon died in 1962, Merton wrote: "He was a man of great comprehension and I was happy to have been numbered among his friends, for this meant entering into an almost prophetic world, in which he habitually moved. It seems to me that mutual comprehension between Christians and Moslems is something of very vital importance today, and unfortunately it is rare and uncertain, or else subjected to the vagaries of politics. I am touched at the deep respect and understanding which so many Moslems had for him, indeed they understood him better than many Christians."[41] Massignon introduced Merton to al-Hallaj, whom the Trappist later described as a "great saint and mystic, martyr of truth and of love."[42]

As Catholics, Massignon and Merton were profoundly struck by al-Hallaj's discussion of the innermost secret heart (*sirr*) of every person—which Massignon called *le point vierge*, "the virgin point"—in a passage that Massignon translated as follows: "Our hearts, in their secrecy, are a virgin alone, where no dreamer's dream penetrates . . . the heart where the presence of the Lord alone penetrates, there to be conceived." At this "primordial point" (*nuqta asliyya*), present in the heart of every human, the reality of God can bring to reality the full latent personality of each human being. Merton later wrote: "This little point . . . is the pure glory of God in us . . . like a pure diamond, blazing with the invisible light of heaven."[43] Catholic faith and Islamic mysticism flow together through the extraordinary story of the tenth-century mystic al-Hallaj.

6

LAW
AND
THE
STATE

In this chapter, we highlight and compare a number of the fundamental issues concerning politics and the state addressed in the philosophical and intellectual debates of these two faith systems. We begin with an analysis of the legal systems of each faith and then move to the philosophical discussion of the roles of faith and reason that has preoccupied major Catholic and Shi'i thinkers. After examining these underlying philosophical foundations, we move to the idea of the polity and the realities of economic and political hierarchy. We conclude with a discussion of the intellectual and political challenges that will inevitably confront Shi'ism and Catholicism in the twenty-first century.

Roman Catholicism and Shi'i Islam over the centuries have been deeply involved in politics. Although neither faith system possesses a clear, accepted position with respect to politics, the following principles can be identified as central to the teachings and practices of both traditions:

1. Catholicism and Shi'ism emphasize the normative foundations of political systems.
2. Both faith systems have developed legal frameworks that stress the preeminence of eternal and divine law.
3. Both have struggled to explain the faith/reason dichotomy.
4. Both preach a special sensitivity to the needs of the poor and the alienated in society.

5. Both have sought to transform their social and political missions during the second half of the twentieth century.

Throughout its history, the Roman Catholic Church has been heavily involved in the political process. The famous comment attributed to Jesus, "Give back to Caesar what belongs to Caesar—and give to God what belongs to God" (Mark 12:17), states an argument classically used for the separation of church and state. The statement does not mean that humankind should or could abandon politics. In the words of one analyst, "This text may not be treated as a pretext for washing our hands of politics. Rather it is an urgent invitation to live the freedom of the daughters and sons of God. The God of Jesus Christ is not in the service of the gods of this world."[1] The emphasis here is on God and His authority, which is superior to that of Caesar. From the time of Jesus, Catholic Christianity has been highly politicized. Resting behind the politics of Catholicism is a reasoned legal framework that links God and humankind.

CATHOLICISM AND A TAXONOMY OF LAW

The idea of an unchanging, eternal law emanating from God or nature has a long heritage reaching back to the philosophers of China and Greece. Natural law theory, however, has been elaborated especially for Christian use by Roman Catholic thinkers. The most sophisticated discussion of the paradigm of law remains the detailed analysis by Thomas Aquinas in the thirteenth century.[2] Although Protestant scholars adopted aspects of natural law theory, they questioned the relationship between eternal law and natural law and often viewed natural law as simply advisory and constantly changing. Furthermore, Protestant thinkers were deeply influenced by positivism and the doctrine of the fall of humankind and argued that the human mind could not consistently distinguish good from bad, right from wrong.

According to Aquinas, there are four major categories of law: eternal law, natural law, divine law, and human law (see figure 1).[3] *Eternal law* is the form of God's wisdom that directs the activities of all creatures. It is the unchanging exemplar of divine wisdom that shapes all actions, movements, and governments. There are two categories of eternal law: natural law and divine law. Both natural and divine law have their origins in eter-

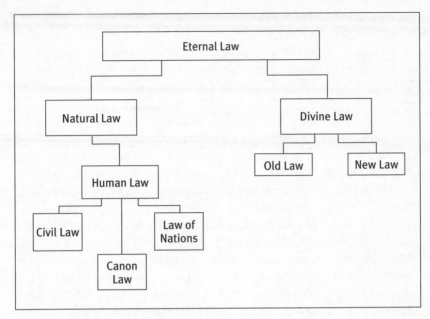

Figure 1. The Thomist Taxonomy of Law
Source: Adapted from J. Budziszewski, *Written on the Heart: The Case for Natural Law* (Downers Grove, Ill.: InterVarsity Press, 1997), 60.

nal law. *Natural law* "is nothing other than the participation of eternal law in rational creatures."[4] It is an emanation of unchanging eternal law perceived by the rational interpretation of this eternal law. St. Paul wrote that "natural law is inscribed in the hearts of all men"; similarly, Romans 2:14–15 states: "When the Gentiles who have no law do by nature what the Law prescribes, these having no law are a law unto themselves. They show the work of the Law written in their hearts." And in the words of Augustine: "Thy law is written in the hearts of men, which iniquity itself effaces not."[5] The particular precepts of natural law are deduced from the cardinal principle that enjoins humankind to do good and avoid evil and to love one's neighbor. These principles (or in Thomist terms, "primary principles") are considered to be innate in human nature.

Divine law is the reflection of eternal law as presented in God's revealed word. Both natural law and divine law are known by reason and revelation, but natural law is revealed through the created nature, whereas divine law is revealed through the created text of the Holy Scriptures. Principles of divine law, for example, are revealed through the prophets and through the Bible. Within the category of divine law, Aquinas distinguishes between "old law," which corresponds to the law of the Old Testament, and "new law," which corresponds to the law of the New Testament.

Human law is the application of the unchanging principles of natural law to the changing circumstances of human life.[6] Because it is derived from natural law, human law fosters religion, promotes justice, and furthers the common welfare. Human law adapts itself to the differing circumstances of time and place. This law is of critical importance in a rapidly transforming world. Natural law theory as applied to the human experience posits a number of inalienable rights, including the rights to life, liberty, worship, property, labor, and assembly.

Deriving from human law is a sophisticated series of ecclesiastical regulations known as canon law. Canon law is the body of law that organizes and regulates the activities of the church. It oversees a wide variety of affairs, ranging from the sacraments to the role and place of the clergy.

In sum, eternal law, natural law, divine law, and human law, though quite distinct from one another, can be compared to a tree. Eternal law represents the deeply embedded system of roots; natural law and divine law are analogous to twin trunks of the tree growing out of the roots; and the different systems of human law are similar to the various limbs of the tree. Growing from both the trunk of the tree and the branches is canon law.[7]

Over the years, the Catholic teachings concerning law based on the theories of Aquinas have been reinforced and invigorated by various popes in their encyclicals. An authority on Aquinas and his ideas, Pope Leo XIII (1878–1903) directed that the Thomist philosophical framework be the recognized intellectual philosophy of the Catholic Church. In this Thomist tradition, Pope Pius XII (1939–58) used natural law theory to anchor teachings concerning such controversial issues as birth control, abortion, and capital punishment. Pius XII presented natural law as the foundation of the social and political doctrine of the church. In his words, when the church struggles "to win and defend her own freedom, she is actually doing this for the true freedom and for the fundamental rights of man. In her eyes these essential rights are so inviolable that no argument of State and no pretext of the common good can prevail against them."[8]

As we have seen, unlike Jesus in his earthly mission, the Prophet Muhammad was called on to build a polity. Islam has been intensely political. Like Christian politics, Muslim politics has developed around a framework of law. It is a cardinal principle in Islam that all just law derives from God. The word for this law, *shari'a*, is derived from *shar'*, or "prescribed by God." The science of *fiqh* (Islamic jurisprudence) is the process of gaining insight into divine law. Law in Islam is a revealed system governing ritual acts, ethics, penal codes, and even commercial matters. According to Muslim beliefs, *shari'a* is "what God and His messenger have prescribed" in the Qur'an (the literal Word of God) and in the acts of His messenger (which were all divinely protected from error). Whereas the Qur'an contains the divine principles of Islam, the *sunna* or practice of Muhammad and his closest associates (for Twelvers, the Imams) and the *hadith* (words and acts) flesh out the details. Sunnis believe that different schools of insight into divine law are permissible. Twelvers make much less than Sunnis of *ijma'*, the doctrine that the majority of the community (or its scholars) are protected from error, as we have seen. One dictum of an Imam can outweigh all interpreters. In the absence of the Imam, scholars must be guided by reason and tradition (*ma'qul wa manqul*). The basic, common foundation of the *shari'a*, however, consists of the Qur'an, the *sunna*, and the *hadith*.

Shari'a in Islam encompasses both divine law and eternal law in the Thomist framework (see figures 2 and 3). In the Islamic philosophy of law, divine law is more important than it is in the Christian Catholic context. The primary reason for this difference in emphasis is found in the fact that the Qur'an, Islam's Word of God, contains many more explicit legal instructions than the Gospels: for example, prescriptions for marriage, divorce, inheritance, warfare, and punishments. In Islamic history, human law came to be referred to as *qanun* in the 'Abbasid state. Legal prescriptions of the ruler were justified by the words of the Qur'an, which proclaimed, "Obey God and obey the messenger and those in authority among you" (4:59). *Shari'a* embodies the prescriptions of the first two, and *qanun* represents the commands of the third, whose authority is usually held to be derived from the obligation to seek what is best for the community and the general interest. The faithful will obey his commands. The word *qanun* and the word for canon law are both derived from the Greek word for "rule" or "norm." In Catholicism, however, canon law is more restricted than *qanun*.

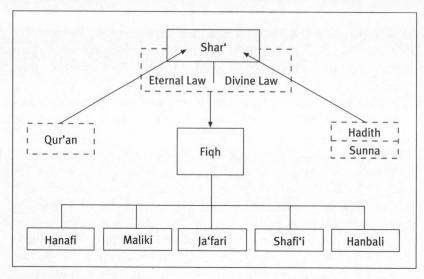

Figure 2. The Muslim Taxonomy of Law

Canon law is the law of the church, whereas *qanun* refers to governmental regulations.

The *shariʿa* has never been monolithic in nature, but it has sought to govern all aspects of a believer's life, personal, ritualistic, ethical, and political. In Islamic history, the systematic codification of the law did not occur until the eighth and ninth centuries. The four major schools of Sunni Muslim law are the Hanafi, Maliki, Shafiʿi, and Hanbali schools. A fifth school of Muslim law is the Shiʿi version known as the Jaʿfari school, named after the sixth Imam, Jaʿfar al-Sadiq (d. 765), who was a scholar of great renown.

Shiʿi Jaʿfari law is very similar to Sunni law, though there are occasional differences, such as in the rules for inheritance. Most important, Shiʿism stresses the role of the Imams as interpreters of the law. This emphasis injected flexibility into the Shiʿi system until the disappearance of the Imam, and even after through his living representatives, the *mujtahids,* who provide *ijtihad,* or interpretation. Every Twelver believer, according to the dominant Usuli school, is required to follow the dictates of a living *mujtahid.* In Sunnism, it was generally held until modern times that "the gates of *ijtihad"* closed with the destruction of Baghdad in the thirteenth century, or even earlier with the emergence of the schools of law. This view was surely

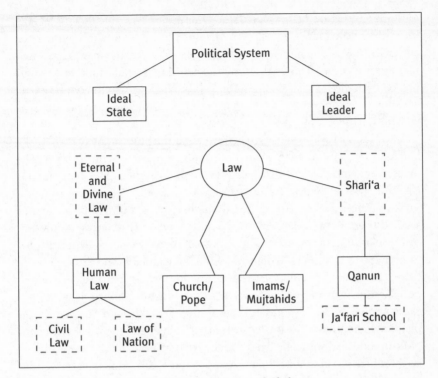

Figure 3. Politics and Law in Catholicism and Shi'ism

overstated because Sunni *muftis* and *shaykhs* still practiced "little *ijtihad*" by issuing *fatwas* (religious rulings) that determined the actual application of the law, and certain jurists insisted on their right to practice *ijtihad* well after that time. Because Usuli Shi'is have insisted that one must be guided by a living *mujtahid*, Twelver Shi'i law continues to be more flexible in its interpretation and application than Sunni law.

Over the years, many great Muslim thinkers have struggled with the fundamental problem of speculative philosophy—the reconciliation of reason with revelation. Revelation laid down certain laws, and the Prophet's implementation of law was itself a form of revelation, a *nass*. The importance of this issue is summarized in a book that focuses on the reason/revelation dichotomy: "The problem of the relationship between revelation and reason is indeed one of the most famous and profound topics in the history of human thought."[9] How were later generations best able to gain insight into the revealed law—by using their minds or by blindly following later authorities? Was the *shari'a* best interpreted using reason or faith, philosophy or revelation? This is the same question that preoccupied Christian intellectuals such as Thomas Aquinas. Like their Christian counterparts, Muslim philosophers arrived at various conclusions concerning the reason/faith issue.

Abu Nasr al-Farabi (870–950) believed that the philosophy of the Greeks had found its true home in Islam. Philosophy is universal truth, and prophets convey symbolic truth. The perfect ruler is the philosopher-king/Imam. Al-Farabi was a Central Asian with Shi'i tendencies whose father was a Turkish officer in the army of the caliphate. He was reared in Baghdad and studied there with Syriac Christian scholars who were deeply influenced by Neoplatonic commentators on Aristotle. He believed that a theistic philosophy must also include dialectical theology (*kalam*) and jurisprudence (*fiqh*). Al-Farabi argued that revelation is important, but reasoned interpretation is even more significant. Among Muslim philosophers, he became known as the "Second Teacher," after Aristotle, and he wrote compendious commentaries on Aristotle that influenced most later Muslim philosophers. Although he lived a reclusive life and had mystical leanings, al-Farabi spent time in Baghdad, Aleppo, and Cairo as he debated fundamental philosophical and political questions of the day.

Abu 'Ali ibn Sina (980–1037) postulated that both reason and revelation are important. Known in the West as Avicenna, he was born near Bukhara to a family with strong Shi'i leanings. A famous physician, whose *Canon of Medicine* was translated into Latin and used widely in European medical schools well into the Renaissance, Ibn Sina was also a statesman and a great philosophical synthesizer. Not only was he an outstanding metaphysician, arguing that the gift of being is linked with the light of intelligence, but he stressed the complementary relationship between knowledge gained through *zahir* and knowledge gained through *batin*. As a faithful Muslim, he believed that God is the Creator. In his view, the rational soul of created humanity ascends by love as far as the Creator. In an oft-repeated anecdote, Ibn Sina and a great Sufi thinker allegedly met privately. After the meeting, Ibn Sina reportedly stated, "All that I know, he sees," and the Sufi master is said to have declared, "All that I see, he knows."

Abu Hamid al-Ghazali (1058–1111) was a brilliant intellectual born in

Khurasan in Iran. He was trained in philosophy and the religious sciences, and he sharply criticized the emphasis on reason and philosophy and argued that only revelation can give sure knowledge in matters that lie beyond the physical world. He claimed that God can be directly "tasted" and experienced, as the Sufis taught, and that this experience is what makes the sciences of religion alive for human beings. Although he was a careful scholar of Aristotelian logic, he postulated that it is impossible to understand metaphysics by reason. Furthermore, he questioned the philosopher's views that God is a universal idea. This, he argued, was not the God of the Qur'an, who spoke to every human individually. In al-Ghazali's judgment, reason is simply unable to comprehend the absolute. Al-Ghazali's attack on philosophy was persuasive to many Sunni thinkers. His emphasis on the *batin* helped enable him to overcome what he considered to be the limitations of rationality but drove many Muslims to abandon philosophy for subjective speculation. In al-Ghazali's view, faith and Sufism are the ultimate proofs of dialectical theology.

Ahmad ibn Muhammad ibn Rushd (1126–98), the great Spanish Muslim philosopher known in Latin as Averroës, confronted the views of al-Ghazali. He held that philosophy is the handmaiden of divine law and that although the *shari'a* rests on revelation, it can be properly understood only when jurists study philosophy. In the words of Philip K. Hitti, "Averroës was a rationalist and claimed the right to submit everything save the revealed dogmas of faith to the judgment of reason; but he was not, as believed by many, the father of free thought and unbelief and the great enemy of faith."[10] The idea that Ibn Rushd taught that there is one truth for science and another for religion was a medieval Latin misunderstanding; for him, truth must always be one. His commentaries on Aristotle were indispensable to Thomas Aquinas as well as to the medieval Spanish Jewish sage, Musa b. Maimun (Maimonides).

Nasir al-Din Tusi (1201–74) was one of the most distinguished of all Twelver theologian-philosophers, an Iranian savant with Sufi inclinations who threw his intellectual weight behind the ideas of al-Farabi and Ibn Sina. An outstanding scientist, mathematician, and astronomer in addition to being a great *mujtahid* and teacher, Tusi oversaw a sophisticated and well-equipped observatory in the Mongol capital of Maragha in thirteenth-century Iran. Like other philosophers before him, Tusi wrote about the virtuous state, which would be guided by a philosopher-king who received inspiration from the Archangel Gabriel, perhaps a dissimulating way of saying that he would be either a prophet or an Imam.

These towering Muslim scientists and intellectuals were all in accord that the *shari'a*, the overarching eternal system of law, was divinely inspired and interpreted both through the lens of reason and through the force of revelation. They differed in the relative emphasis they placed on each source. Tusi, of course, was a Shi'i, and al-Farabi and Ibn Sina had Shi'i inclinations. Al-Ghazali and Ibn Rushd were Sunni sages. These Muslim thinkers also did not agree on the role of Sufism and the *batin* in the interpretation of Islamic law. Although the debate occurred within the worldview of Islam, it was closely intertwined with a similar discussion that took place in the intellectual history of Christianity.

Spain and Sicily acted as bridges over which Muslim ideas were transmitted to Christian Europe. Islamic philosophy and science helped Christianity lift itself out of the Dark Ages. Once Toledo, in formerly Muslim Spain, was conquered in 1085, the Catholic authorities made use of its libraries by setting up a center of translation to render Muslim works into Latin—including the Qur'an and *hadith*. The Arabic translations of Greek science and philosophy made the ideas of such seminal thinkers as Aristotle available to Western medieval Christian thinkers. Aquinas had an extensive knowledge of the works of Ibn Sina and Ibn Rushd. Ibn Rushd's writings, as we have seen, served to reintroduce Aristotelianism to the West. Indeed, Ibn Rushd, whose philosophy and commentary dominated the intellectual world between the twelfth and sixteenth centuries, was better known in Christian Europe than in the Islamic world. Marshall Hodgson writes: "Cultural exchange between Islamdom and the Occident in High Medieval times was drastically one-sided. . . . By and large, Muslims found almost nothing that they thought worth learning from the Occident. . . . In contrast, Occidentals were absorbing cultural practices and conceptions of many diverse sorts from Islamdom, and this absorption was of far-reaching importance to the growth of their culture." [11]

The fertilization of Christian minds by ideas from great Muslim intellectuals brought Muslims and Christians to analogous positions in addressing the major philosophical ideas of the day. In confronting such central issues as the complex relationship between reason and revelation, they also studied the science of politics and the ideal state. The Platonic and Aristotelian writings emphasized that the right governing of the *polis* was a central question of philosophy and among the highest of sciences. In the words of a leading scholar of Islamic political thought, "There can be no doubt about the political significance of philosophy; and the philosophical qualification of the ideal ruler of the ideal state is as necessary as his ability to exercise authority and wield effective power."[12]

Besides Nasir al-Din Tusi, three other Muslim philosophers discussed above wrote about the issues of politics and political leadership as philosophical concerns. The contributions of al-Farabi, Ibn Sina, and Ibn Rushd followed directly from their philosophical perspectives. Influenced by both Aristotle and Plato, al-Farabi compared the political community to the human body. In his judgment, the ultimate goal is the health of each part of the body, and the perfect leader represents the heart of the body. The perfect ruler is the philosopher-king, whose goal is the happiness of all members of the community. According to al-Farabi, the king "is the first chief, and it is he in whom are combined six conditions: a) wisdom; b) perfect practical wisdom; c) excellence of persuasion; d) excellence in producing an imaginative impression; e) power to fight the holy war (jihad) in person; and f) that there be nothing in his body to prevent him attending to the holy war. . . . It is for this man to rule according as he thinks right and wishes."[13]

Ibn Sina built on the philosophical foundations established by al-Farabi. He agreed that the ideal state would be established by a wise philosopher-king, a prophetic figure. This leader would promulgate wise laws and provide for a succession, which would be best established by appointment from the previous incumbent. The community would owe these successors obedience, and those who refused would be treated as infidels. Members of the community would be guided by the *shari'a*, the divine law given to them through their prophet. The Muslim caliph/successor is the representative of the Prophet Muhammad, and he must have "a high intelligence which will enable him to acquire practical wisdom (as distinct from theoretical wisdom), and also an expert knowledge of the *shari'a* in which nobody must surpass him."[14] Ibn Sina also argued that if the caliph should become a tyrant, the people had an obligation to dispose of him.

Ibn Rushd consummated the thinking of al-Farabi and Ibn Sina. He preferred Aristotle to Plato, partly because of the Aristotelian emphasis on the role of law. In his dismissal of al-Ghazali's refutation of philosophers, he accepted many of al-Ghazali's criticisms of the Neoplatonists and sought to restore the "true Philosophy," that of Aristotle. His political philosophy blended conclusions of Aristotle's *Nichomachean Ethics* and Plato's *Republic*, on which he wrote a commentary. He could not refer to Aristotle's *Politics* because it had not been translated into Arabic, a problem that was common among all philosophers who used the Arabic texts. Ibn Rushd was "more conscious than Al-Farabi [and Ibn Sina] of the supremacy of the *shari'a* as the ideal revealed law, and of its political function as the ideal constitution of the ideal state."[15] Ibn Rushd, like al-Farabi and Ibn Sina, held that politics was a branch of philosophy and shared the same goal as religion: the happiness of humankind in this world and the next. He agreed "with Aristotle when he stresse[d] that the chief function of the ruler is his guardianship of justice: 'When he guards justice, he guards equality.'"[16] Ibn Rushd was strongly critical of tyranny, a system that undermines the rule of law. A perfect state can exist, ruled by the ideal ruler, the philosopher-king, who rules according to divine law.

These leading Muslim philosophers share many important characteristics. They all confronted directly the tension between faith and reason and the relation of both to the *shari'a*. All of these Muslim intellectuals made room for Sufism and the experiential in developing their theories of law, politics, and philosophy. Even Ibn Rushd conceded that mysticism may help to attain rational knowledge, but for him it could not replace it. Like their Greek teachers, they saw politics as one of the noblest branches of philosophy. They sought to define the ideal state and the ideal government. In their discussions, these Muslim sages emphasized the importance of justice and equity within the framework of divine and human law. In so doing, they proposed a balance between ruler and ruled. They condemned both tyranny and anarchy. Finally, their discussions presaged the debate that was to surround the issue of reform in a rapidly changing world.

THE CATHOLIC DEBATE ON FAITH AND REASON

The Christian medieval Scholastic thinkers, men such as St. Bonaventure (1221–74), Albertus Magnus (1206–80), and, especially, Thomas Aquinas (1225–74), addressed the issues of faith, reason, and politics in the same general time frame as their Muslim counterparts. Only twenty-seven years passed between Ibn Rushd's death and Aquinas's birth, and Tusi was a contemporary of both Aquinas and Bonaventure—coincidentally, Tusi, Aquinas, and Bonaventure all died in the same year, 1274. In analyzing the position and philosophy of the Catholic Church on the issues of reason, faith, and politics, we will again focus on the work of Thomas Aquinas. The Thomist intellectual framework, so important among Catholics, remains the most comprehensive and systematic of any Christian theological system.

After falling into some obscurity in the centuries after the death of its founding genius, Thomist philosophy came back into the mainstream of Catholic religious thought in the mid-nineteenth century. In the 1840s, Italian Jesuits returned to the philosophy of Aquinas, but the real resurrection of Aquinas's framework occurred in the latter two decades of the century through the powerful intervention of Pope Leo XIII. In his encyclical *Aeterni Patris* of August 4, 1879, Leo XIII urged his readers "to restore the golden wisdom of St. Thomas, and to spread it far and wide for the defense and beauty of the Catholic faith, for the good of society, and for the advantage of all the sciences."[17] The pope himself emphasized the Thomist contribution to the debate about faith and reason. In elegant language, Leo XIII summarized the conclusions of Aquinas concerning this age-old debate: "Again, clearly distinguishing, as is fitting, reason from faith, while happily associating the one with the other, he both preserved the rights and had regard for the dignity of each; so much so, indeed, that reason, borne on the wings of Thomas to its human height, can scarcely rise higher, while faith could scarcely expect more or stronger aids from reason than those which she has already obtained through Thomas."[18] In the view of Aquinas, faith and reason were linked symbiotically. Reason prepared the mind to receive the realities of faith.

Aquinas's strong emphasis on reason and rationality led some Catholic intellectuals to conclude that he was subordinating the role of revelation. These individuals believed that Scholasticism had serious weaknesses. They argued, for example, that it "relied too heavily on reason and logic. The Bible and the writings of the Fathers very often took second place to Aristotle and Scholastic colleagues."[19] Other commentators criticized Aquinas for exactly the opposite reason. In their judgment, he overemphasized the role of revelation at the expense of reason. In making this argument, these scholars pointed to Aquinas's writings that postulate that the truths known by reason are distinct from higher truths known by faith alone. Furthermore, according to Aquinas, reason should exist in the service of faith, or in the words of one scholar, "In Thomism, reason is the slave of faith, as philosophy is subordinate to theology and civil authority to ecclesiastical."[20]

Leo XIII's restoration of Thomism was not merely an intellectual or doctrinal decision. Given the upheaval of the nineteenth century and the incoherence that marked the Catholic Church at the time, the pope turned to the teachings of Aquinas in a calculated search for political and social stability. Unlike his predecessor, Pius IX, who sought to protect the church by papal fiat, Leo XIII hoped to co-opt the opposition and to silence the clamor of socialism and revolution by focusing attention on social justice. The fact that Leo XIII undoubtedly believed in the progressive ideas he presented in the encyclical *Rerum Novarum*, for example, does not mean that he was unaware of the political implications of his policy. He sought to protect the Catholic status quo and the hierarchical power of the papacy within that status quo. William McSweeney, therefore, is only slightly overstating the argument when he writes: "At the level of social organization, his [Leo XIII's] strategy was to demonstrate that the church had already had a solution to the problems posed by socialists and that the interests of the workers and their emancipation from enslavement to material conditions were better served by Catholicism than by the godless creeds of socialism or communism."[21]

The popes following Leo XIII also stressed the importance of Thomism. Challenged frontally by the rise of "modernism," the Catholic Church sought to anchor its theology in the bedrock of Thomist philosophy. Despite a deemphasis on the philosophy of Aquinas during Vatican II in the 1960s, Pope John Paul II returned to Scholastic philosophy in his 1998 encyclical, *Fides et Ratio* (Faith and reason).[22] In this document, the pope revived the age-old debate concerning the relationship between philosophy and revelation. In his view, faith and reason are not incompatible, and he deplores "a growing separation between faith and philosophical reason." In particular, he postulates that the overreliance on faith leads to nihilism and what he terms "fideism." In presenting his arguments, the pope, sensitive to the renaissance of Scholastic philosophy during the papacy of Leo XIII, urges Catholic intellectuals to once again rediscover Aquinas. The reliance on "Neothomist" thought has endured to the twenty-first century.[23]

Although Thomas Aquinas did not produce a systematic and comprehensive treatise on politics, he did address the subject numerous times in his writing. Like Aristotle and the Muslim philosophers, he began with the premise that human beings are social and political animals. At the heart of his political philosophy is the system of law described above. This system defines the relationship between the realm of the divine and the world of humankind. Also, it evaluates the various forms of political rule and emphasizes the significance of issues such as justice and equity. According to Aquinas, "Natural law is like a bridge, thrown as it were across the gulf which divides man from his divine Creator."[24]

Aquinas was a political realist who took a moderate and measured stand on issues concerning the individual and the group, the ruler and the ruled, political order and disorder, and justice and injustice. Because he built his intellectual framework on a scaffolding that stressed a world of relentlessly ordered and graded hierarchy, he harbored a visceral preference for conservative organization. This view was reinforced as the philosopher grew older and witnessed growing incoherence and disorder in the world around him. In the *Summa contra Gentiles*, he argued that everyone was born unequal and that society was composed of individuals of unequal talent, wealth, prestige, and power. This was the nature of things. Aquinas would have agreed with Chrysippus, the Stoic philosopher and dialectician who once stated that "some seats in the theatre are always better than others."[25]

Aquinas supported kingly rule and criticized sedition and rebellion. He disapproved of tyrannicide. In general, he placed a high value on obedience to authority, and like St. Paul, he counseled citizens to be submissive to the political leader of the day. In his words, the welfare of society "lies in the preservation of its unity, which is called peace." The principal responsibility of the ruler is to maintain unity and order. In this task, "the rule of one man is more useful than the rule of many."[26]

Despite this position, Aquinas tempered his political ideas in several ways. In so doing, he revealed his commitment to the Aristotelian emphasis on moderation and the golden mean. Like the Greek philosophers, he accepted a taxonomy of government that consisted of monarchy, aristocracy, and democracy. Although he emphasized the primary importance of monarchy, he in fact argued that the ideal government would consist of a mixture of the three forms. Monarchy was the best guarantor of unity; aristocracy promoted administrative excellence; and democracy provided popular support and participation. He was aware that a monarchy could easily degenerate into tyranny: "Just as the government of a king is the best, so the government of the tyrant is the worst."[27] Indeed, tyranny was cause for civil disobedience. He believed that "disobedience was the right answer to the precepts of wicked power." Aquinas was "a liberal constitutionalist, who maintained the moral excellence of a regime where political prudence was widespread and as many citizens as possible assumed responsibility for popular decisions under a common law."[28]

Like the Muslim philosophers, Aquinas postulated that the goal of humankind is happiness, which can be attained only through group life. He wrote, "The good of the multitude is greater and more divine than the good of any one man."[29] The individual alone cannot attain happiness. At the same time, however, the collectivity exists for the good of the individual, not the other way around. An individual's rights are inherent and inalienable. Regardless of an individual's material circumstances, that individual has "the right to preserve his life, to marry and to bring up children, to develop his intelligence, to be instructed, to hold to the Truth, to live in Society."[30]

Aquinas wrote extensively about the virtues of justice and equity. To him, equity was the highest form of justice. Equity was a universal principle that contained moral meaning and captured the essence and spirit of the law and not just the written legal code. Thomism taught that all humans are equal before the law; indeed, the *demos*, the *populus* (the masses, the public), maintains an equality-based moral privilege that is ultimately founded on eternal law. This moral-based equality is what Aquinas termed equity.

The Thomist view of politics contains several basic themes. First, the goal of politics is to attain happiness. This happiness is best achieved through membership in a group, a community. The core of the community is found in the institution of the family. Political leadership is best realized through the institution of monarchy. In an era of anarchy and incoherence, Aquinas understood that strength at the center of a political system is important for community survival. At the same time, he decried the excesses of monarchy and acknowledged that corrupt and tyrannical leaders are subject to deposal. In his writings on law, justice, and equality, he was sensitive to the rights of the *populus*. A realist par excellence, Aquinas pursued a worldview of balance and moderation, a mixture of authority and liberty, a policy of prudence that embraced both divine-based morality and worldly reality. As a Dominican, Aquinas was part of a religious order that was organized according to democratic principles. The Dominicans were a more relaxed and less hierarchical group than other orders. They tended to reach decisions through consensus and the broad participation of the membership. Generally, the leaders of the order were elected. The organization of the Dominicans included both democratic decision making and strong but consultative leadership.

Thomas Aquinas was also part of the Catholic Church, however, an institution that was organized hierarchically, with the pope at the apex of power and the archbishops, bishops, and priests in the ranks below. Aquinas had no difficulty in reconciling the two organizations. The Catholic Church was a beneficent organization that received its raison d'être from the One God through the instruments of eternal and divine law. The church was devoted to the health and well-being of a community in which justice and equity were central virtues.

RELIGION AND THE STATE

Over the centuries, the relationship between the Catholic Church and secular authorities has waxed and waned. With the rise of the nation-state, there has generally been a formalized space between the two realms. Although never hesitant to speak out on issues of faith and morals, the church has been reluctant to become too closely involved with the secular authorities that guide the state. Political quietism has prevailed. When the church fathers have become entwined with the state, however, it has often been in a supportive role. In modern times in various Third World settings such as Latin America, the Catholic hierarchy has thrown its weight behind power and privilege. This policy came under heavy criticism in the second half of the twentieth century when Catholic clerics themselves frontally challenged the church's identification with ruling elites, which were often oppressive.

Historically, Islam, like Christianity, has witnessed periods when the clerical class, the 'ulama, allied itself with the governing establishment. The alliance with the pomp and circumstance of wealth and power began in the time of the caliphate of 'Uthman and the Umayyads. Like the Catholic Church, Islam was the locus of tension between a commitment to the poor and oppressed on the one hand and an alliance with the ruling elements on the other. The history of Shi'i Islam, in particular, reflects this dialectic.

As a minority group often distrusted by the Sunni establishment, Twelver Muslims carefully avoided confrontation with the governing powers of the day. Most of their Imams pursued a policy of political quietism. Throughout their history, however, Shi'i believers sporadically broke loose from their quietist moorings and, carrying a banner proclaiming the equality of all humanity before its Creator, challenged the political and religious establishment of the time. Scholars have sometimes termed these movements "extremist" or "radical" Shi'ism. The social and political teachings of Islam have, like Catholicism, stressed the principles of unity (*tawhid*) and community (*umma*). In the words of Seyyed Hossein Nasr, "Unity is the alpha and omega of Islam."[31] The concept of *tawhid* encompasses the unity of God, the indivisible coexistence of the *zahir* and *batin* in the individual, and integration of society as a whole. Politically, the Prophet built integrative patterns into a divided and conflictual society prone to disintegration. Through a universal message delivered by a great leader, peoples of many quarreling tribes were attracted to a single community. The conquest of a Muslim empire carried this message to many races and peoples.

The principles of unity and community define the essence of Islam. In different terms, in the teachings of both Catholicism and Islam, the group takes precedence over the individual. In Catholic piety, the church and the community of the faithful are equivalent to the Islamic *umma*. Yet a major concern of modern people, Catholic or Shi'i, is individual liberty. This includes not only the liberty to do as one pleases, which will quickly run counter to the ideas of divine law in each tradition, but also the liberty to be responsible for one's own actions within the confines of reason. The issue is important in both communities, and here Rome and Tehran often seem to speak the same language.

Both Catholicism and Shi'ism have clearly grown in response to their specific histories, and both face challenges in the modern world. Historically, it has been easier for them to adjust to authoritarian governments than it has been for them to adjust to freedom because tyrannical rulers did not touch the sources of their spiritual authority, whereas freedom might be feared as a threat to the very foundations of faith. Each tradition has thus had to wage battle against obscurantists in its own ranks while at the same time attempting to defend itself against the secular charge that it is no longer cogent or relevant.

Roman Catholicism had to face the challenge much earlier than Shi'ism because its strength was chiefly in Western Europe and the Americas, where the ferment of nationalism and of revolutions against old political structures was intense in the nineteenth century. Great harm had been done to the church by absolutist regimes and the French Revolution. The Italian national *risorgimento*, moreover, directly threatened the papacy as the temporal monarchy that ruled central Italy. In working for the freedom of the church from the domination and interference of the liberal state, the rulers of the church drew on its tradition to greatly accentuate the spiritual power of the papacy. In particular, the sixteenth-century work of the Jesuit Robert Bellarmine (canonized in 1930) concerning the absolute and infallible spiritual monarchy of the pope proved useful.[32] This Ultramontanism and the revival of Scholasticism and Thomism were both centered in Rome and championed by the Jesuits. The long reign of Pius IX (1846–78) saw the loss of the Papal States to the Kingdom of Italy alongside continual centralization of the church. His 1864 encyclical *Quanta cura* (What care) insisted that the idea that society should be governed without reference to religion and without distinction between true and false religion must be condemned. It ended with his notorious "Syllabus of Errors," in which he listed eighty "errors" that seemed to include freedom of the press, sovereignty of the people, freedom of conscience and religion, and the very idea that the papacy could reconcile itself with progress, liberalism, and modern civilization. Great perplexity among the bishops and their faithful ensued, as well as waves of anticlericalism and anti-Catholic sentiment in one country after another.[33] Bishop Dupanloup of Orléans asserted in an irenic argument that for prudential reasons the church might properly permit considerable freedom of religion, the press, and popular sovereignty, as in the United States. Roman Catholics have agreed that *Quanta cura* was not an infallible document. Few, however, would argue that the acts of the Council of the Vatican that was convened by the pope in December 1869 did not partake of the infallibility of the assembled church. The gathering included 200 bishops from outside Europe, 49 from the United States, and 60 from the Eastern churches in union with Rome.

The constitution, *Pastor Aeternus*, passed by virtually all of the council fathers (the dissidents had left Rome rather than offend the pope or be held anathema by the majority), contained the canon:

> We teach and define that it is a dogma divinely revealed: that the Roman Pontiff, when he speaks *ex cathedra,* that is when in discharge of the office of Pastor and Doctor of all Christians, by virtue of his supreme apostolic authority he defines a doctrine regarding faith or morals to be held by the Universal Church, by the divine assistance promised him in Blessed Peter, is possessed of that infallibility with which the Divine Redeemer willed that his Church should be endowed for defining faith or morals: and that therefore such definitions of the Roman Pontiff are irreformable of themselves, and not from the consent of the Church. But if anyone, which God forbid, presumes to contradict this Our definition — *let him be anathema.*[34]

A semiofficial tract written in 1871 by the general secretary of the council and commended by the pope laid down careful conditions for the exercise of infallibility in such terms as to win over the minority that disagreed. These gave rise to the observation that the pope could now be infallible as long as he defined nothing, but the papacy had still been provided with a formidable weapon. The net effect of all of these centralizing moves, nonetheless, was not rebellion but clearly a deepening and strengthening of the quality of spiritual life of ordinary Catholics. The controversial beatification of Pius IX in September 2000 may be understood in this context.

This statement of absolute papal power continues to perplex the Catholic Church. Even if one subscribes fully to the text of *Pastor Aeternus,* there is still the question of how the Petrine supremacy is to be understood and exercised in modern times, particularly as the Roman church seeks to mend the breach with the apostolic churches of the East. In this spirit, Pope John Paul II has asked the bishops and theologians of the world to join him in seeking "the forms in which this ministry [the papacy] may accomplish its service of love."[35]

In Shi'i Iran, the final collapse of the Safavid regime in the 1720s had fostered receptivity to the modern idea of the "State of Iran," although the idea of Iran as a polity among a family of states was only partly embraced even by the servants of the state in the nineteenth century.[36] Shortsighted rulers in the nineteenth century greatly increased the national debt to Britain and Russia, both of which hoped to gain "interests" in Iran that would justify their making the country a protectorate. At the same time, the Qajar dynasty ruling the country failed to strengthen itself through the creation of a modernized army and bureaucracy capable of enforcing its will on the 'ulama, as had occurred in Turkey and Egypt. As a result, the clerics could call on their traditional allies in the merchant and entrepreneur class, the bazaaris, and through them on the urban masses, to stand against the rulers. The 'ulama thus successfully opposed the "absolutism" and illegitimacy of the power of the shahs, whose concessions to foreign commercial interests were damaging the economic prospects of Iranian merchants and taxpayers.[37] It was even possible for the 'ulama to oppose the construction of a railway (in 1872) on the grounds that it would open the country to an exploiting horde of non-Muslim foreigners. Thus it was that the 'ulama could emerge as champions of the national consciousness. This situation was facilitated by the triumph of the Usulis, which had been building since the eighteenth century, who gave their mujtahids much more power than that enjoyed by Sunni 'ulama. "Liberty" for Iranians came to be defined not as freedom of conscience but freedom from tyranny, foreign incursions and exploitation, and the threat of a Western-inspired secularization such as was occurring in the Ottoman Empire.

A hero for the Muslim world of the nineteenth century emerged in the person of Jalal ad-Din al-Asadabadi (1838–97), an Iranian scholar who gained acceptance in the majority Sunni world by claiming to be an Afghan Sunni and was hence called "al-Afghani." He was the founder of Muslim anticolonialism and traveled to India, Afghanistan, Turkey, Iran, Egypt, and Europe, utilizing his considerable rhetorical and persuasive skills as a writer and preacher to awaken the younger generation to the necessity of a pan-Muslim (Shi'is and Sunnis) revival of thought and action in the face of Western colonialism and selfish domestic rulers. He backed all movements in support of constitutional liberties and did not shrink from Ibn Sina's doctrine that it is a duty to remove a tyrannical ruler by force, if necessary.[38] He was also active in Freemasonry and was grand master of the Star of the East Lodge in Cairo. His readiness to associate with members of other religions in his political activities probably owed much to his Masonic background.[39] His influence on the intellectual history of the modern Islamic world has been profound. Virtually every movement for Islamic reform in modern times has used some of his ideas.

Yet even before Jalal ad-Din was active, the Shiʿi ʿulama of Iran and their popular following had won victories in a struggle with the shahs of the Qajar dynasty. In 1826, they were able to call for a religious war against Russia. In 1872–73, they demanded the revoking of the wide concessions given to British financier Julius Reuter for the exploitation of minerals and forests in Iran and the construction of railways. The ʿulama feared that the growth of foreign influence in the country would pose a direct threat to their administration of justice and the national quality of life, which is exactly what happened later with the presence of large numbers of foreigners in Iran. Although this view was characterized by others as xenophobic and obscurantist, the ʿulama were defending real principles for a Shiʿi Islamic society and campaigning against the shah's attempt to bolster his own powers with foreign help.

Subsequently, the ʿulama were active in the struggle to repeal the monopolistic British control of tobacco in 1891–92. Without their leadership and support, the opposition to the tobacco monopoly would certainly have failed. Finally, the ʿulama were prominent in the movement that led to the granting of a constitution in August 1906.[40] Although the Iranian constitutional revolution was organized primarily by the *bazaaris*, their old allies, the ʿulama, worked with them and mobilized the lower classes to support the demand for a constitution.

The general demand for modernizing reform was supported by many of the higher ʿulama. When Reza Khan came to power after his coup d'état in February 1921, he seemed to many to be the charismatic embodiment of the desired reformer, the strong man who would restore Iran's unity, independence, and pride.

If we compare the response of Twelver Shiʿism to the challenge of secularism and modernity with that of Roman Catholicism, we will observe that the already centralized Roman church found its remedy in strengthening the central power of the papacy, though it has not been fully comfortable with the result. The Shiʿi ʿulama, who had no pope and whose Imam was "absent," turned to the masses and the *bazaaris* for strength.

Once Reza Khan was crowned shah in April 1926, however, he turned to consolidating his power in the traditional manner. From 1934 until 1941, when he was forced to abdicate by invading Russian and British armies, he moved toward an alliance with European fascism. Those ʿulama who opposed such modernizing measures as his new law code interdicting the veil for women and his interference with custom did so at their peril. To many, *taqiyya,* the time-honored practice of dissimulation, seemed the best part of courage.

Reza Shah's son, Muhammad Reza Shah, was confronted by the rise of a nationalist leader, Muhammad Musaddiq, supported by both the modern secular middle class and the traditional religious *bazaari* class and its allies among some of the *'ulama.* The most prominent of these was Ayatollah Abu al-Qasim Kashani. Kashani's religious right Society of Muslim Warriors, composed mainly of young lower-echelon *bazaaris,* called for the implementation of the *shari'a,* the repeal of Reza Shah's secular laws, and protection of the national sources of production. Kashani's group was even willing to make an alliance with the communist Tudeh Party to support Musaddiq against the shah and Britain. On August 19, 1953, Musaddiq was overthrown by a coup in favor of the shah, with the well-documented assistance of the Central Intelligence Agency and British intelligence. With classic Marxist pragmatism, the Tudeh deserted Musaddiq on the grounds that the time was not ripe and that his National Front had "bourgeois" leadership. Many *bazaaris* and allies of the *'ulama* drew lessons from this experience. Since the ensuing dictatorship of the shah depended on his political and military ties with the United States, the later leaders of the Iranian Revolution were ready to target the United States as their principal enemy.

After Ayatollah Khomeini, the charismatic leader of the revolution, attacked the shah's "mistakes" and incited riots in Iran's major cities, he was forced into exile in the shrine-cities of Iraq and later in France. The way had been paved for the extraordinary emergence of an *ayatollah* at the head of the revolutionary forces who would topple the monarchy, take the American embassy personnel hostage, and set up a clerical Shi'i regime. We will say more about these fundamental issues in chapter 7.

The concepts of *tawhid* and *umma* interlock with the issues of political authority, social equality, and the distribution of wealth and power. Leading Shi'i theoreticians, for example, have carried the idea of *tawhid* far beyond the conventional emphasis on the oneness of God. For Iranian sociologist Ali Shariati, for example, *tawhid* refers to a special "worldview," a perspective both unifying and unitarian that negates all contradictions and divisions in society. *Tawhid* is designed to overcome "legal, class, social, political, racial, ethnic, territorial, cognatic, genetic, intrinsic, and even economic" divisions. The pursuit of *tawhid* is the pursuit of "absolute equality."[41] In this view, the *umma* is a seamless web of Muslim believers in which the poor and dispossessed have the same rights as the rich and the privileged. Ideally, equality prevails. In fact, in both Catholicism and Shiʻi Islam, the role of *tawhid* and *umma*, unity and community, has limitations. The ideas tend to remain utopian in character.

Ultimately, the question of the distribution of power and wealth is a political issue. In both Shiʻi Islam and Roman Catholicism, there has long been a strong public commitment to justice and the recognition that all human beings remain equal in the eyes of God. Pope Pius XII, not as well known for social sensitivity as Pope Leo XIII and other papal leaders, has written that social justice ought "to regulate suitably the sharing and using of wealth, so that it is not concentrated excessively in one place while it is lacking entirely in another. Wealth is like the blood in the human body; it ought to circulate around all members of the social body."[42]

7

AUTHORITY, JUSTICE, AND THE MODERN POLITY

The teachings of Christianity and Islam sharply criticize the preoccupation with material goods and the accumulation of wealth, while stressing the transitory nature of life on earth. According to Mark 10:25, "It is easier for a camel to pass through a needle's eye than for a rich man to enter the Kingdom of God." In words attributed to Imam ʿAli: "This world is sweet and green, surrounded by lusts and liked for its immediate enjoyments. It excites wonder with small things, is ornamented with false hopes and decorated with deception. Its rejoicings do not last and its afflictions cannot be avoided. It is deceitful, harmful, changing, perishable, exhaustible and destructive."[1]

On the Christian side, it is written in James 5:1–4: "As for you, you rich, weep and wail over your impending miseries. Your wealth has rotted, your fine wardrobe has grown moth-eaten, your gold and silver have eroded, and their corrosion shall be a testimony against you; it will devour your flesh like a fire." In the Islamic tradition, a *hadith* attributed to the Prophet states: "Rejoice you poor emigrants; you will enter paradise half a day before the rich, and that half day is as five hundred years."

In the Christian tradition, according to Isaiah 58:7–10, "Share your bread with the hungry, shelter the oppressed and the homeless; clothe the naked when you see them and do not turn your back on your own." Similarly, in Islam, according to Imam ʿAli, "Fear God regarding the lowest class, the wretched, needy, suffering and disabled who have no means at their disposal. . . . Be heedful for God's sake of those rights of theirs which He has entrusted to you. Set aside for them a share of your treasury."[2]

Both Christian/Catholic and Muslim/Shi'i traditions have emphasized the principles of equality and justice. Both traditions, for example, have strongly condemned usury (*riba*) and taught that because all wealth came from God, those who were disproportionately wealthy were expected to share their possessions with the poor and less fortunate. The charging of interest, therefore, was criticized by Islamic and Christian social commentators. Aquinas, for example, abhorred usury and considered it sinful, unnatural, and unjust. The Dominican scholar devoted several pages of the *Summa Theologica* to this subject. The Qur'an also condemns usury: "O you who have faith, do not devour *riba*, making it double and redouble, and fear God that you may succeed" (3:130). Muslim scholars and jurists considered usury to be a pernicious and forbidden practice.

Shi'i and Catholic doctrine taught that the state was intimately involved in establishing and implementing such basic principles as equality and justice. Yet models of the state and politics were never clearly enunciated by either Christians or Muslims. Furthermore, these teachings existed as ideals that were not always realized in either religious system. There has been a noticeable gap between ideals and realities in both traditions. The situation is made more complex because neither faith system is monolithic in its beliefs and practices. Diverse voices represent diverse interpretations in both traditions.

In order to understand the role of church and state, one must focus not only on the ideals of the particular religions but also, painful though it may be, on historic practice. Although Catholicism and Shi'ism stress individual equality and social justice, in reality, both religions have not always acted to promote these principles. The gap between word and deed can be seen in many cases in the relationship between the religion and the particular political system in which that religion resides. How do Catholics and Shi'is view politics and the state? How does each tradition seek to meet the challenge of modernity while at the same time preserving its own roots and essence?

CATHOLICISM, POLITICS, AND THE STATE

The history of Catholic political thought reveals the absence of a single, accepted, preferred mode of politics. Although they share a general sense of the contours and configuration of an ideal state, different Catholic leaders have supported different types of political structures at different times. In general, the church has avoided extreme types of political systems even though it has learned to coexist with practically any kind of secular state.

Through time, the Catholic hierarchy has resisted political systems that were either individualist or collectivist in their approach. The Catholic leadership has criticized states that have sought to maximize the autonomy of individuals within society. In these political systems, the freedom and independence of the individual take precedence over the collectivity, that is, the common good, in a way that sacrifices the state to the narrower self-interest of the individual. At the same time, the church has deeply distrusted collectivist models such as socialism and Marxism. In these cases, the state seeks to eliminate or cripple the autonomy of the individual. The fact that the socialist/Marxist approach also promoted atheism led the Catholic Church to condemn adamantly this form of political system.

Even though the church distrusted individualism and collectivism, it was forced to confront the social and political reasons for the appeal of these systems. On the one hand, there was a strong, almost universal drive in support of the rights of the individual. On the other hand, the state came to exist as a mechanism designed to provide the basic social, economic, and political needs of the people.

In order to offset the appeal of individualist and collectivist politics, the Catholic hierarchy sought to develop a political system that promoted the interests of both the individual and the community. This political type sprang from the intellectual soil cultivated by the ideas of Aristotle and Thomas Aquinas and fertilized by the encyclicals of Popes Leo XIII, Pius XI, Pius XII, and John XXIII. According to these thinkers, the community ultimately takes precedence over the individual because it is only in the community that human beings can attain their moral good. Thus there is a need for a strong state that can protect the community and the communal well-being.

The tilt in Catholic thinking about the state has been decidedly in the direction of state interventionism and authoritarianism. Pope Leo XIII, for example, author of the seminal 1891 encyclical *Rerum Novarum,* spoke out in favor of justice for the working classes of society. In so doing, however, he favored strong state control and, within the state, a privileged place for the church. Even his social policies "were designed for the same end: the restoration of the power and influence of the church in the secular world through a disciplined laity."[3]

Leo XIII introduced liberal ideas in order to protect the place of the church, which was under siege at the time. This is why one observer writes that he "betrayed the Catholic intelligentsia."[4] Fearing the demise of the church in an era of rapid social change, Leo XIII struggled to preserve order by administering carefully apportioned doses of reform. He confronted the forces of transformation through the introduction of controlled reformation.

Leo XIII favored a strong central government in order to ensure the implementation of his reforms. As part of his political strategy, he recognized the inherent dangers of a disproportionately powerful state that would smother the rights and independence of the individual. In order to provide a protective zone of autonomy for the individual and for individual rights, Leo XIII introduced assistance or aid (*subsidium*) to help protect the rights of the individual from undue encroachments by the state. In the encyclical *Quadragesimo Anno* (1931), Pius XI institutionalized Leo XIII's idea and explicitly proposed the idea of "subsidiarity."

In the words of Pius XI, subsidiarity is defined as "a fundamental principle of social philosophy, fixed and unchangeable, that one should not withdraw from individuals and commit to the community what they can accomplish by their own enterprise and industry. So, too, it is an injustice and at the same time a grave evil and a disturbance of right order, to transfer to the larger and higher collectivity functions which can be performed and provided for by lesser and subordinate bodies."[5] Although many claimed that this kind of intervention by the state was "revolutionary" and "went flatly against liberalism,"[6] it was accepted and adopted by the popes who succeeded Leo XIII. The continuing relevance of this principle is seen in the fact that it was emphasized in Pope John XXIII's important encyclical *Mater et Magistra* (1961).

The principle of subsidiarity protects the rights of individuals within a larger society and gives them a certain autonomy that enables them to pursue their own goals. The central authority must respect this autonomy and intervene only when the smaller units are unable to protect themselves. In particular, the state must promote social justice and the common good. If justice and the rights of individuals are abused and the common good is threatened, then the state may intervene. At the same time, however, "the state has no right to substitute a bureaucratic apparatus for the functioning of the free associations, nor has it, by reason of social perfectionism, a right to meddle continually in petty tutelage in the affairs of its citizens."[7]

Catholicism stresses the priority of the community over the individual. It is quite comfortable with the existence of a strong central authority or state. The state and the church should exist to promote the common good. In this context, the Catholic Church has found it possible to coexist with many different kinds of political systems: monarchical, military, theocratic, democratic. It has existed alongside authoritarian and totalitarian systems such as communist, socialist, and fascist governments. In such situations, the principle of subsidiarity is smothered by the realities of central power. It is simply ignored by the political authorities and is only feebly referred to by church leaders.

In the real world of religion and politics, order, stability, hierarchy, and authority may take precedence over autonomy, participation, and individual rights. In this situation, the victims are principles of natural law such as preservation, procreation, human dignity, social justice, and the common good. Despite the writings and progressive ideas of several popes in the last century and church pronouncements in support of justice and principles such as subsidiarity, Catholic authorities have often lacked the will and capacity to curb the excessive preemption of power by both religious and secular political elites. Lacking power and the apparatus of force, the church has had to rely on the goodwill of the state to promote the common good. According to St. Paul, it is the state that "carries the sword; not for glory's sake or for superhuman pride and lust, but for the sake of the order of the common good."[8]

But what happens when the state wields the sword in the interest of the few and the corrupt or when the political elite promotes injustice rather than redressing it? History suggests that in these circumstances, the church often temporizes, accommodates, and compromises.

Church leaders have sometimes worked more closely with state leaders than with their own coreligionists. The church has often been a committed defender of the status quo. It has not always successfully come to grips with the challenge of modernity. In instances where the church has ignored oppressive government or where it has tacitly cooperated with such government, it has found itself increasingly alienating the masses of practicing Catholics. This situation is exacerbated by the doctrinaire and unyielding position the church has taken with respect to such critical issues as contraception, clerical celibacy, and women's rights. The church's unwillingness to rethink these important issues has alienated millions of Catholic believers.

Among Catholics, social and political movements have sprung up to question and challenge the old system. Many of the individuals who question the church are from what Harvey Cox terms the "underside" of society; they exist in the cracks and at the periphery of human existence. Those at the bottom of society challenge both church and state in much of the world. Cox theorizes that the new challenging forces "will come not from the center but from the bottom and from the edge. They will come from those sectors of the modern social edifice that for various reasons—usually to do with class or color or gender—have been consigned to its lower stories and excluded from the chance to help formulate its religious vision."[9] The new proactive forces will be recruited from those who have been "touched and trampled upon" by an oppressive and authoritative modernity. These pressures have been strongly felt by the Vatican leadership. Former tactics that relied on papal pronouncements and principles such as subsidiarity have failed to quell the forces bubbling up from below in new and unprecedented ways. Two results of this challenge were the convening of Vatican II and the emergence of a movement known as liberation theology. Although the suffering and disaffected masses became increasingly alienated from the church, the leaders of Vatican II and supporters of liberation theology were drawn from the intelligentsia and middle classes of society.

THE CATHOLIC CHURCH AND LIBERATION THEOLOGY

In the 1960s, a new movement known as liberation theology developed at the grass roots of many Catholic societies. Liberation theology challenged both the state and the church on the grounds that key principles of natural law such as justice, equality, and popular participation were being neglected by the Catholic establishment. The leaders who formulated the theology of liberation were largely Latin Americans and included Peruvian priest Gustavo Gutierrez, Uruguayan Jesuit Juan Segundo, Argentine priest Enrique Dussel, Spanish Jesuit Jon Sobrino, and Brazilian professor Father Leonardo Boff. Gutierrez can be termed the father of liberation theology because he first sketched out the ideas of the new approach at a meeting in Chimbote, Peru, in 1968. In August 1968, over 100 Catholic bishops gathered in Medellín, Colombia, where they prepared the basic documentary justification for a theology of liberation. Gutierrez's ideas provided the intellectual foundation for this important meeting.[10] It is significant that liberation theology grew strongest in those regions where Catholic bishops had often ignored or cooperated with oppressive governments.

According to liberation theologians, political leaders had forgotten the basic principles of the Christian message, a message that emphasized the fact that all human beings were equal in the eyes of God. The poor and the oppressed suffered from institutionalized violence while the church allegedly stood by and did little. Gutierrez and his colleagues argued "that a responsible commitment within class conflict is an expression of love for one's neighbor. They are not fomenting hatred, as critics contend; class conflict already exists. Through solidarity in struggle with the poor, class division must be transcended in a new type of society."[11]

The liberation theology movement attacked injustice, inequality, oppression, and corruption by formulating a Christian message that emphasized the need to organize politically at the lower reaches of society. If the establishment church and the state failed to confront the problems of the poor and the dispossessed, then the people and sympathetic clerics felt they had little choice but to take matters into their own hands. In so doing, they took a page out of the papal teachings on social justice and subsidiarity and organized their own popular organizations at the grass roots of society. These base communities (*comunidades de base*) became "radical subsidiaries" that sought to introduce fundamental reform into society. The proponents of base communities were operating well within the Catholic social tradition because these communities were in fact intermediate groups established within the context of the principle of subsidiarity. Although the leaders of liberation theology were often privileged, highly educated clergy, the movement rested on the foundation of popular discontent. Because liberation theology generated support from below, it can be described as a "populist" movement.

In analyzing society, liberation theology leaders reached two main conclusions. First, they noted the marked differences among social classes in society. They were concerned by the inequality and exploitation that prevailed, especially in the Third World and Latin America. Second, having reached this conclusion, the advocates of liberation theology determined that they had to act to reform the situation. In their terms, they saw the need to combine their theory with "praxis." The most important instruments of their strategy were the base communities that would challenge the establishment's oppressive status quo. These communities spread across Latin America and could be found in Europe and the Philippines as well.

Base communities are termed "base" because they represent the bottom of society. They are anchored deeply in the grass roots of society and are effective precisely because they rely on the highly personal, face-to-face, informal interactions among families, friends, and neighbors. This kind of personal networking maximizes the chances for the communities to achieve their goals. Face-to-face relations provide special incentives for group members to contribute to the group's objectives. Group members cannot disappear in anonymity, nor can they remain passive, as is often the case in religious congregations that interact electronically. Although television evangelists are able to reach huge audiences, the commitment of their membership cannot match the esprit and contributions of those who meet one another at gatherings such as church socials and other religious events.

Both the Catholic and secular political establishments were badly shaken by the rapid growth and increasing popularity of liberation theology. The church had already decided in the early 1960s to attempt to introduce some basic reform because it feared it was becoming increasingly irrelevant. Pope John XXIII, recognizing the rot in the foundation and rafters of the Catholic Church, convened the Vatican II meetings, which overlapped with the liberation theology movement. During the same time frame, a related social movement known as the "option for the poor" burst on the scene.

Originating in Latin America in the early 1970s, the option for the poor asked the church and the faithful to commit themselves to the pursuit of justice for the poor. The three goals of the option for the poor are to oppose state-sponsored oppression, to work closely with the poor to resist this oppression, and to support a church that includes the poor in the decision making. In this program, one is expected to choose an option to "engage actively in a struggle to overcome the social injustices that mar our world. To be genuine it must come from a real experience of solidarity with the victims of our society."[12]

Although the church leaders came to accept the principles of Vatican II, they were less enthusiastic about the phrase "option for the poor" and often outright hostile concerning the activities of liberation theology supporters. Publicly, Vatican leaders have often agreed with the diagnosis of liberation theology. They admitted the problem of a visible gap between the haves and the have-nots. Pope John XXIII spoke eloquently about this problem. His successor, Paul VI, wrote an encyclical in 1967 entitled *Populorum Progressio* (On the development of peoples) that sharply criticized the abandonment of the poor. Indeed, Paul VI's message provided some of the inspiration for the development of liberation theology. The reaction to this theology is seen in the *Wall Street Journal*'s comment that *Populorum Progressio* was nothing but "warmed over Marxism."[13]

Twenty years later, Pope John Paul II wrote an encyclical designed to renew the message of *Populorum Progressio*. In *Sollicitudo Rei Socialis* (The social concerns of the church), John Paul II quoted from *Populorum Progressio*, which recognized the right of every individual "to be seated at the table of the common banquet, instead of lying outside the door like Lazarus, while the dogs come and lick his sores."[14]

In *Sollicitudo Rei Socialis*, John Paul II wrote of the church's responsibilities to the poor: "Faced by cases of need, one cannot ignore them in favor of superfluous church ornaments and costly furnishings for divine worship; on the contrary, it could be obligatory to sell these goods in order to provide food, drink, clothing, and shelter for those who lack these things."[15] Despite these words, observers have noted that the pontiff held no auctions offering the precious holdings of the Vatican in exchange for resources to improve the lives of the destitute. On the contrary, John Paul II moved quietly and effectively against liberation theology. His Eastern European background and personal experience with communism made him wary of the relationship he perceived between liberation theology and Marxism. He thus developed a two-pronged approach designed to bring the movement of liberation theology under tight control.

First, the pope co-opted many of the ideas and programs of liberation theology. Examples include his various papal announcements lamenting the situation of the poor and stressing their privileged position. In his writings, Pope John Paul II sent out encouraging messages stressing the importance of the base communities and the theology of liberation. At the same time, however, he packed these messages with so many limiting conditions that, in the words of Anselm Min, his commitment to the cause of liberation "died the death of a thousand qualifications."[16] John Paul II's unprecedented travels across the world, in which he used his great personal charisma to preach to the poor, also helped steal the appeal of liberation theology.

Besides pursuing this "soft" approach, Pope John Paul II implemented a "hard" program whereby he sought to weaken liberation theology by excommunicating clerics sympathetic to the new theology and by using his power of appointment to place more conservative bishops and cardinals in key positions. In a highly publicized visit to Mexico in January 1999, the pope told the bishops of North and South America not only to take care of the poor but also to minister to the rich: "Love for the poor must be preferential, but not exclusive. . . . Pastoral care for the leading sectors of society has been neglected."[17] In the pope's opinion, the rich also needed help.

When Pope John Paul II visited Mexico, an article in the *New York Times* flatly stated that the suppression of liberation theology had been a "central campaign of his 20-year papacy. Fighting one of the most bitter religious battles of modern times, the Vatican has closed seminaries, censored Church texts and discredited hundreds of Latin American Church leaders who taught the insurgent interpretation of Christianity."[18]

Despite this papal policy, the death knell of liberation theology has hardly been sounded. The preferential option for the poor remains strong, and various forms of base communities are still active across Latin America and elsewhere. The appeal of liberation politics is also evidenced by the fact that many of its ideas have been co-opted by the establishment church. The movement has survived both the notable success of Protestant evangelicals and the collapse of Marxism.

In the tradition of Leo XIII, Paul VI, and others, Pope John Paul II has spoken loudly for the poor while at the same time undercutting political movements such as liberation theology. The struggle has been one about authority. Who would lead the battle in the name of the poor and the dispossessed? Leo XIII in the nineteenth century took up the banner for the poor and has gone down in history as the "working man's pope." Both Leo XIII and John Paul II, among others, however, promoted reform in order to protect the authority of the church. Doctrinally, however, these church leaders gave up little ground and inflexibly reinforced the church's iron stance on issues such as birth control, homosexuality, a celibate and male priesthood, women's rights, and abortion.

John Paul II, in particular, has followed the lead of Pope Paul VI, an outstanding leader and progressive thinker. Paul VI continued the work of Vatican II, promoted ecumenism, led a campaign for world peace, and decried much of the pomp and circumstance that had come to encrust the papacy. Referring to the church as "troubled and tormented,"[19] Paul VI did much to strengthen the institution. Many judge him severely, however, because of his 1968 encyclical *Humanae Vitae*, which launched a frontal attack on birth control. Catholic intellectual Gary Wills describes *Humanae Vitae* as "the most disastrous papal document of this century," a "petty and parochial" letter "that dealt the most crippling blow to organized Catholicism of our time."[20]

Although Wills's judgment may seem overly harsh, it demonstrates alarm about a church leadership that appears to be stubbornly clinging to the past while its flock moves ahead. In the words of Wills, *Humanae Vitae* "is not really about sex. It is about authority. Paul decided the issue on that ground alone. He meant to check the notion that Church teaching could change."[21] Advisers close to Paul VI warned that to alter the church's position on birth control would be an admission that its past policy had been mistaken. Also, to change church policy on an issue as important as birth control would encourage demands for reform concerning other key issues facing the Vatican.

The preferred style of politics of the Catholic Church is congruent with the Vatican's view of politics and the state more generally. Centralized authority is the preferred authority. Pope John Paul II, for example, consistently appointed bishops who were devoted to "a Romanocentric, top-down version of the Church."[22] In exercising and protecting this papal authority, church leaders have been willing to utilize methodologies of reform and participation whenever they were deemed appropriate. The participatory principle of subsidiarity is as relevant to politics within the church as it is to nation-state politics outside the church.

Traditionally, the popes have committed themselves to protecting the status quo in the Catholic Church. In so doing, the effect has been to reinforce their own positions of authority. When confronted with serious challenges to church doctrine, they have given up ground grudgingly. In the last three decades of the twentieth century and beginning of the twenty-first century, however, change has exploded so rapidly and deeply that the Vatican has found itself on the defensive. The masses of Catholic believers have increasingly challenged the papal leadership and have begun to demand equality, justice, effective participation, and improved living conditions. The laity has in essence ignored the papal injunctions concerning birth control and has become increasingly supportive of a married priesthood. Leading papal figures such as Leo XIII, Paul VI, and John Paul II have selectively supported reform in order to protect both papal and church authority.

In the twenty-first century, humankind exists in a world caught in the midst of fundamental transformation. Old systems have collapsed and crumbled, and new systems have not yet been developed and put in place. Individuals everywhere find themselves caught in situations of incoherence. Those systems and structures that refuse to confront the challenges of the day face extinction. The Catholic Church understood these realities very well and began dismantling the traditional system through the activities of Vatican II. A new system, however, has yet to emerge. In the words of one observer: "The burst of theological creativity that followed Vatican II was purchased at the price of coherence. The binding vision broke into puddles of quicksilver and slipped away. . . . An organization premised on timelessness is ill-equipped to manage change."[23]

Papal policy has reflected inconsistency and uncertainty in this challenging age. Popes have been both flexible and doctrinaire. Popes Paul VI and John Paul II, for example, opened channels of communication while at the same time shutting off debate on current issues such as birth control and female ordination. Although John Paul II "ringingly proclaimed the equality of women and the importance of women to the Church," his doctrinal office ruled that the impossibility of women's ordination is an infallible truth of the faith.[24]

Given the intellectual and populist challenges that confront the church today, past strategies that emphasize authority and infallibility seem likely to fail. It is significant that Pope John Paul II has taken the unprecedented action of apologizing for past actions of the church. In effect, this policy has functioned to restrict papal infallibility. Nor is there much hope for policy that promotes incremental revision at the expense of fundamental structural change. The Catholic Church is likely to remain troubled and tormented for some time to come.

Overlapping closely with the development of liberation theology in the Catholic world was the dramatic appearance of an activist, populist Shiʻi movement in the Muslim world. This powerful Islamic movement appeared in the late 1960s after the 1967 Arab-Israeli War and gained momentum and strength with the coming of the Iranian Revolution in the late 1970s.

THE POLITICS OF POPULIST SHIʿISM

The poor and the oppressed are as prevalent in Muslim societies as they are in Christian cultures. The widening gap between the haves and have-nots has become a chasm. This social inequity has caused increasing dissatisfaction and discontent among the masses of Muslim citizens. Sunnism and Shiʿism both face these deepening social, economic, and political problems. It is the Shiʿis, however, who have experienced pain and poverty most deeply and who are most motivated to do something about it. Having existed throughout history as a minority that has endured considerable discrimination, the Shiʿis have responded by either retreating into a form of quietism or rising in rebellion against the establishment of the day.

Shiʿi leaders hold diverse views concerning politics and the state. One knowledgeable source speaks of a "plurality of poles," different leadership styles, and "alternate outlets of activism."[25] Traditionally, the Shiʿi community has practiced the politics of quiescence in order to protect itself from the hostile forces in the majority communities. When pushed and cornered, however, the Shiʿis have sporadically resorted to rebellion. According to one Sunni source, "The history of the Shia down through the ages is a history of constant revolutions, most of them crushed. Yet every generation of Shiites gathers its revolutionary strength until its revolution fails, then awaits the next generation, or more auspicious circumstances, with the same result."[26]

Shiʿism of the Khomeini mold in Iran represents a trend that institutionalizes a new activist role for Shiʿi leaders in society. In Iran, many of the grand *ayatollahs* disagreed strongly with Khomeini and his focus on Islamic government. *Mujtahids* such as Muhammad Reza Golpayegani in Qum and Abol Qasim Khoʿi in Najaf warned against clerical intervention in the affairs of state. Those who accepted the close relationship between clerics and the secular state often questioned the place of the *faqih*, the learned jurisprudent who in Khomeini's view represented the ultimate power in Shiʿi society. Clerics such as Husayn ʿAli Montazeri stressed a wider political participation and criticized the concept of the *faqih*, which undercut democratic politics.

Khomeini's vision, however, proved to be popular not only in Iran but also in countries such as Lebanon, Iraq, Bahrain, and Saudi Arabia. In these countries, charismatic leaders in the Khomeini mold increasingly began to appear on the scene. In Lebanon, the key figure was Imam Musa al-Sadr, an outstanding leader who was born in Iran of Lebanese heritage. Imam Musa gained great popularity as the leader of a movement to improve the living conditions of the Shiʿis, but he mysteriously disappeared during a trip to Libya in August 1978. Most observers believe he was assassinated. Another example of a politicized *mujtahid* was Muhammad Baqir al-Sadr, who courageously condemned the oppressive dictatorship of Saddam Hussein in Iraq. In April 1980, al-Sadr and his sister, Bint al-Huda, were executed by Saddam's police. In Bahrain, a country that is over 70 percent Shiʿi, the regime has harshly attacked Shiʿi leaders such as Shaykh ʿAli Salman and Shaykh ʿAbd al-Amir Mansur al-Jamri, who was also harassed and jailed by the Bahraini secret police. Finally, in Saudi Arabia, a Shiʿi cleric named Shaykh Hasan al-Saffar has established a reform movement urging his coreligionists to fight for political involvement, civil society, and minority rights. Hasan al-Saffar condemns dependency and corruption. In the words of Mamoun Fandy: "In this respect, al-Saffar's theology of liberation is similar to liberation theology in Latin America. It privileges praxis over theory."[27]

These Shiʿi leaders represent a new kind of cleric. They have not hesitated to become involved in politics. Like Khomeini, they have been political activists and have confronted the secular political elites who have controlled their societies. At the same time, the establishment politicians have recognized that these Shiʿi popular leaders represent a threat to the general status quo and the authority of the regimes themselves. These governments have responded to the perceived threat by imprisoning and executing the Shiʿi leaders. In so doing, they have angered and alienated Shiʿi populations across the Middle East.

Because of the success of the Iranian Revolution, the power and appeal of Ayatollah Khomeini, and the significance of Iran in the world of Shiʿism, in this section we focus primarily on Shiʿism in Iran. Shiʿi Islam has been the state religion in Iran since 1501, when Shah Ismaʿil founded the Safavid dynasty. Over the years, various royal dynasties have risen and fallen until 1978, when the Shiʿi masses rose to overthrow a secular, monarchical political system. As a result of the revolution, the Shi'i *'ulama* took control of the political system.

The Iranian Revolution was a classic revolution in the genre of the French and Russian Revolutions. Class conflict and social divisions tore the old system to pieces as the deprived masses rose to challenge the Pahlavi monarchy. Organized primarily by the religious leaders and composed of peasants, workers, low-level government officials, *bazaaris,* and disaffected members of the middle class, the revolution overthrew the shah's government in a fourteen-month period between January 1978 and February 1979.

After the shah's departure, an internal political struggle ensued. The result was a victory for the religious forces, who easily disposed of the Western-educated professionals and secular liberals. The religious leaders had their bases of power among the people, and with the people, they had struggled to survive in harsh conditions. The Shi'is' message of equality and their willingness to sacrifice their lives to improve their living conditions and protect their religious beliefs explain much about the revolution.

Before the Iranian Revolution of 1978–79, Shi'ism coexisted in many countries with secular regimes. Its principles concerning government and society remained only ideals discussed and debated among members of the *'ulama.* Among the influential voices in the discussion of the shape of the Islamic Republic were intellectuals such as Ali Shariati, Morteza Mutahhari, and Mehdi Bazargan. In the end, however, the most distinguished and influential figure, whose ideas determined the establishment of the Islamic Republic, was the charismatic leader of the revolution, Ayatollah Ruhollah Khomeini. Khomeini presented his ideas about politics and the state most extensively in his books *Kashf al-Asrar* (The discovery of secrets) and *Hokumat-i Islami* (Islamic government). Today, the Islamic Republic stands as an empirical example of Shi'i political rule. The essence of this rule can be summarized in the following nine characteristics:

1. All power and authority are believed to emanate from God.
2. There is no distinction between mosque and state, between the religious and the secular.
3. The community of the faithful (the *umma*) takes precedence over any constituent parts thereof, whether they be individuals, families, tribes, or nation-states.

4. The divine law that has been revealed to humankind through the Prophet and the Imams takes precedence over all human law.

5. The interpretation of the *shari'a* is entrusted to the guardianship (*velayat*) of learned jurisprudents (*fuqaha*), who are themselves members of the *'ulama*.

6. A special leader (*faqih*) oversees the political system. This leader (also sometimes referred to as the *rahbar*) must be learned, righteous, and accepted by the people.

7. Within the context of the existence of the *faqih*, political participation is an important right of the people.

8. The principle of political participation is institutionalized in an Islamic constitution that provides for a national representative assembly known as the Islamic Majlis.

9. The cardinal principles of justice and equality demand that the masses of the poor and the deprived (*mustaza'fin*) be accorded special consideration within the Islamic Republic.

In sum, the Islamic Republic is a system of Islamic populism in which ultimate authority resides in God and His representatives (*fuqaha*) on earth, while important residual power rests with the people, who participate in elections and the ongoing business of politics. In Khomeini's words: "Islamic government is a government of law. In this form of government, sovereignty belongs to God alone and law is His decree and command."[28] Khomeini goes on to point out that the ruler of an Islamic government must both understand the law and exercise justice impartially.

Leading scholars of Iran and Shi'ism have correctly identified Khomeini as a populist rather than a fundamentalist. The term "fundamentalist" connotes an image of "inflexible orthodoxy, strict adherence to tradition, and rejection of intellectual novelty. . . . In the political arena, however, Khomeini, despite his own denials, was highly flexible, remarkably innovative, and cavalier toward hallowed social traditions. He is important precisely because he discarded many Shii [*sic*] concepts and borrowed ideas, words, and slogans from the non-Muslim world. In doing so, he formulated a brand-new interpretation of state and society. The final product has less in common with conventional fundamentalism than with Third World populism, especially in Latin America."[29]

Populism is an anti-establishment, multiclass movement in which the masses in society rally around a charismatic leader who reflects and promotes their interests. In Shiʿi Iran, Khomeini mobilized the people using a religious political philosophy that stressed equality and justice.

Khomeini spoke in terms of class conflict and emphasized the unjust plight of the *mustazaʿfin* (the oppressed), who were the victims of the *mustakbarin* (the arrogant). In his last will and testament, he stressed the rule of law that focused on equity and social justice (*adeli-yi ijtemaʾi*). He warned the political leaders "to appreciate the value of the people of this nation, do not shirk in serving them, particularly the oppressed, the deprived and the ill-treated, who are the light of our eyes and are everyone's benefactors, and these are the people who made the Islamic Republic possible through their sacrifices." [30]

During the war with Iraq, the *ayatollah* praised the Iranian soldiers: "To which class of society do these heroic fighters of the battlefield belong? Do you find even one person among all of them who is related to persons who have large capital or had some power in the past? If you find one, we will give you a prize. But you won't." [31] He warned high-ranking government officials that "whenever the people consider that one of you is climbing to the upper rungs from the middle classes or are seeking power and wealth for yourselves, they must throw you out of their ranks. . . . It was Imam ʿAli who said that his torn shoes were more valuable than a position in government." [32]

The Shiʿi Islamic state emphasizes justice and the law within the overarching doctrine of doing good and avoiding evil. According to Khomeini, "If the duty of enjoining the good and avoiding the evil is properly performed, all other duties will automatically fall into place." [33] "This principle and the emphasis on law and justice resemble the Catholic focus on natural law. Unlike Western natural law scholars, however, who were concerned with the relation of justice to society, scholars of Islamic jurisprudence concentrated their efforts on the concept of justice in relation to God's will and related it to the destiny of man." [34]

Although God is the originator of all laws, humankind must interpret and apply these laws. Khomeini draws a distinction between divine law (*qanun-i khodaʿi*) and human law (*qanun-i bashari*). Because human law can be distorted and unfair, Shiʿi Islam places a special emphasis on the *fuqaha* and the *mujtahids*. These learned clerics, as we have seen, are the guides and guardians of the faithful. Despite reserving a role for these savants,

Khomeini's Islamic government has protected the right of the people to participate in politics. One of the political institutions that Khomeini emphasized was the Majlis, a legislative body chosen in national elections. According to Khomeini, the former shah "wanted a Majlis with its representatives selected and approved by him. He could not tolerate deputies elected by the people because they criticized him for usurping power. In the Islamic Republic, we will have a Majlis that is elected by the people, and would not be a rubber-stamp [farmayeshi] Majlis."[35]

During the rule of the shah, the Shi'i clerics worked closely with the masses of people. The influence of the 'ulama among the people was enormous, despite the fact that the shah's secular state controlled the police, the military, and the entire governmental apparatus. The shah attempted to cloak himself in religious legitimacy by surrounding himself with a group of establishment clerics. Many members of the 'ulama, however, opposed the oppressive government of the shah. This group of clerics represented populist Shi'ism at work. The establishment Shi'ism of the palace, represented by figures such as the Imam Jum'eh, was easily overrun by the revolution.

It is this new type of government with its tilt toward a clerical leadership that we term populist Shi'ism. Khomeini's personality and the existence of the faqih in the end, however, provided the system with a sharp authoritarian edge. The Shi'i model à la Khomeini contains a centralized authoritarianism that outstrips participatory mechanisms such as the Majlis. This system has not been conducive to democratization. The dialectical push and pull between center and periphery, between harsh authoritarianism and democratic participatory politics, is seen in contemporary Iran in the tension that exists between the faqih, Seyyed 'Ali Khamene'i, and the president, Muhammad Khatami. This dialectic also exists in the Catholic Church in the struggle between the papal center and the more progressive forces of many of the bishops, priests, and laity.

CATHOLICISM, SHI'ISM, AND POPULISM

Although there are significant differences between the modern Shi'i and Catholic approaches to the state and politics, there are also a number of striking similarities. One major difference concerns the line drawn between church and state. In Catholicism, there is no equivalent to the faqih and the *faqih's* final authority in temporal and spiritual matters. The pope exercises special authority only in matters of faith and morals. Furthermore, the leaders of the Catholic Church have tended to oppose various attempts by the clergy to enter into government and politics. Despite these kinds of differences, Catholics and Shiʿis share certain characteristics in the realm of politics.

In the 1960s, the establishment Catholic Church found itself challenged by the masses of the faithful, who increasingly let it be known that they found the social, political, and religious status quo unacceptable. During this same time period, Iranian activists began to challenge the authority of the secular regime of the shah. Sensing the depth of the disaffection, both the Catholic leadership and the shah's regime in Iran attempted to co-opt the ideas of the growing opposition. Vatican II and the "white revolution" in Iran had similar goals. They sought to protect the status quo by administering carefully apportioned doses of reform. Pope John XXIII assembled the Second Vatican Council in October 1962, and the shah announced the establishment of his "white revolution" in January 1963.

The growing power of liberation theology in the world of Roman Catholicism developed into a movement in the late 1960s and early 1970s. Similarly, the populist opposition to the shah crystallized in the mid-1960s and hardened in the early 1970s. Elsewhere, violence shook the world and peaked in the riots and demonstrations of 1968. The United Nations proclaimed the 1960s the "decade of development" and announced a massive campaign to narrow the gap between rich and poor. The campaign failed miserably, and the gap has only increased in subsequent decades. Both Catholicism and Shiʿism have had to confront the problems that have developed from this explosive situation.

Catholicism and Shiʿism exhibit relevant similarities in eight areas:

1. the fundamental tension between faith and reason
2. the normative nature of politics, politics based on systems of law derived from divine precepts
3. the preeminent importance of the concepts of unity and community
4. the rejection of both Western liberal and Eastern Marxist models of the state

5. the coexistence of two realms of power in society—the authority of the institution at the center and the participatory interests of the people at the periphery
6. the increasing concern for the downtrodden and oppressed in society and the world at large
7. the institutionalization of almsgiving and charity
8. the failure to integrate women into the authority structure of both faith systems

Both Shi'i and Catholic thinkers have long had a lively debate about the relationship between faith and reason. In the end, both traditions have concluded that revelation and reason are essential ingredients in their faiths. Although the emphasis has differed from one scholar to another, the general conclusion is that reason (or philosophy) can lead to the truths of revelation, which are of central concern in religious systems. Thomas Aquinas himself was not always consistent concerning this issue. Ultimately, he concluded that faith and reason "were both valid and divinely legitimated sources of human knowledge" and implied that revelation acted "as a kind of negative check on reason."[36] Nor were the great Islamic thinkers always in agreement here. While al-Ghazali severely questioned the role of philosophy, other Muslim sages such as Ibn Rushd defended its place, and we have seen that Shi'ism always emphasized it.

Flowing naturally from the faith/reason issue is the principle of law that guides and directs human political activity. Indeed, the Islamic and Catholic Christian communities emphasize the existence of a divine rule that guides the legal system. The law is the tent pole of the political system. In Islam, the divine law (shari'a) provides the totality of human guidelines. The shari'a is superior to all human law, and its application to human conditions is known as the practice of fiqh. According to Catholic teaching in the Thomist tradition, unchanging eternal law subsumes both natural law and divine law. Natural law concerns the rational application of eternal law, whereas divine law emphasizes the revelational component. Human law, it follows, is the application of the unchanging principles of natural law to the changing circumstances of human life. In the Islamic Republic of Iran, the state is organized according to the shari'a, which is held to contain all of the basic principles that activate the social and political systems. In Catholicism, the emphasis on divine law and natural law exists primarily as the philosophical foundation for the political thought of practicing Catholics.

In Catholicism, the good of the community takes precedence over the well-being of the individual member of the community. The same is true in Islam, which emphasizes the *umma*, the Islamic community that knows no borders or boundaries. Union, unity, and community take precedence over individualism, dispersion, and the division of peoples into families, tribes, and even nation-states. In the thinking of Ayatollah Khomeini and other theoreticians of the Islamic Republic of Iran, the individual, the self (*nafs*), should never take precedence over the common good. As we have seen, the Muslim concept of *umma* corresponds roughly to the Catholic concept of the church.

Given the priority of the common good, the community, and the *umma* and given the belief that human law is derived from a higher system of law (divine law), it follows that both visions of politics emphasize the centralized authority of the state. This centralization, however, has two checks: it must be applied in keeping with higher moral principles, and it must reserve a degree of autonomy for the people. This principle of subsidiarity in the Catholic tradition is paralleled by the principle of participatory populism inherent in the Shiʿi philosophy of politics.

The presence of the *faqih* in the Shiʿi state provides for a stronger model of authoritarianism in Shiʿism than the model of authoritarianism that exists in Catholicism. Centralized papal control cannot begin to match the power of the Shiʿi *faqih*. Nonetheless, both *mujtahids* and popes have struggled to protect their authority, an authority increasingly under siege. In so doing, they have adopted many similar tactics and strategies, including the use of carefully apportioned reform in order to avoid radical political change. The centralization of Catholicism is greatly envied in Islam — Shiʿi Islam especially — but the degree of direct political control is absent in Roman Catholicism.

Both Catholicism and Shiʿism have rejected the alternatives of Western liberalism and Eastern socialism. With the collapse of the major experiment in planned socialist economics in the Soviet Union in the 1980s and 1990s, the socialist model was severely tarnished. At the same time, Catholicism has generally thrived in Western industrial environments. In sum, Shiʿi Islam and Roman Catholicism both attempt to walk the narrow path between centralization and participation, between authority and liberty. In this delicate journey, both traditions lean in the direction of central control.

The centralizing tilt toward authoritarianism in both Shi'ism and Catholicism can be easily abused. Just as *mujtahids* can counsel obedience and subservience in the face of oppression, so too can the Catholic clerics discourage the faithful from challenging decisions from the center. Furthermore, both clerical groups can recommend acceptance of the secular status quo in various national contexts. Until the appearance of Khomeini, the *'ulama* often sought to preserve the political and religious status quo through various strategies. One of the most effective was to preach reform in an effort to avoid the need to transform. In the latter half of the twentieth century, such strategies increasingly failed. Authoritarianism infused with political oppression led to social and political upheaval. In Catholicism, these movements, with their "option for the poor," came to be known as liberation theology, while in Shi'i Iran, they were referred to as a populist Islam that represented the rights of the downtrodden (*mustaza'fin*).

Khomeini's *mustaza'fin* were paralleled in Catholic Latin America, for example, by the *oprimidos* or the *masas popularas*. Just as Shi'is emphasize the lives of Imam 'Ali and Imam Husayn, who are believed to have suffered and to have challenged oppression, so too do liberation theologians stress the life and suffering of Jesus, who championed the cause of the deprived and dispossessed. Whereas 'Ali "lived in simplicity and poverty like the poorest of people," maintaining great "compassion for the needy and poor,"[37] Jesus "empt[ied] himself, taking the nature of a slave" and "being rich became poor" (Philippians 2:6; 2 Corinthians 8:9). Imams 'Ali and Husayn, like Jesus, are thought to have suffered and to have died redemptive deaths. These transcendental acts of martyrdom were believed to have taken place as part of "the struggle against human selfishness and everything that divides men and enables them to be rich and poor, possessors and dispossessed, oppressors and oppressed."[38]

Roman Catholicism and Shi'i Islam have rich heritages of charity and almsgiving. Through a wide variety of organizations and institutions, the church has encouraged charitable giving in order to help improve the lives of the poor. Millions of the poor and impoverished representing numerous religions and nationalities have benefited from Catholic charities over the years.[39] Catholics are urged by the church to practice charity, which is considered one of the cardinal virtues of the faith. An excellent example of Catholic charity in action is the Catholic Relief Services, founded in 1943 by Catholic bishops in the United States. In 1995, Pope John Paul II stated: "In a world scarred by religious divisions and national rivalries, Catholic Relief Services testifies to the unity of the human family and to the equal and inalienable dignity of each and every person. . . . With courage and compassion, Christians must be ever attentive to the cry of the poor, serving the Lord who is present in their suffering."[40] Other Catholic charitable organizations range from the Society of St. Vincent de Paul to the Knights of Columbus and the Little Sisters of the Poor.

In the world of Shi'ism, charity is also an integral part of the teachings of the religion. The concept of *zakat* is defined as almsgiving based on the *shari'a* and is considered to be one of the five pillars of Islam. Although the practice of *zakat* applies to both Shi'is and Sunnis, there is an additional dimension in the Shi'i experience. The believer is expected to pay *khums*, or one-fifth of one's surplus income after necessary expenditures are paid. As part of the *khums*, Shi'is pay what is known as *sahm-i Imam* (share of the Imam), which is used to support needy clerics. The Shi'i *mujtahids*, therefore, have significant resources, and they play a key role in distributing wealth where it is most needed.

In both Catholicism and Shi'ism, the leading clerics, whether they be bishops or *mujtahids*, oversee the acquisition and distribution of charitable funds. This institutionalization of charitable giving is one method of redistributing the wealth in society. The strong emphasis on charity and almsgiving follows naturally from teachings that stress equality and social justice. Despite the commitment to charity, which has undoubtedly had an impact on alleviating the suffering of the poor, Catholic and Shi'i almsgiving has not solved the problems of poverty. If anything, it has moderated the pain and suffering and helped awaken the social consciousness of the masses. Thus, movements such as liberation theology and populism have sought to fill the void in the face of modern malaise.

Central to the challenges confronting both Shi'ism and Catholicism is the situation of women. Although many Shi'i women staunchly supported the Iranian Revolution, women have not always fared well in the Islamic Republic. They feel powerless because when they try to interpret the Qur'an and traditions in ways more representative of the equality and dignity they are sure God intended, they are told they have no right to determine such questions. Shi'i women are rarely *mujtahids,* and the Islamic educational system overwhelmingly favors males, even though there is no inherent reason why Shi'i women should not be *mujtahids.*[41] Hence, although women wield considerable power in Islamic society, they lack authority. This is especially apparent in the field of family law, which remains "the cornerstone of the system of male privilege set up by establishment Islam."[42] Seyyed Hossein Nasr correctly points out that the roles of men and women are complementary, not competitive. Men and women stand as equals before God. In the everyday realm of politics and social life, however, the Shi'i woman is not equal to the man.

Catholic women, like Shi'i women, lack the authority of men. As long as the church follows the traditions of the apostles, who apparently did not ordain women, women's way to the priesthood seems barred. Just as there were no female Imams, there have been no female popes. "Deaconesses" in the early church ministered to women and children, though they did not serve at the altar. Women have, of course, also served as nuns and abbesses and have been scholars and even "doctors of the Church." No formal barrier blocks their access to the role of chancellor or administrator of a parish or diocese. Nonetheless, women in the Catholic tradition lack the rights and authority to become priests, bishops, and popes and are unable to say Mass. Scholars of the early church often viewed women as inferior and ritually impure. In the history of both Shi'ism and Catholicism, there has been a de facto segregation of men and women.

In Roman Catholicism and Twelver Shi'ism, opportunities for women to play a meaningful public role have not kept pace with the changes that have marked the modern world. Although women wield considerable power and influence in both traditions, they continue to lack authority. By keeping the door of authoritative leadership closed to 50 percent of the population in each society, the Catholic and Shi'i hierarchies alienate many of their believers and weaken their organizational structure.

The theoreticians of liberation theology have encountered situations in which the principle of subsidiarity has proven to be ineffective in the face of overwhelming state power. In states where military juntas and oligarchies have ruled capriciously and arbitrarily, Catholic clergymen have become involved in challenging governing establishments in an attempt to redress the imbalance between centralized authoritarianism and popular participation. In so doing, they have developed a theology that stresses a prophetic—as opposed to institutional—form of involvement of the church with the state. This perspective brings them closer to the philosophy of Shi'i populism. The approach of liberation theology is more scriptural than scholastic, more historical-dialectical than philosophical.

Based on a powerful source of divine legitimacy that suffuses all human activity and working within a framework of law and social justice, both Catholic-inspired liberation theology and Shi'i populism reserve a special autonomy and dignity for the individual and the popular masses. When such autonomy and dignity are seriously threatened, the religious leaders, whether Shi'i *'ulama* or Catholic clerics, have increasingly indicated a willingness to engage in political activism, invoking the model of the Imams and Jesus.

The congruence of religion and politics is seen in Shi'i Islam. In Roman Catholicism, the gap between the two realms is slowly beginning to narrow as Third World citizens turn to intermediaries and representatives of Jesus for aid and succor. Because social, political, and economic problems are global in scope, Shi'i Islam and Roman Catholicism face similar challenges. They must confront the challenge of modernity while at the same time preserving their valued traditions. The strategies that these faith systems adopt will determine not only the relevance of their heritages but also the capacity of much of humankind to survive with justice, dignity, and understanding.

CONCLUSION:
THE COMPARATIVE
POLITICS OF
RELIGION

By comparing two religious traditions that at first sight appear to be quite different and distinct, this book seeks to advance our understanding of both faith systems. One may be a convinced Roman Catholic or a believing Twelver Shi'i, a practicing member of another tradition or a follower of no tradition and still benefit from this comparative exercise. This approach provides a useful way to convey information, and it can freshen the discussion of the respective religions. Beyond these goals, however, this study attempts to serve a more general purpose. It seeks to treat religion — a defining aspect of human experience — as an integral part of society and politics. And it attempts to do so in the context of a rapidly transforming world. By carefully comparing Roman Catholicism and Shi'i Islam as these systems confront similar problems in a similar world, one may better understand the human predicament.

By the beginning of the twenty-first century, leading religious voices increasingly have been raised in invitations for dialogue and cross-denominational communication. On the Catholic-Muslim front, for example, Pope John Paul II stated in 1999:

> Like Christians and Jews, Muslims look upon the patriarch Abraham as a model of unconditional submission to the will of God, and they know that in the one God we find our origin, our teacher, our guide and our last end. . . . Through dialogue with Muslims, we come to a better knowledge

of one another. Today Christians and Muslims are called to cooperate in defending human dignity, moral values and freedom. By working for reconciliation and peace, in humble submission to God's will, the two religions can be signs of hope, making the world more aware of the wisdom and mercy of God, who created the human family and continues to govern and guide it.[1]

In this book, we have presented and discussed similarities in Shi'i and Roman Catholic belief and practice, including the following:

1. an emphasis on the significance of the passion of innocent victims who in free acts of moral solidarity offered their lives for their followers and are seen as atoning for them
2. the belief that God's grace and gifts are mediated through sacred personages (Imams and saints) who act as intercessors
3. the centrality of a sorrowful mother figure at the heart of a holy family that represents the social foundation of the faith system
4. the influence of Platonic and Aristotelian thought on theologians who have debated the relationship between revelation and reason
5. the importance of mystical movements
6. the role of martyrdom and redemptive suffering
7. the recognition of legal systems based on the premise that all power derives from God
8. the drive for the establishment of social and political systems that will provide justice, liberty, and security

The Aristotelian premise that humans are social animals and that politics is an architectonic science is accepted by both Catholics and Shi'is. Their stories have a heavy political component. Both have accepted perforce that political rule may not be the rule of the most excellent, that *din* (religion) and *dawla* (state), though intertwined, must at times be distinct. Both abhor anarchy as destructive of the good things that God desires for humanity, and both have sometimes been forced to compromise with tyranny, although such a compromise rarely has been made willingly.

All societies are confronted with social problems such as the gap that divides rich and poor, the tension between liberty and authority, and the struggle between justice and inequity. These seminal issues will continue to plague religious and political thinkers in an imperfect world. Beginning with their common premise that all power emanates from God, both Twelver Shiʿism and Roman Catholicism have developed ideal models of the state that combine strong central authority with concern for the moral freedom of the individual. In Catholicism, the organic model is one in which the preeminence of the community is balanced against the principle of subsidiarity that protects the rights of the individual. In Twelver Iran today, the balance is between the guardianship of the learned jurisprudent (*faqih*) and an apparatus of popular participation that includes elections and an Islamic Majlis. In both cases, in the real world of politics, there has been a tendency for these systems to tilt in the direction of authoritarianism.

Despite this tilt, the Roman Catholic and Twelver Shiʿi traditions have maintained a special sensitivity to the needs of the individual and the importance of human rights and social justice. In the Third World, this concern is expressed in great sympathy for the oppressed (the *oprimidos* in Spanish, the *mustazaʿfin* in Persian and Arabic). At its peak, the Catholic movement of liberation theology active in Latin America was not unlike Shiʿi populism in the Middle East. There is a dialectical tension between "establishment religion" and "populist religion" and between centralizing authority and social justice, with its concerns for individual freedom. The direction of the dialectic varies through time depending on the social forces and the political leadership of the day.

In the piety of both traditions, there is a pervasive emphasis on the rights of the poor. Going back to the time of Jesus and his disciples and to Imam ʿAli and his descendants, there has been a deep commitment to the oppressed, the dispossessed, and the distressed. As long as this remains the case, there will be little doubt that both Twelver Shiʿism and Roman Catholicism will be under pressure to represent a God who desires justice and equality.

The social and political power of these religious traditions is witnessed by the history of martyrs, who made the ultimate sacrifice for their convictions. In both faith systems, the mark of the martyr crosses the divide between the *zahir* and the *batin*. The strength of the *batin* is the power of love, sacrifice, and redemption. It is the inner force represented by Jesus, Husayn, and al-Hallaj. These traditions teach that "dying power" can be more influential and meaningful than "killing power." The power and relevance of martyrdom are seen in the message delivered by Ayatollah Khomeini to the pope's special envoy shortly after the Iranian Revolution when the United States was threatening to invade Iran: "Our nation looks forward to an opportunity for self-sacrifice and martyrdom. Now let us suppose that in the absence of all reasoning Mr. Carter or perhaps the superpowers should agree to send military forces here. Well, then we have a population of thirty-five million people, and once we are all martyred, then our enemies can do whatever they want to with this country."[2]

The power of love, self-sacrifice, and martyrdom is sometimes diluted and compromised in the "real" world, where the forces of greed, corruption, injustice, and oppression often prevail. The religious establishment may reflect pomp and circumstance, wealth and affluence, luxury and clientism—the desire to preserve a status quo that has become not just episodically but systematically unjust. It is in response to this establishment mind-set that the masses of people threaten to rise to challenge the system.

In the Catholic case, the problems that arose when the intelligentsia began to fundamentally question church doctrine were addressed by socially sensitive encyclicals, the dramatic events of Vatican II, and the pope's emphasis on global travel to meet firsthand the poor and the afflicted. The thunder of liberation theology was muffled through a carefully developed policy of co-optation planned by Pope John Paul II, the most widely traveled pope in history. He used his leadership to weaken the explosive revolutionary thrust of liberation theology and disengage it from its Marxist connotations. John Paul II did not, however, demolish the movement because he himself knew well that Jesus had preached a "preferential option for the poor."[3]

In Iran, Twelver Shi'ism challenged the secularizing regime of the Pahlavi political elite in the late 1970s. Led by a charismatic Shi'i *mujtahid*, Ayatollah Ruhollah Khomeini, who espoused a populist ideology, the Shi'i masses and their leaders took control of a modern political system. The oppressive policies of the shah, his establishment clerics, and his Western-trained army and police failed completely.

As the revolutionaries became the establishment, ruling Iran for over two decades, the new Shi'i leaders found themselves confronted by a punishing ninety-five-month war with an invading Iraqi army backed by the United States, Russia, Europe, and several of the wealthy Arab Gulf states and a costly economic embargo instituted by the United States. Furthermore, the revolutionary Shi'i political leaders found that they themselves were challenged by their own postrevolutionary *mustaza'fin*.

Challenges to the political status quo that are generated by populist religious movements—whether Christian or Muslim, Catholic or Shi'i—develop most powerfully during periods of economic hardship, social anomie, and political oppression. The force of so-called religious fundamentalism, for example, is strongest in these times of trouble. Individuals grasp religion during periods of crisis and incoherence. The research of one erudite Jordanian scholar demonstrates that religious revivalism arises historically during periods of unusually pronounced insecurity. The greater the insecurity, the more fervently people turn to religion.[4] Both Christianity and Islam were born during times when society was mired in deep malaise and harsh transition. Jesus of Nazareth and Muhammad of Mecca appeared on the world stage when corruption and oppression were rampant, when the lower and middle classes found themselves sinking deeper into poverty and impotence, and when hopelessness and despair pervaded their lives and culture.

In the latter half of the twentieth century, many Catholics turned to their religion for help, and in so doing, they struggled to shape their faith to their immediate needs. At the same time, many Twelver Shi'i Muslims looked to their religious leaders for support and succor. There is every reason to expect that populist religious faith will represent a major ideological force in the twenty-first century, a century certain to be an age of transformation. At this time in history, it is important that the widely diverse world communities and cultures strive to communicate with, tolerate, and, most important, understand one another.

NOTES

INTRODUCTION

1. The quotations pertaining to the March 1999 meeting between Pope John Paul II and Hojjat ol-Islam Muhammad Khatami are drawn from various newspapers and press releases in the authors' possession.
2. Edward Lodge Curran, *Great Moments in Catholic History* (New York: Grosset and Dunlap, 1938), 32.
3. Usama ibn-Munqidh (d. 1188), quoted in Philip K. Hitti, *Islam and the West* (Princeton, N.J.: D. Van Nostrand, 1962), 167.
4. Quoted in G. H. Jansen, *Militant Islam* (New York: Harper and Row, 1979), 14.
5. Pakistani Supreme Court justice Muhammad Shahabuddin, quoted in Ralph Braibanti, "Cornelius of Pakistan: Catholic Chief Justice of a Muslim State," *Islam and Christian-Muslim Relations* 10 (1999): 118. This work is an excellent analysis of the life and influence of A. R. Cornelius.
6. Several thousand Twelver Shi'is live in the Kharab quarter of Damascus. In Syria, a Twelver is referred to as a *rafid* (pl., *ruffad*), or "rejecter" of the first three caliphs. In Kenya, there are an estimated 10,000 Twelvers, most of whose ancestors migrated to Africa from India in the late nineteenth century.

CHAPTER ONE

1. Few religions require assent to doctrine. Such assent does not make one a Shinto, a Hindu, or even a Jew. A Muslim needs to believe only in the one God and that Muhammad is His messenger. The short Apostles' Creed that was used in Rome may date to as early as 150.
2. Proverbs 1–9; Job 28; Ecclesiasticus 24; Wisdom of Solomon 7:22–8:1.
3. John 1:4, 5, 9.
4. Ibid., 14:6.
5. The primacy of Peter is fundamental to the Catholic communion. Needless to say, this primacy is recognized not only in the West; that is, not all Catholics are "Roman." The historic churches of the East all have branches

in communion with the pope (or universal father) of Rome as head of the universal church. They may have different hierarchies, liturgical and sacramental forms, and canon laws, but they are all as "Catholic" as the pope himself because they are united under his primacy. Here we will focus mainly on the church of the West, the Church of Rome, which has lived not only with the primacy of Peter (and his successor, the bishop of Rome) but also with the direct rule of the papacy as ecclesial governor. Eastern Catholic churches are governed by other hierarchs who accept the pope as their spiritual head.

6. The Roman Church also has hierarchs called patriarchs, for example, the patriarch of Venice. Their actual function differs little from that of any other archbishop.

7. "Pope" is derived from the Greek *papa*, meaning universal father. The title was given to two of the leading patriarchs—of Alexandria and Rome—and is still used by their successors.

8. This was the famous *filioque*, which described the Holy Spirit as proceeding not only "from the Father," as the original creed had stated, but also "from the Son." The truth of the statement (which had been around a long time and had both proponents and critics) was not called into question as much as the unilateral action of the pope.

9. Quoted by Pope Pius X in *Iucunda Sane* (Healthy youth), March 12, 1904.

10. Ibid.

11. Charles the Great (Charlemagne) descended from the Frankish chief minister Pépin of Herstal (d. 714), whose grandson Pépin assumed royal power after 749 with the approval of Pope Zachary. Pépin protected Pope Zachary from his enemies, the Lombards of north Italy. Charles was anointed emperor in Old St. Peter's Basilica in 800 by Pope Leo III, and he swore to defend the Church of St. Peter. He was not recognized by the Byzantine emperor, who believed that the pope had committed treason against the true Roman Empire.

12. See note 8. The formula seems to have originated in Visigothic Spain.

13. See Joseph H. Lynch, *The Medieval Church* (New York: Longman, 1992), 82.

14. Ibid., 108–13.

15. The Christian theologians of the East were much less categorical. Grace is important, but there is also the activity of the divine Logos, which permeates all of creation. Humankind's predicament is therefore serious indeed but not fatal. Humankind is always made in the image (*icon*) of God.

16. This movement was led by the followers of Cornelis Jansen, the theologian bishop of Ypres (d. 1638), whose views on salvation brought them papal

condemnation in 1653, 1708, and 1713, as well as the enmity of the Jesuits and of Louis XIV in France.

17. See Robert Wuthnow, *Loose Connections: Joining Together in America's Fragmented Communities* (Cambridge: Harvard University Press, 1998), in which problems and solutions are articulated.

18. This is the famous *Hadith al-Ghadir,* so-called from the Ghadir or salty pool of Khumm in the desert where the Prophet told the caravan to stop.

19. "Man kuntu mawlahu, fa-'Ali mawlahu." Many hold that he added, "Allahumma wali man walahu wa 'adi man 'adahu" (O God, be the friend of those who befriend him, and the enemy of those who antagonize him).

20. Shi'is often accuse 'A'isha of having concealed Muhammad's attempts at the end to reinforce his choice of 'Ali.

21. Because the name was later also adopted by followers of the Prophet's uncle 'Abbas, Shi'is held that it could be used only for *shi'at 'Ali,* "partisans of 'Ali."

22. Obviously, a great deal can be said about this matter on both sides. Both believe they are justified; both produce statements and witnesses to back their point of view. A great Sunni jurist of the eighth century, Abu Hanifa of Kufa, stated about the argument, "We leave this dispute to God, who knows matters secret and hidden" (*Al-Fiqh al-Akbar,* in *Majmu'at Shuruh al-Fiqh al-Akbar* (Hyderabad: Osmania University Press, 1321], 5).

23. The word *imam* means "leader," literally "the one in front," and is also used to refer to anyone who leads the prayer. It is used in Sunnism to refer to a very eminent scholar, for example, the leader of a school of jurisprudence.

24. The ancestor of the kings of Jordan laid claim to the title after 1924, but the claim was not generally conceded.

25. The Isma'ilis also follow this practice when ordered by their leaders.

26. Certain sayings ascribed to Muhammad foretell the coming of such a "Guided One." At various times in Muslim history up to the present, claimants to the title have appeared. The Fatimid caliphate of the Isma'ili Shi'is was established by a claimant known as 'Ubaydallah the Mahdi in 908 in North Africa, and it survived until 1171 in Egypt. A caliphate was established in Morocco in 1132 by a dynasty that followed a Mahdi named Ibn Tumart and ruled until 1212 over Muslim Spain and North Africa as far west as Tripoli. The dynasty ended only in 1276.

27. The name means "withdrawers" and was first applied to those who refused to be drawn into the political quarrels of the early community. It later came to be used for those who sought guidance in reason rather than internecine wrangling, though the rationalists themselves became a wrangling

faction. Historically, the Mu'tazila had close ties with the Zaydi Shi'is, and the Sunni scholars of Yemen still refer to the Zaydis as "Mu'tazila."

28. Qur'an 96:3–8.

29. See Hossein Modarressi Tabataba'i, *An Introduction to Shi'i Law: A Bibliographic Study* (London: Ithaca Press, 1984), 4. Modarressi points out that although this is true, one eminent modern authority argues that in practice all such rules of reason are to be found in the Qur'an and the traditions of the Prophet and the Imams.

30. Their names have been preserved both by Ibn Babuyi (or Babawayh) al-Saduq of Qum (d. 991), who was a traditionist and no friend of theological reasoning, and by Ibn al-Mu'allim al-Shaykh al-Mufid (d. 1022), who argued for theological reasoning. Some of them are Hisham b. al-Hakam, Hisham b. Salim, Zurara b. A'yan, Mu'min al-Taq, and Yunus b. 'Abd al-Rahman, all of whom lived in the eighth century.

31. These are Muhammad b. Ya'qub al-Kulayni (d. 941) and Muhammad b. 'Ali b. Husayn ibn Babuyi (or Babawayh) al-Saduq (d. 941). See Modarressi Tabataba'i, *Introduction*, 23.

32. W. Madelung, "Al-Mufid," in *Encyclopaedia of Islam* 2 (Leiden: E. J. Brill, 1991), 7:312–13; Modarressi Tabataba'i, *Introduction*, 40–43. His *Kitab al-Irshad*, with lives and traditions of the Prophet and the Imams, has been translated into English by I. K. A. Howard (Elmhurst, N.Y.: Tahrike Tarsile Qur'an, 1981).

33. "Sharif" is not a name but a title given to a descendant of the Prophet.

34. Along with the collections of al-Kulayni and Ibn Babuyi, these make up the "four books" of Shi'i *hadith*.

35. Nasir al-Din Tusi's *Tajrid al-Kalam* (Theology laid bare) "has preserved its authority among masters of this discipline for more than seven centuries," and Muhaqqiq al-Hilli "is considered to be the foremost Shi'ite jurist" ('Allamah Tabataba'i, *Shi'ite Islam*, translated by Seyyed Hossein Nasr [Albany: State University of New York Press, 1975], 110).

36. The study of the principles and derivations of jurisprudence in Twelver Usuli thought is an ongoing process, far from being laid down in the past once and for all. See Modarressi Tabataba'i, *Introduction*.

37. More than intellectual debate is involved. Shi'is must pay the *khums*, or one-fifth of each year's profits, to the Imam or, in his absence, to their *mujtahid*, to be used for community purposes. *Mujtahids* also control bequests, pious endowments, and trusts. They cannot use the money for private purposes, but they can, for example, choose sites, contractors, and personnel for a school or foundation. Leading *mujtahids* may have great economic power and political influence.

38. Modern works that have contributed greatly to our understanding of the Usuli-Akhbari debate include Mangol Bayat, *Mysticism and Dissent: Socio-religious Thought in Qajar Iran* (Syracuse: Syracuse University Press, 1982); Said Amir Arjomand, *The Shadow of God and the Hidden Imam* (Chicago: University of Chicago Press, 1984); and Abbas Amanat, "In Between the Madrasa and the Marketplace: The Designation of Clerical Leadership in Modern Shi'ism," in *Authority and Political Culture in Shi'ism*, edited by Said Amir Arjomand (Albany: State University of New York Press, 1988), 98–112.

39. Ayatullah Mirza Hasan al-Haeri al-Ehghaghi al-Usku'i, interview by James Bill, Imam Sadiq Mosque, Kuwait, October 4, 1983. Born in 1897, Mirza Hasan was still active in 2000.

40. Important old Twelver communities are found in southern Iraq, southern Lebanon, the Arab sections of the Persian Gulf, and southern and central India (the Dakkhan and Awadh). Smaller groups may be found elsewhere, for example, in Central Asia, Anatolia, and the Caucasus.

CHAPTER TWO

1. Hostile and adulatory accounts may be found of almost all the leading Shi'i personages and events, reflecting the religious division. Wherever possible, we have selected the accounts found in sources acknowledged not only by Shi'is but also by Sunnis and found in the Sunni collections of *hadith* and *akhbar*. A good summation of these sources is found in W. M. Watt, "Fatima," in *Encyclopaedia of Islam 2* (Leiden: E. J. Brill, 1991).

2. Al-Bukhari, *Jami' al-Sahih* (Leiden: E. J. Brill, 1868–1908), 2:435–36.

3. Shaykh al-Mufid, *Kitab al-Irshad*, translated by I. K. A. Howard (Elmhurst, N.Y.: Tahrike Tarsile Qur'an, 1981), 46–48.

4. Al-Tabari, *Ta'rikh*, ser. 1, pp. 1402–3, translated by W. Montgomery Watt and M. V. McDonald in *History of al-Tabari* (Albany: State University of New York Press, 1987), 7:119–20; al-Mufid, *Al-Irshad*, 52–61.

5. Ibn Ishaq and Ibn Hisham, *The Life of Muhammad*, translated by A. Guillaume (Pakistan: Oxford University Press, 1955), 454–56; al-Mufid, *Al-Irshad*, 65–72.

6. See al-Tabari, *Ta'rikh*, ser. 1, pp. 1577–81, in *History of al-Tabari*, and al-Mufid, *Al-Irshad*, 85–87.

7. The name refers to not only people from the area of South Arabia now called Yemen but also anyone from the southern division of tribes who might live there, in Oman, or anywhere; for example, the Aws and Khazraj tribes of the oasis of Madina were also called "Yemenis." According to Arab

genealogical tradition, all of these tribes were descended from Qahtan, or Joktan, the descendant of Abraham.

8. As usual, accounts vary about the reason. 'Ali is said to have ordered his people not to shed the blood of Muslims, but in the issue, he was attacked and found himself forced to fight. The most reasonable account, given by the historian al-Tabari (translated by Adrian Brockett in *History of al-Tabari* [Albany: State University of New York Press, 1997], 16:122–24), indicates that 'Ali and the rebels were near agreement that those guilty of 'Uthman's murder should be punished when some of those on his side began to attack the men of Zubayr, Talha, and 'A'isha's army.

9. Al-Tabari, *Ta'rikh*, ser. 1, p. 3282. One of 'Ali's warriors is quoted as saying that these were his orders before every battle (translated by G. R. Hawting in *History of al-Tabari* [Albany: State University of New York Press, 1996], 17:30).

10. Ziyad was one of 'Ali's ablest officers, but his mother had been a prostitute in the town of Ta'if. After 'Ali's death, Mu'awiya attached Ziyad to his cause by having witnesses swear that in pre-Islamic times his father had been Mu'awiya's own father, the aristocratic Abu Sufyan, chief of the Clan of Umayya and leader of the Meccan enemies of Muhammad, who had often been in Ta'if on business. The Prophet had married Abu Sufyan's daughter, Umm Habiba, in part to show Abu Sufyan that he would lose nothing by coming to Islam. 'Ubaydallah was Ziyad's son.

11. The best accounts of the battle of Karbala are preserved in al-Tabari's *Ta'rikh*, translated by I. K. A. Howard in *History of al-Tabari* (Albany: State University of New York Press, 1990), esp. 19:74–76, and in the collection of accounts by Abu Mikhnaf translated in ibid., 83–161. Even at this remove, they bring tears to the eyes.

12. Al-Tabari, *Ta'rikh*, ser. 2, p. 371. In a similar story, Yazid b. Mu'awiya was the man with the cane and the companion was Abu Barza al-Aslami (ibid., 283, 383).

13. Al-Mufid, *Al-Irshad*, 383.

14. Some of them have been translated by William C. Chittick in *A Shi'ite Anthology*, edited by Sayyid Muhammad al-Tabataba'i (Qum: Ansariyan Publications, 1982), 113–22.

15. Ibn Babuya, *A Shi'ite Creed*, edited and translated by A. A. A. Fyzee (New York: Oxford University Press, 1942), 96.

16. See al-Kardari, *Manaqib Abi Hanifa* (Beirut: Dar al-Ahnaf, 1981), 37–38.

17. Offspring by a slave handmaiden, such as Abraham and Jacob had, are of course fully legitimate in Islamic law. The legal term for the child's mother is *umm walad*, usually translated as "concubine."

18. See al-Masʿudi, *Muruj al-Dhahab* (Paris: Société Asiatique, 1869), 5:467–71.

19. See E. Kohlberg, "Muhammad b. ʿAli Zayn al-ʿAbidin," in *Encyclopaedia of Islam 2* (Leiden: E. J. Brill, 1991), 7:397–400.

20. Quoted in al-Mufid, *Al-Irshad*, 416.

21. Ismaʿilis regard Imam Jaʿfar as the fifth Imam, not the sixth, since they hold that Imam Hasan was really only practicing *taqiyya* to draw the hunters from Husayn, who was the true heir of ʿAli. Thus Ismaʿil is their sixth Imam, and Muhammad his heir, the seventh. The number seven has figured prominently in their gnostic religious system, and they are often called "Seveners."

22. See al-Tabari, *Taʾrikh*, ser. 3, p. 446, translated by John A. Williams in *Early ʿAbbasi Empire* (Cambridge: Cambridge University Press, 1989), 2:47, and Abu al-Faraj al-Isfahani, *Maqatil al-Talibiyin* (Matbaʿ Najaf, Iraq, 1935).

23. E. Kohlberg, "Musa al-Kazim," in *Encyclopaedia of Islam 2*, 7:645–48.

24. Al-Tabari, *Taʾrikh*, ser. 3, p. 533, in *Early ʿAbbasi Empire*, 2:126.

25. For a discussion of the accounts and the sources, see Kohlberg, "Musa al-Kazim."

26. See al-Mufid, *Al-Irshad*, 477–78.

27. See Ibn Babuyi, *Shiʿite Creed*, article 38.

28. Al-Mufid, *Al-Irshad*, translation, 495.

29. Ibid., 523. See also J. Eliash, "Hasan al-ʿAskari," in *Encyclopaedia of Islam 2* (Leiden: E. J. Brill, 1971), 3:246–47.

CHAPTER THREE

1. Qurʾan 19:31.

2. For a thorough discussion of the fundamental differences between Islamic and Christian beliefs, see Robert L. Fastiggi, "The Incarnation: Muslim Objections and the Christian Response," *Thomist* 57 (July 1993): 457–93.

3. Qurʾan 4:171.

4. Hebrews 4:15.

5. Imam ʿAli, *Nahj al-Balagha*, sermon 159, p. 324. This collection of sermons attributed to Imam ʿAli dates from the early eleventh century and has been published as *Nahjul Balagha* (The peak of eloquence), translated by Sayed Ali Reza (Elmhurst, N.Y.: Tahrike Tarsile Qurʾan, 1986). A similar statement about Jesus is attributed to the ascetic Hasan of Basra in the early eighth century.

6. Hamid Enayat, *Modern Islamic Political Thought* (Austin: University of Texas Press, 1982), 183.

7. This is from the Gloria prayer in the Roman Catholic eucharistic liturgy.

8. *The Miracle Play of Hasan and Husayn,* translated by Sir Lewis Pelly (London, 1879; reprint, Farnborough, England, 1970), 103.

9. Jaroslav Pelikan, *Mary through the Centuries* (New Haven: Yale University Press, 1996), 2.

10. Luke 1:26.

11. Qur'an 3:42, 43, 45, 46.

12. Ali Shariati, *Fatima Is Fatima,* translated by Laleh Bakhtiar (Brooklyn: Muslim Students Council, n.d.), 136.

13. Ibid., 134.

14. Mahmoud Ayoub, *Redemptive Suffering in Islam: A Study of the Devotional Aspects of Ashura' in Twelver Shi'ism* (The Hague: Mouton, 1978), 35.

15. D. A. Spellberg, *Politics, Gender, and the Islamic Past: The Legacy of 'A'isha Bint Abi Bakr* (New York: Columbia University Press, 1994), 40, 160.

16. L. Veccia Vaglieri, "Fatima," in *Encyclopaedia of Islam* (Leiden: E. J. Brill, 1965), 2:847–48.

17. Mary's other six dolors are the flight into Egypt, Christ lost in the temple, Christ carrying the cross, the crucifixion, Christ being taken down from the cross, and Christ's burial. See J. C. Gorman, "Sorrows of Mary," in *New Catholic Encyclopedia* (New York: McGraw-Hill, 1967), 13:441–43. This great emphasis on Mary's sorrows is almost entirely a Roman Catholic phenomenon. It accompanies the devotion to the crucifix, the crucified Christ, while the Eastern church has focused more on the transfiguration and resurrection of Jesus.

18. Ayoub, *Redemptive Suffering,* 48.

19. Louis Massignon, "Die Ursprünge und die Bedeutung des Gnostizismus im Islam," in *Eranos Jahrbuch 1937* (Zurich: Rhein-Verlag, 1938), 64–65, quoted in David Pinault, "Zaynab bint 'Ali and the Place of Women in the Households of the First Imams in Shi'ite Devotional Literature," in *Women in the Medieval Islamic World,* edited by Gavin R. G. Hambly (New York: St. Martin's Press, 1998), 75.

20. Luke 1:46–55.

21. Pelikan, *Mary through the Centuries,* 3, 178–79.

22. Shariati, *Fatima Is Fatima,* 164–65.

23. "Imam" in this context means "The Leader," not to be confused with the general use of the term throughout the Islamic world to refer to a prayer leader. The interpretation of the Imamate differs considerably from one Shi'i sect to another. Our discussion focuses on the Twelver or Ithna 'Ashariya sect, the dominant sect in Iran.

24. Seyyed Hossein Nasr, *Ideals and Realities of Islam*, rev. ed. (Chicago: Kazi Publishing, 2000), 159.

25. 'Allamah Tabataba'i, "The Imams and the Imamate," in *Shi'ism: Doctrines, Thought, and Spirituality*, edited by Seyyed Hossein Nasr, Hamid Dabashi, and Seyyed Vali Reza Nasr (Albany: State University of New York Press, 1988), 165.

26. There are twenty-three days rather than twenty-four because the twelfth Imam is in occultation and therefore has no death to be commemorated.

27. Imam 'Ali is buried at Najaf in Iraq, and Imam Hasan at Madina, as well as Imams Zayn al-'Abidin (IV), Baqir (V), and Sadiq (VI). Imam Husayn is buried at Karbala, and Imams Kazim (VII) and Taqi (IX) are buried at Baghdad. Imam Rida (VIII) is buried at Mashhad in Iran, and Imams Naqi (X) and Hasan al-'Askari (XI) are buried at Samarra in Iraq. The *sardab* or cellar where Imam Mahdi (XII) disappeared is in the same area. Visitation to these shrines is sought perhaps even more eagerly than visitation to the Prophet's tomb in Madina, although the tombs of Sayyida Fatima and the Imams at Mecca have been largely effaced by the Sunni Wahhabi sect, which dominates in Saudi Arabia.

28. Abu al-Hasan al-Hujwiri, *Kashf al-mahjub*, translated by R. A. Nicholson (London: Luzac, 1911), 210, 213.

29. Carra de Vaux, "Wali," in *Encyclopaedia of Islam*, 4:1110. For an illuminating discussion of the role of saints in Islam, see G. E. von Grunebaum, *Muhammadan Festivals* (London: Curzon Press, 1976), 67–84.

30. The medieval Sunni traveler Ibn Jubayr of Valencia (d. 1217) visited the shrine in Sunni Cairo in 1187 and wrote: "We observed men kissing the blessed tomb, surrounding it, throwing themselves upon it, smoothing with their hands the *kiswa* [covering] that was over it, moving round it as a surging throng, weeping and entreating Glorious God to bless the hallowed dust, and offering up humble supplications such as would melt the heart and split the hardest flint. A solemn thing it was, and an awe-inspiring sight" (*Travels of Ibn Jubayr*, translated by R. J. C. Broadhurst [London: Jonathan Cape, 1952], 37).

31. See Henri Corbin, "Le sens de l'Imam pour la spiritualité Shi'ite," in *Aspects du shi'ism duodecimain* (Paris: Gallimard, 1971), 285.

32. This is not a general phenomenon in Shi'ism. The Zaydi Shi'is of Yemen are generally hostile to the cult of saints or to any idea that they can have intercessory powers.

33. Ayoub, *Redemptive Suffering*, 199.

34. *Catechism of the Catholic Church* (Liguori, Mo.: Liguori Publications, 1994), section 956, 249.

35. Ibid. (emphasis added).
36. Quoted in Lawrence S. Cunningham, *The Meaning of Saints* (San Francisco: Harper and Row, 1980), 29.
37. Ibid., 30.
38. Walter M. Abbott, ed., *The Documents of Vatican II* (New York: Herder and Herder, 1966), 82–83.
39. *Catechism of the Catholic Church*, section 2683, p. 645.
40. P. Molinari, "Intercession of Saints," in *New Catholic Encyclopedia*, 12:497.
41. F. X. Lawlor, "Infallibility," in ibid., 7:497.

CHAPTER FOUR

1. Murtada Mutahhari, "Shahid," in *Jihad and Shahadat: Struggle and Martyr-dom in Islam*, edited by Mehdi Abedi and Gary Legenhausen (Houston: Institute for Research and Islamic Studies, 1986), 126. Ayatollah Mutahhari, who wrote so sensitively about martyrdom, died a martyr himself when he was assassinated in May 1979.
2. Lacey Baldwin Smith, *Fools, Martyrs, Traitors: The Story of Martyrdom in the Western World* (New York: Alfred A. Knopf, 1997), 146.
3. Ibid., 10.
4. See Ignatius of Antioch, in *Ancient Christian Writers*, (New York: Paulist Press, 1946), 82.
5. See E. L. Petermann, "Redemption," in *New Catholic Encyclopedia* (New York: McGraw-Hill, 1967), 12:158–59.
6. Ibid., 160.
7. Mahmoud Ayoub, *Redemptive Suffering in Islam: A Study of the Devotional Aspects of Ashura' in Twelver Shi'ism* (The Hague: Mouton, 1978), 15.
8. Samuel Z. Klausner, "Martyrdom," in *The Encyclopedia of Religion* (New York: Macmillan, 1987), 9:231.
9. Quoted in Mahmoud Ayoub, "Foreword," in Abedi and Legenhausen, *Jihad and Shahadat*, vii.
10. *Jerusalem Post*, February 15, 1985, quoted in Augustus Richard Norton, *Amal and the Shi'a* (Austin: University of Texas Press, 1987), 113. Norton has explained the Nabatiyya incident to the authors. He views it as a major political event of the time and one that "dripped with evocative symbolism."
11. Klausner, "Martyrdom," 232.
12. J. P. Christopher et al., *The Raccolta: A Manual of Indulgences* (New York: Benziger Brothers, 1957), 80. This source, "authorized by the Holy See," contains 125 pages of Catholic prayers and devotions to the Blessed Virgin.

13. Dr. H. Hakim-Elahi, interview by James Bill, Tehran, Iran, November 12, 1966.

14. Quoted in G. E. von Grunebaum, *Muhammadan Festivals* (London: Curzon Press, 1976), 93. For a superb collection of articles describing the *ta'ziyya*, see Peter Chelkowski, ed., *Ta'ziyeh: Ritual and Drama in Iran* (New York: New York University Press, 1979).

15. See von Grunebaum, *Muhammadan Festivals*, 92, 94.

16. Dr. Josef Ziegler, University of Mainz, quoted in *The Oberammergau Passion Play* (Carbondale: Southern Illinois University Press, 1984), 2.

17. F. J. Courtney, "Flagellation," in *New Catholic Encyclopedia*, 5:955.

18. See Abu al-Faraj al-Isfahani, *Maqatil al-Talibiyin* (The slaying of the Talibis) (Matba' Najaf, Iraq, 1935), for biographies of the scores of descendants of Abu Talib who lost their lives for political reasons, including those who died in prison. This work was composed in 923.

19. Hamid Enayat, *Modern Islamic Political Thought* (Austin: University of Texas Press, 1982), 182–83.

CHAPTER FIVE

1. Al-Ghazali, *Al-Mustasfa min 'ilm al-usul* (Cairo: Bulaq Press, 1894), 1:5–6.

2. For reference to these two *hadith*, see Muhammad 'Ata al-Rahim, *Jesus: A Prophet of Islam* (Karachi: Begum Aisha Bawany Waqf, n.d.), 223.

3. 'Ali ibn Abu Talib, *Nahjul Balagha* (The peak of eloquence), translated by Sayed Ali Reza (Elmhurst, N.Y.: Tahrike Tarsile Qu'ran, 1986), 324.

4. A *laura* was a loosely organized cluster of cells, each of which was occupied by a monk or hermit, that was overseen by a particular superior.

5. Margaret Smith, *The Way of the Mystics* (New York: Oxford University Press, 1978), 256.

6. See al-Tabari, *Ta'rikh* (Cairo edition, 1962), 3:226–27; corresponds to Leiden edition, ser. 1, p. 1850.

7. Al-Bukhari, *Jami' al-Sahih* (Leiden: E. J. Brill, 1868–1908), 3:410–11.

8. It is, of course, a temptation for men to use their power to tyrannize and exploit women. Muslim mystics condemn this. According to Rumi: "Tenderness, kindness and affection are human, but harshness and lust are animal in nature. Woman is a ray of God, no earthly beloved. She is creative: one may say she is uncreated" (*Mathnavi* [Tehran, n.d.], 1:2433–36, translation by John Williams).

9. The early Sufis who were believing and practicing Shi'is include Ma'ruf al-Karkhi, Yahya ibn Mu'adh al-Razi, Ta'us al-Yamani, Bahlul Majnun, Malik

ibn Dinar, and Mansur ibn ʿAmmar. See John Alden Williams, ed., *Themes of Islamic Civilization* (Berkeley: University of California Press, 1971), 329.

10. See ʿAli Hujwiri, *Kashf al-Mahjub*, translated by R. A. Nicholson (London: Luzac, 1911), 74–80.

11. Quoted in Hamid Enayat, *Modern Islamic Political Thought* (Austin: University of Texas Press, 1982), 22.

12. See Goethe's *West-Oestlicher Diwan* (Zurich: Manesse, 1952).

13. *Diwan-i Hafiz* (Brockhaus edition, 1854), no. 79, translated by John Alden Williams. Churchbells and the cross are both regarded with repugnance by strict Muslims, but the sincere devotee must realize how much he has in common with believers of other creeds.

14. This is apparently a reference to the esoteric teacher, the *shaykh* or *pir*, whose motives are pure and who is thus entitled to obedience.

15. "Qasr-i Amal," in *Diwan-i Hafiz*, no. 32, translated by John Alden Williams.

16. See Ervand Abrahamian, *Khomeinism* (Berkeley: University of California Press, 1993), 7.

17. See William Hanaway's translations of five *ghazals* written by Khomeini in the 1980s, "Five Mystical Ghazals by the Ayatollah Khomeini," *Iranian Studies* 30 (Summer/Fall 1997): 273–76.

18. W. T. Stace and R. C. Zaehner, quoted in Geoffrey Parrinder, *Mysticism in the World's Religions* (London: Sheldon Press, 1976), 153–54.

19. Kenneth L. Woodward, *Making Saints* (New York: Simon and Schuster, 1990), 158.

20. Ibrahim b. Adham, quoted in John Alden Williams, *The Word of Islam* (Austin: University of Texas Press, 1994), 113–15.

21. Khidr or Khadir, "Evergreen," the immortal mentor of the saints, himself a great saint, was held to be the figure described in the Qurʾan 18:61–83 as a mentor to Moses. Moses is seeking the confluence of the Two Seas (manifestation and being) but passes by his goal, not perceiving it. He then asks whether he can follow Khidr, who says Moses will not be able to bear his company. Moses promises to be silent and learn. As they travel, Khidr performs three apparent outrages, and each time Moses objects. Finally Khidr parts company with him, showing him that each time a good was brought from an apparent evil. In Sufism, Moses represents the law and Khidr represents the esoteric greater wisdom.

22. According to the Qurʾanic nativity of Jesus, "So Mary conceived him, and withdrew to a distant place, and the birthpangs came upon her by the trunk of the palm-tree. She said, 'Would I had died ere this, and become a nothing, forgotten!' But he who was below her [Jesus] called to her, 'No, do not sorrow! Your Lord has set below you a rivulet. Shake also the palm-trunk,

and dates fresh and ripe shall fall upon you. Eat, drink, and be comforted'" (19:22–26). On thirteenth- and fourteenth-century Persian bowls and tiles, the tree of life is depicted with a pool beneath it (apparently suggested by this verse), and in the pool there are fish. Since the fish are living in the water of life, Rumi says, they are as immortal as Khidr; they are images of the Sufi adepts who live in the Divine Source.

23. A. J. Arberry, trans., *Mystical Poems of Rumi* (Chicago: University of Chicago Press, 1968), 32.

24. See Miguel Asin Palacios, *St. John of the Cross and Islam,* translated by H. W. Yoder and E. H. Douglas (New York: Vantage Press, 1981).

25. John of the Cross, *Spiritual Canticle,* in *The Collected Works,* nos. 14, 15, p. 412, quoted in Maria Jaoudi, *Christian and Islamic Spirituality* (New York: Paulist Press, 1993), 72–73.

26. E. Allison Peers, *Blanquerna* (London: Jarrolds, 1929); Anthony Bonner, *Selected Works of Ramon Lull,* 2 vols. (Princeton: Princeton University Press, 1985). "The Book of the Lover and the Beloved" is translated by E. Bonner in A. Bonner's *Doctor Illuminatus* (Princeton: Princeton University Press, 1993), 188–237.

27. "Lull's Influence," in Bonner, *Doctor Illuminatus,* 57–71.

28. Deuteronomy 21:22–23.

29. The Arabic word *faqir,* "poor man," is commonly used for a Sufi, one who may be physically needy but in all conditions knows his total dependence on God and his own poverty before Him. The Persian word is *darvish,* which is most common in English in its Turkish form, *dervish.*

30. Frithjof Schuon, *The Transcendent Unity of Religions* (Wheaton, Ill.: Theosophical Publishing House, 1984), 121.

31. Seyyed Hossein Nasr, *Traditional Islam in the Modern World* (London: Kegan Paul, 1987), 254.

32. "There were repercussions even in Roman Catholic theology in that Massignon's advocacy of al-Hallaj's cause raised the question of the recognition of genuine mysticism beyond the Church's formal boundaries" (Sidney H. Griffith, "Merton, Massignon, and the Challenge of Islam," in *Merton and Sufism: The Untold Story,* edited by Rob Baker and Gray Henry [Louisville, Ky.: Fons Vitae, 1999], 54).

33. The Qarmati or Carmathian movement was a breakaway Mahdist Isma'ili Shi'i reform movement that swept across the tenth-century Muslim world advocating social reform in general and justice and equality in particular. The Qarmati movement appealed to all classes, sects, and religions but found special acceptance among peasants, bedouins, and semiskilled workers.

34. Annemarie Schimmel, *Mystical Dimensions of Islam* (Chapel Hill: University of North Carolina Press, 1975), 68. This excellent source includes an analysis of the life and ideas of al-Hallaj (ibid., 62–77).
35. Williams, *Word of Islam*, 121.
36. Quoted in Herbert Mason, *The Death of al-Hallaj* (Notre Dame, Ind.: University of Notre Dame Press, 1979), 76–77. Just as Massignon has brought the person and message of al-Hallaj into the consciousness of the Western world, Mason has brought the personality and ideas of Massignon to the attention of the English-speaking public. Beyond providing this service, Mason is an outstanding scholar of Sufism in his own right. See, for example, Herbert Mason, *Testimonies and Reflections: Essays of Louis Massignon* (Notre Dame, Ind.: University of Notre Dame Press, 1989.
37. Nasr, *Traditional Islam*, 254–55.
38. Some of Merton's lectures are transcribed and discussed in Bernadette Dieker, "Merton's Sufi Lectures to Cistercian Novices, 1966–69," in Rob Baker and Gray Henry, eds., *Merton and Sufism: The Untold Story* (Louisville, Ky.: Fons Vitae, 1999).
39. Thomas Merton, *The Hidden Ground of Love: The Letters of Thomas Merton on Religious Experience and Social Concerns*, edited by William H. Shannon (New York: Farrar, Straus, Giroux, 1985), 51, 67.
40. We have drawn much material from Baker and Henry, *Merton and Sufism*. See also Paul Hendrickson, "One of Us," *Washington Post*, December 27, 1998, p. F1.
41. Merton, *Hidden Ground*, 53.
42. Ibid., 44.
43. Griffith, "Merton, Massignon, and the Challenge of Islam," 63, 67.

CHAPTER SIX

1. José Cardeñas Pallares, *A Poor Man Called Jesus: Reflections on the Gospel of Mark* (Maryknoll, N.Y.: Orbis Books, 1990), 76.
2. For Aquinas's treatise on law, see *Summa Theologica*, questions 90–97, in *Basic Writings of Saint Thomas Aquinas*, edited by Anton C. Pegis (New York: Random House, 1945), 2:742–805.
3. Professor J. Budziszewski has shared his ideas concerning natural law theory with us.
4. Thomas Aquinas, *Summa Theologica*, question 91, article 3, in Pegis, *Basic Writings*, 2:750.

5. Quoted in T. A. Wassmer, "Natural Law," in *New Catholic Encyclopedia* (New York: McGraw-Hill, 1967), 10:251–62.

6. Some scholars postulate that human law is different from civil law and positive law. According to J. Budziszewski, civil law is one type of human law; the other is the law of nations. Positive law is simply law presented or "posited" by someone (personal correspondence, February 6, 1999).

7. The core of this analogy is presented in Wassmer, "Natural Law," 256.

8. Pius XII, address at International Convention of Humanistic Studies, 1949, quoted in ibid., 259.

9. A. J. Arberry, *Revelation and Reason in Islam* (London: George Allen and Unwin, 1971), 7.

10. Philip K. Hitti, *The Arabs: A Short History*, 5th ed. (New York: St. Martin's Press, 1968), 143.

11. Marshall G. S. Hodgson, *The Venture of Islam* (Chicago: University of Chicago Press, 1974), 2:362.

12. Erwin I. J. Rosenthal, *Political Thought in Medieval Islam: An Introductory Outline* (Cambridge: Cambridge University Press, 1958), 140. Rosenthal also writes that it is extremely important "to see political science in the context of philosophy as a whole" (ibid., 122).

13. Al-Farabi, "The Virtuous City," in *Themes of Islamic Civilization*, edited by John Alden Williams (Berkeley: University of California Press, 1971), 115.

14. Rosenthal, *Political Thought*, 153.

15. Ibid., 176.

16. Ibid., 186.

17. Pope Leo XIII, *Aeterni Patris* (Of the Eternal Father), August 4, 1879, in *The Great Encyclical Letters of Pope Leo XIII* (New York: Benziger Brothers, 1903).

18. Ibid.

19. Richard P. O'Brien, *Catholicism* (Minneapolis, Minn.: Winston Press, 1966), 1:52.

20. William McSweeney, *Roman Catholicism: The Search for Relevance* (New York: St. Martin's Press, 1980), 71.

21. Ibid., 76.

22. For an analysis of *Fides et Ratio* and for extensive excerpts of the encyclical, see *New York Times*, October 16, 1998, pp. 1, 10.

23. In the new *Catechism of the Catholic Church*, published in 1994, for example, Aquinas is cited fifty times in the notes. For a superb discussion of the development of "Neothomism" and "Neoscholasticism," see James C. Livingston, *Modern Christian Thought* (Upper Saddle River, N.J.: Prentice-Hall, 1997), 1:342–55. Livingston has knowledgeably explained to the authors the place of Thomism in the development of Christian thought.

24. A. P. D'Entreves, ed., *Aquinas: Selected Political Writings* (Oxford: Basil Blackwell, 1948), xiii.

25. Thomas Gilby, *The Political Thought of Thomas Aquinas* (Chicago: University of Chicago Press, 1963), 193.

26. Thomas Aquinas, *On Kingship: To the King of Cyprus,* edited by I. Th. Eschmann (Toronto: Pontifical Institute of Medieval Studies, 1949), 11–12.

27. Ibid., 13.

28. Gilby, *Political Thought,* 156, 198–99.

29. Aquinas, *On Kingship,* 40.

30. Aquinas, *Summa Theologica,* vol. 1, question 94, article 2, quoted in Maurice De Wulf, *The System of Thomas Aquinas* (New York: Dover, 1959), 118.

31. Seyyed Hossein Nasr, *Ideals and Realities of Islam,* rev. ed. (Chicago: Kazi Publishing, 2000), 16.

32. See Bellarmine's *Controversies against the Heresies of Our Times (1586–93).* On this period, see the admirably organized work, Livingston, *Modern Christian Thought,* esp. 1:13.

33. British prime minister William Gladstone and American president Abraham Lincoln wondered if they could count on the loyalty of their Catholic citizens. In Germany, the Jesuits had been expelled by 1872 and diplomatic relations with the Vatican had been severed. Four years later, two-thirds of the bishops of the Kingdom of Prussia had been imprisoned or driven from their dioceses, and 1,400 German parishes had no pastors, as part of the *Kulturkampf.* Far from disintegrating, the Catholic resistance to Chancellor Bismarck's policies forced him to seek peace with the church while he struggled with the Social Democrats.

34. J. Neuner and H. Roos, *The Teaching of the Catholic Church* (Staten Island, N.Y.: Alba House, 1967), 388.

35. Pope John Paul II, *Ut Unum Sint* (That they may be one), 1995. This encyclical was followed by a remarkable document from the Congregation for the Doctrine of the Faith in December 1998, "Reflections on the Primacy of Peter," which acknowledges that the practice of the primacy is historically conditioned, hence changing. Just as this world is passing, "the immutable nature of the primacy of Peter's successor has historically been expressed in different forms of exercise appropriate to the situation of a pilgrim church in this changing world."

36. See Said Amir Arjomand, *The Turban for the Crown* (New York: Oxford University Press, 1988), 27–33.

37. Nikki Keddie, ed., *Scholars, Saints, and Sufis: Muslim Religious Institutions in the Middle East since 1500* (Berkeley: University of California Press, 1978), 212–15.

38. He was never fully accepted by the Shi'i *'ulama*, despite the similarity of their goals with his. His acceptance among Sunni scholars was greater, but he died under house arrest in Istanbul, where he had sought the patronage of Sultan 'Abd al-Hamid II (Ignaz Goldziher/Jacques Jomier, "Djamal al-Din al-Afghani," in *Encyclopaedia of Islam 2* [Leiden: E. J. Brill, 1965], 2:416–19). See also Hamid Algar, *Religion and State in Iran, 1785-1906* (Berkeley: University of California Press, 1969).

39. See Algar, *Religion and State*, 195.

40. The constitutional revolution in neighboring Russia in 1905 in the aftermath of the Russo-Japanese War had an undeniable impact. *Mullahs* were exhorted in the growing popular Iranian press to follow the example of the Russian clergy, which on "Bloody Sunday" had helped mobilize the masses. Political ferment was particularly strong in Tabriz, close to Turkey and the Caucasus. See M. Reza Ghods, *Iran in the Twentieth Century* (Boulder, Colo.: Lynne Rienner, 1989), 28–30.

41. Hamid Enayat, *Modern Islamic Political Thought* (Austin: University of Texas Press, 1982), 156.

42. Pope Pius XII, "Dilecti Filii," letter to the German bishops, October 18, 1949, quoted in Jean Yves Calvez and Jacques Perrin, *The Church and Social Justice* (Chicago: Henry Regnery, 1961), 149.

CHAPTER SEVEN

1. 'Ali ibn Abu Talib, *Nahjul Balagha* (The peak of eloquence), translated by Sayed Ali Reza (Elmhurst, N.Y.: Tahrike Tarsile Qur'an, 1986), sermon 110, p. 257.

2. Imam 'Ali, "Letter to Malik Ashtar, Governor of Egypt," in W. C. Chittick, *Conduct of Rule in Islam* (London: Muhammadi Trust, n.d.), n.p.

3. William McSweeney, *Roman Catholicism: The Search for Relevance* (New York: St. Martin's Press, 1980), 79.

4. Ibid., 80.

5. Pope Pius XI, *Quadragesimo Anno* (On the fortieth year), 1931, quoted in R. E. Mulcahy, "Subsidiarity," in *New Catholic Encyclopedia* (New York: McGraw-Hill, 1967), 13:762.

6. Jean Yves Calvez and Jacques Perrin, *The Church and Social Justice* (Chicago: Henry Regnery, 1961), 329.

7. Heinrich A. Rommen, *The State in Catholic Thought* (New York: Greenwood Press, 1945), 304.

8. Ibid., 293.

9. See Harvey Cox, *Religion in the Secular City* (New York: Simon and Schuster, 1984), 21.

10. For a summary of the ideas of Gutierrez, see Gustavo Gutierrez, *A Theology of Liberation* (Maryknoll, N.Y.: Orbis, 1973).

11. Phillip Berryman, *Liberation Theology* (New York: Pantheon, 1987), 26.

12. Donal Dorr, *Option for the Poor* (Maryknoll, N.Y.: Orbis, 1992), 3.

13. See *New York Times*, February 20, 1988, 5.

14. Pope John Paul II, *Sollicitudo Rei Socialis* (Social concern), 1987, quoted in ibid., 4. The reference is to Luke 16:21.

15. Ibid., 5.

16. Anselm K. Min, *Dialectic of Salvation: Issues in Theology of Liberation* (Albany: State University of New York Press, 1989), 119. In this thoughtful critique of the Vatican's encounter with liberation theology, Min writes that liberation theology is responding to "the screaming demand of these billions of 'non-persons' for liberation from the conditions which literally kill them." Min then raises the question: "Is the church going to treat the problem of global poverty simply as one of the corporal works of mercy, something which may make us better Christians but without which we could still be Christian, something which is therefore ultimately peripheral to the Gospel?" (ibid., 159–60).

17. See "Pope Urges Bishops to Minister to the Rich," *New York Times*, January 24, 1999, p. 10.

18. See Sam Dillon, "Ecatepec Journal: A Rebel Creed, Stifled by the Pope, Flickers Still," *New York Times*, January 21, 1999, p. 4.

19. Quoted in Frank Korn, *From Peter to John Paul II: An Informal Study of the Papacy* (Canfield, Ohio: Alba Books, 1980), 214.

20. Gary Wills, *Papal Sin: Structures of Deceit* (New York: Doubleday, 2000), 73–74.

21. Ibid., 74.

22. Charles R. Morris, *American Catholic* (New York: Times Books, 1997), 334.

23. Ibid., 373.

24. Ibid., 334.

25. Hamid Enayat, *Modern Islamic Political Thought* (Austin: University of Texas Press, 1982), 94.

26. *Atadamon*, quoted in Peter Theroux, *The Strange Disappearance of Imam Moussa Sadr* (London: Weidenfeld and Nicolson, 1987), 9.

27. Mamoun Fandy, *Saudi Arabia and the Politics of Dissent* (New York: St. Martin's Press, 1999), 214.

28. Imam Khomeini, *Islam and Revolution: Writings and Declarations of Imam Khomeini*, translated by Hamid Algar (Berkeley: Mizan Press, 1981), 56.

29. Ervand Abrahamian, *Khomeinism* (Berkeley: University of California Press, 1993), 17. For another thoughtful discussion of Shi'i populism, see Manochehr Dorraj, *From Zarathustra to Khomeini: Populism and Dissent in Iran* (Boulder, Colo.: Lynne Rienner, 1990). Dorraj writes that Khomeini "thrived on the strong populist streak in the Iranian political culture and seized power on the basis of a popular mandate" (ibid., 165–66). For a superb biography of Khomeini, see Baqir Moin, *Khomeini: Life of the Ayatollah* (New York: St. Martin's Press, 1999).

30. *Imam Khomeini's Last Will and Testament* (Washington, D.C.: Iranian Interests Section of the Islamic Republic of Iran, n.d.), 28.

31. *Tehran Times*, February 10, 1982, p. 6.

32. Ibid.

33. Imam Khomeini, *Islamic Government* (Rome: European Islamic Cultural Center, n.d.), 110. For an informed discussion of this principle, see Hamid Dabashi, *Theology of Discontent* (New York: New York University Press, 1993), 454–55.

34. Abdulaziz A. Sachedina, "The Creation of a Just Social Order in Islam," in *State Politics and Islam*, edited by Mumtaz Ahmad (Indianapolis, Ind.: American Trust Publications, 1986), 125.

35. Quoted in Bahman Baktiari, *Parliamentary Politics in Revolutionary Iran* (Gainesville: University Press of Florida, 1996), 63.

36. Paul Sigmund, "Law and Politics," in *The Cambridge Companion to Aquinas*, edited by Norman Kretzman and Eleonore Stump (Cambridge: Cambridge University Press, 1993), 219.

37. 'Allamah Tabataba'i, *Shi'ite Islam*, translated by Seyyed Hossein Nasr (Albany: State University of New York Press, 1975), 214.

38. Gutierrez, *Theology of Liberation*, 300.

39. Beyond Washington, D.C., the various networks of Catholic charities consisted of 1,400 social agencies and more than 200,000 volunteers, who assisted more than 11 million needy Americans through social service programs. See Dorothy M. Brown and Elizabeth McKeown, *The Poor Belong to Us: Catholic Charities and American Welfare* (Cambridge: Harvard University Press, 1997), 197.

40. Copy of speech by Pope John Paul II delivered in Baltimore on October 8, 1995.

41. Female *mujtahids* are not unknown in Iran. A record of the lives and deeds of certain female *mujtahids* is found in I'timad al-Saltaneh, *Khayrat-i Hisan* (Tehran, 1925; in Persian).

42. Leila Ahmad, *Women and Gender in Islam* (New Haven: Yale University Press, 1992), 242.

1. Pope John Paul II, "Remarks at Weekly General Audience," May 5, 1999, quoted in *Catholic Observer*, May 14, 1999.
2. Copy of Ayatollah Khomeini's message to the papal envoy.
3. Shiʻi ideologues in Iran have closely observed and strongly praised liberation theology in the Catholic world. At the same time, they have strongly condemned the papacy for its failure to support the liberation movement. In the words of one Shiʻi analyst: "The thought represented by the Pope and the Vatican believes in supporting and affirming the colonialist and hegemonic powers and in the unconditional reconciliation of the oppressed and the oppressors. In other words, they believe in the submission of the oppressed to the oppressors" ("The Growth of Liberation Theology in the Christian World," *Kayhan International*, January 16, 1988, p. 6).
4. Dr. Fathi Abboudi, interview by James Bill, Amman, Jordan, December 4, 1985.

GLOSSARY OF SHIʿI TERMS

Ahl al-Bayt: "People of the House of the Prophet," hence those descended lineally and mystically from the family of ʿAli and Fatima.

Akhbaris: Twelver Shiʿis who prefer a fundamentalist adherence to the *akhbar,* or account of the words and actions of the Prophet and the Imams, to any analogical reasoning about the *akhbar* intended to lead one to general principles (*usul*).

ʿAshura: the "tenth" of the month of Muharram, cognate with 10 Tishri, or Yom Kippur, a general day of fasting to atone for sin and the day of Imam Husayn's martyrdom.

ayatullah: literally "sign of God," a title accorded to Shiʿi scholars of the highest rank by other *ayatullahs.*

Babis: an offshoot of the Shaykhis who followed Mirza ʿAli Muhammad, who first claimed to be the *bab* or door to the twelfth Imam and then claimed to be the Mahdi. He was executed in 1850. The Bahaʾi faith then developed from this movement.

baraka: divine blessing, present in holy persons, places, and objects.

Buyids: a family of Shiʿi warlords from the mountains southwest of the Caspian Sea who gained dictatorial powers in the ʿAbbasi caliphate from 945 to 1055. While ostensibly honoring Sunnism, they favored Muʿtazilis and Zaydi and Twelver Shiʿis.

dhikr: "mentioning," repeating the names of God, often in a special service. The *dhikrs* of the Sufi orders of Islam are many and various.

fatwa: a religious ruling, delivered in Twelver Islam by a *mujtahid.*

faqih: jurisprudent, or one who has achieved *fiqh* or insight into the *shariʿa.*

Ghadir al-Khumm: the "Deceiver" of Khumm, a salty pool in the desert where the Prophet is said to have announced that ʿAli was to be his successor.

ghayba (Persian *ghaybat*): the hidden state in which the twelfth Imam exists until his return.

hadith: an account of words and/or acts of the Prophet, preserved by chains of reliable authorities. Shiʿis also transmit *hadith* of the Imams.

al-Hallaj: Sufi martyr crucified in Baghdad in 922 for claiming union with God.

Hanafi: Sunni school of jurisprudence, named after Abu Hanifa of Kufa, who urged careful attention to the precedents of learned jurisprudents in arriving at law.

Hanbali: Sunni school of jurisprudence, named after Ahmad ibn Hanbal of Baghdad, who held that one should follow only the Qur'an and plausible *hadith* of the Prophet in arriving at law, without regard to reason or tradition.

hikma ilahiyya: "divine wisdom," Twelver theosophy/mystical philosophy.

hujjat al-Islam: "proof of Islam," the title for a rank of *mujtahid,* below that of *ayatullah.*

ijtihad: "exertion" to get at the meaning of texts, hence "interpretation" of religion.

ikhtiyar: free choice of one's actions.

imam: in a general sense, any leader of Muslim prayer. In Islamic law, the Imam is the leader of the religion. Twelver Shi'is believe there have been only twelve Imams, all from the family of the Prophet, and the twelfth, though absent from sight, is still the Imam today.

imamzada (Farsi): a lineal or mystical descendant of the twelve Imams, hence a saint. Also used for the saint's tomb or shrine.

Ishraqiyya: the "Illuminationist" philosophy of Shaykh Yahya al-Suhrawardi (executed 1191).

Ja'fari: the name usually given to the Twelver school of jurisprudence, after Imam Ja'far al-Sadiq.

karamat: charisms or divine gifts, hence the saints' power to perform remarkable actions.

Karbala: the Shi'i holy city that has grown up around the tombs of Imam Husayn and his companions in Iraq, where they met martyrdom.

khums: a tax of one-fifth of the spoils of war or of the year's profits, which must be paid by every Twelver to the Imam or, in his absence, to one's *mujtahid.*

Mahdi: the "Guided One," said to have been mentioned by Muhammad as the one who would bring the final triumph of true Islam over all of its enemies shortly before the end of the world. For Twelvers, this is the twelfth Imam.

Maliki: Sunni school of jurisprudence, named afer Malik ibn Anas, a scholar who held that one should endeavor to follow the tradition of Madina.

marja' al-taqlid: "source of imitation," a preeminent interpreter of divine law to whom other *ayatullahs* turn for guidance.

Mashhad: the Shi'i holy city that has grown up around the tomb of Imam Rida (Reza) in eastern Iran, near the earlier city of Tus.

mujtahid: one who has "exerted himself" and is competent to interpret religion for others.

muqallid: one who is not competent to interpret religion and must rely on others' authority.

mustadaʿfin (Persian *mustazaʿfin*): the oppressed.

mustakbirin: people who "make themselves great," the arrogant and oppressive.

muʿtazila: early Muslim rationalists, both Sunni and Shiʿi, who believed that all of religion must be based on reason alone and who furthered the study of Greek philosophy.

Nahj al-Balagha (The peak of eloquence): a compilation of addresses and letters attributed to Imam ʿAli, collected by the Sharif al-Radi (d. 1016).

Najaf: the Shiʿi holy city that has grown up around the tomb of Imam ʿAli in Iraq.

Shafiʿi: Sunni school of jurisprudence, named after al-Shafiʿi, who argued that reason, sound *hadith*, learned consensus, and prevailing customs should all be considered in arriving at insight into *shariʿa*.

shariʿa (related to *sharʿ*): what God and His messenger have laid down, hence Islamic law.

Shaykhis: a small subsect of esoteric Twelvers who place their reliance on the "fourteen inerrant ones," that is, the Prophet, Fatima, and the twelve Imams, and on great *shaykhs* who, being "perfect Shiʿis," can speak for these figures.

Shiʿi: partisan of ʿAli and the "people of the house" (*ahl al-bayt*).

Sufis: Muslim mystics.

Sunnis: those who follow the *sunna* or way of the majority of Muslims, for example, by choosing Abu Bakr, ʿUmar, and ʿUthman over ʿAli.

taqiyya: "warding off evil," the Twelver and Ismaʿili Shiʿi doctrine and practice of dissimulation to avoid threats to life, limb, and property by persecutors. It is not permitted by Zaydi Shiʿis.

ʿulama (sing. *ʿalim*): "learned men," a generic term for Muslim clerics.

Usulis: Twelver Shiʿis who go beyond the *akhbar* by using analogical reasoning and interpretation to establish underlying principles.

wali (pl. *awliyaʾ*): an empowered friend of God, hence also a saint.

ziyarat: "visits" to the tombs or shrines of holy persons such as prophets, imams, and saints.

SELECT BIBLIOGRAPHY

Abbott, Walter M., ed. *The Documents of Vatican II*. New York: Herder and Herder, 1966.

Abedi, Mehdi, and Gary Legenhausen, eds. *Jihad and Shahadat: Struggle and Martyrdom in Islam*. Houston: Institute for Research and Islamic Studies, 1986.

Abrahamian, Ervand. *Khomeinism*. Berkeley: University of California Press, 1993.

Ahmad, Mumtaz, ed. *State Politics and Islam*. Indianapolis, Ind.: American Trust Publications, 1986.

Akhavi, Shahrough. *Religion and Politics in Contemporary Iran: Clergy-State Relations in the Pahlavi Period*. Albany: State University of New York Press, 1980.

Algar, Hamid. *Religion and State in Iran, 1785–1906*. Berkeley: University of California Press, 1969.

'Ali ibn Abu Talib. *Nahjul Balagha* (The peak of eloquence). Translated by Sayed Ali Reza. Elmhurst, N.Y.: Tahrike Tarsile Qu'ran, 1986.

Amir Arjomand, Said. *The Shadow of God and the Hidden Imam*. Chicago: University of Chicago Press, 1984.

——. *The Turban for the Crown: The Islamic Revolution in Iran*. New York: Oxford University Press, 1988.

——, ed. *Authority and Political Culture in Shi'ism*. Albany: State University of New York Press, 1988.

Arberry, A. J. *Revelation and Reason in Islam*. London: George Allen and Unwin, 1971.

——, trans. *Mystical Poems of Rumi*. Chicago: University of Chicago Press, 1968.

Ayoub, Mahmoud. *Redemptive Suffering in Islam: A Study of the Devotional Aspects of Ashura' in Twelver Shi'ism*. The Hague: Mouton, 1978.

Baker, Rob, and Gray Henry, eds. *Merton and Sufism: The Untold Story*. Louisville, Ky.: Fons Vitae, 1999.

Bayat, Mangol. *Mysticism and Dissent: Socioreligious Thought in Qajar Iran*. Syracuse: Syracuse University Press, 1982.

Beinert, Wolfgang, and Francis Schussler, eds. *Handbook of Catholic Theology*. New York: Crossroad, 1995.

Bill, James A. *The Eagle and the Lion: The Tragedy of American-Iranian Relations.* New Haven: Yale University Press, 1988.

Brunner, Rainer, and Werner Ende, eds. *The Twelver Shia in Modern Times.* Leiden: E. J. Brill, 2001.

Budziszewski, J. *Written on the Heart: The Case for Natural Law.* Downers Grove, Ill.: InterVarsity Press, 1997.

Burckhardt, Titus. *An Introduction to Sufism.* London: Thorsons, 1995.

Calvez, Jean Yves, and Jacques Perrin. *The Church and Social Justice.* Chicago: Henry Regnery, 1961.

Carol, Juniper B. *Mariology.* 2 vols. Milwaukee, Wis.: Bruce, 1955, 1957.

Catechism of the Catholic Church. Liguori, Mo.: Liguori Publications, 1994.

Chelkowski, Peter, ed. *Taʿziyeh: Ritual and Drama in Iran.* New York: New York University Press, 1979.

Chopp, Rebecca S. *The Praxis of Suffering.* Maryknoll, N.Y.: Orbis, 1989.

Cole, Juan R. I., and Nikki R. Keddie, eds. *Shiʿism and Social Protest.* New Haven: Yale University Press, 1986.

Coulson, N. J. *A History of Islamic Law.* Edinburgh: Edinburgh University Press, 1964.

Cox, Harvey. *Religion in the Secular City.* New York: Simon and Schuster, 1984.

Cunningham, Lawrence S. *The Meaning of Saints.* San Francisco: Harper and Row, 1980.

Dabashi, Hamid. *Theology of Discontent.* New York: New York University Press, 1993.

Davidson, Herbert A. *Alfarabi, Avicenna, and Averroës on Intellect.* New York: Oxford University Press, 1992.

De Wulf, Maurice. *The System of Thomas Aquinas.* New York: Dover, 1959.

Dorr, Donal. *Option for the Poor.* Maryknoll, N.Y.: Orbis, 1992.

Dorraj, Manochehr. *From Zarathustra to Khomeini: Populism and Dissent in Iran.* Boulder, Colo.: Lynne Rienner, 1990.

Eaton, Gai. *Islam and the Destiny of Man.* Cambridge: Islamic Texts Society, 1994.

Ellis, Kail C., ed. *The Vatican, Islam, and the Middle East.* Syracuse: Syracuse University Press, 1987.

Enayat, Hamid. *Modern Islamic Political Thought.* Austin: University of Texas Press, 1982.

Esposito, John L. *Islam: The Straight Path.* New York: Oxford University Press, 1989.

Esposito, John L., and John O. Voll. *Islam and Democracy.* New York: Oxford University Press, 1996.

Fandy, Mamoun. *Saudi Arabia and the Politics of Dissent.* New York: St.
Martin's Press, 1999.

Fischer, Michael M. J. *Iran: From Religious Dispute to Revolution.* Cambridge:
Harvard University Press, 1980.

Fischer, Michael M. J., and Mehdi Abedi. *Debating Muslims.* Madison:
University of Wisconsin Press, 1990.

Frank, R. M. *Al-Ghazali and the Ash'arite School.* Durham, N.C.: Duke
University Press, 1994.

Fuller, Graham E., and R. Rahim Francke. *The Arab Shi'a: The Forgotten
Muslims.* New York: St. Martin's Press, 1999.

Gause, F. Gregory. *Oil Monarchies: Domestic and Security Challenges in the Arab
Gulf States.* New York: Council on Foreign Relations, 1994.

Gilby, Thomas. *The Political Thought of Thomas Aquinas.* Chicago: University
of Chicago Press, 1963.

Gilson, Etienne. *Reason and Revelation in the Middle Ages.* New York: Charles
Scribner's Sons, 1938.

———. *The Spirit of Thomism.* New York: P. J. Kenedy, 1964.

Gude, Mary Louise. *Louis Massignon: The Crucible of Compassion.* Notre Dame,
Ind.: University of Notre Dame Press, 1996.

Gudorf, Christine E. *Catholic Social Teaching on Liberation Themes.*
Washington, D.C.: University Press of America, 1981.

Gutierrez, Gustavo. *A Theology of Liberation.* Maryknoll, N.Y.: Orbis, 1973.

Hairi, Abdul-Hadi. *Shi'ism and Constitutionalism in Iran.* Leiden: E. J. Brill,
1977.

Hassan, Farooq. *The Concept of State and Law in Islam.* Washington, D.C.:
University Press of America, 1981.

Hodgson, Marshall G. S. *The Venture of Islam.* 3 vols. Chicago: University of
Chicago Press, 1974.

Hourani, Albert. *A History of the Arab Peoples.* Cambridge: Harvard University
Press, 1991.

Hyman, Arthur, and James J. Walsh, eds. *Philosophy in the Middle Ages: The
Christian, Islamic, and Jewish Traditions.* New York: Harper and Row, 1967.

Jafri, S. H. M. *The Origins and Early Development of Shi'a Islam.* London:
Longman Group, 1981.

Johnston, William. *The Inner Eye of Love: Mysticism and Religion.* New York:
Fordham University Press, 1997.

Keddie, Nikki, with Yann Richard. *Iran: Roots of Revolution.* New Haven: Yale
University Press, 1980.

———, ed. *Scholars, Saints, and Sufis: Muslim Religious Institutions in the Middle
East since 1500.* Berkeley: University of California Press, 1978.

Kerr, Malcolm. *Islamic Reform*. Berkeley: University of California Press, 1966.

Khomeini, Imam. *Islam and Revolution: Writings and Declarations of Imam Khomeini*. Translated by Hamid Algar. Berkeley: Mizan Press, 1981.

————. *Islamic Government*. Rome: European Islamic Cultural Center, n.d.

Knowles, David. *The Evolution of Medieval Thought*. Baltimore: Helicon Press, 1962.

Korn, Frank. *From Peter to John Paul II: An Informal Study of the Papacy*. Canfield, Ohio: Alba Books, 1980.

Kraeling, Emil G. *The Disciples*. New York: Rand McNally, 1986.

Kramer, Martin, ed. *Shi'ism, Resistance, and Revolution*. Boulder, Colo.: Westview Press, 1987.

Kretzman, Norman, and Eleonore Stump, eds. *The Cambridge Companion to Aquinas*. Cambridge: Cambridge University Press, 1993.

Lapidus, Ira. *A History of Islamic Societies*. New York: Cambridge University Press, 1988.

Lings, Martin. *Muhammad*. Cambridge: Islamic Texts Society, 1988.

————. *A Sufi Saint of the Twentieth Century*. 2d ed. Berkeley: University of California Press, 1971.

Livingston, James C. *Modern Christian Thought*. Vol. 1. Upper Saddle River, N.J.: Prentice-Hall, 1997.

Lynch, Joseph H. *The Medieval Church*. New York: Longman, 1992.

McBrien, Richard P. *Catholicism*. 2 vols. Minneapolis: Winston Press, 1980.

McNamara, Kevin, ed. *Vatican II: The Constitution of the Church*. London: Geoffrey Chapman, 1968.

McSweeney, William. *Roman Catholicism: The Search for Relevance*. New York: St. Martin's Press, 1980.

Mahdi, Muhsin. *Alfarabi's Philosophy of Plato and Aristotle*. New York: Free Press, 1962.

Mallat, Chibli. *The Renewal of Islamic Law: Muhammad Baqer as-Sadr, Najaf, and the Shi'i International*. Cambridge: Cambridge University Press, 1993.

Mason, Herbert. *The Death of al-Hallaj*. Notre Dame, Ind.: University of Notre Dame Press, 1979.

————. *Testimonies and Reflections: Essays of Louis Massignon*. Notre Dame, Ind.: University of Notre Dame Press, 1989.

Massignon, Louis. *Essay on the Origins of the Technical Language of Islamic Mysticism*. Translated by Benjamin Clark. Notre Dame, Ind.: University of Notre Dame Press, 1997.

Matthee, Rudolph P. *The Politics of Trade in Safavid Iran*. Cambridge: Cambridge University Press, 1999.

Mazzaoui, Michel. *The Origins of the Safawids*. Wiesbaden: Franz Steiner, 1972.

Merton, Thomas. *Contemplation in a World of Action*. Garden City, N.Y.: Doubleday, 1971.

———. *Run to the Mountain: The Story of a Vocation*. Edited by Patrick Hart. New York: Harper San Francisco, 1995.

Min, Anselm K. *Dialectic of Salvation: Issues in Theology of Liberation*. Albany: State University of New York Press, 1989.

Modarressi Tabataba'i, Hossein. *An Introduction to Shi'i Law: A Bibliographic Study*. London: Ithaca Press, 1984.

Momen, Moojan. *An Introduction to Shi'i Islam*. New Haven: Yale University Press, 1985.

Moosa, Matti. *Extremist Shiites: The Ghulat Sects*. Syracuse: Syracuse University Press, 1988.

Mottahedeh, Roy. *The Mantle of the Prophet*. New York: Pantheon, 1985.

Mutahhari, Murtaza. *Fundamentals of Islamic Thought*. Translated by R. Campbell. Berkeley: Mizan Press, 1985.

Nakash, Yitzhak. *The Shi'is of Iraq*. Princeton: Princeton University Press, 1994.

Nasr, Seyyed Hossein. *Ideals and Realities of Islam*. Rev. ed. Chicago: Kazi Publishing, 2000.

———. *Islamic Life and Thought*. Albany: State University of New York Press, 1981.

———. *Traditional Islam in the Modern World*. London: Kegan Paul, 1987.

Nasr, Seyyed Hossein, Hamid Dabashi, and Seyyed Vali Reza Nasr, eds. *Shi'ism: Doctrines, Thought, and Spirituality*. Albany: State University of New York Press, 1988.

Nicolson, Reynald A. *The Mystics of Islam*. London: Routledge and Kegan Paul, 1966.

Noble, Thomas F. X., and Thomas Head. *Soldiers of Christ*. University Park: Pennsylvania State University Press, 1995.

Norton, Augustus Richard. *Amal and the Shi'a*. Austin: University of Texas Press, 1987.

Parrinder, Geoffrey. *Mysticism in the World's Religions*. London: Sheldon Press, 1976.

Pelikan, Jaroslav. *Mary through the Centuries*. New Haven: Yale University Press, 1996.

Peters, F. E. *Aristotle and the Arabs*. New York: New York University Press, 1968.

Pinault, David. *The Shiites: Ritual and Popular Piety in a Muslim Community.* New York: St. Martin's Press, 1992.

Rajaee, Farhang. *Islamic Values and World View.* Lanham, Md.: University Press of America, 1983.

Richard, Yann. *Shi'ite Islam: Polity, Ideology, and Creed.* Translated by Antonia Nevill. Cambridge, Mass.: Blackwell, 1995.

Rommen, Heinrich A. *The State in Catholic Thought.* New York: Greenwood Press, 1945.

Rosenthal, Erwin I. J. *Political Thought in Medieval Islam: An Introductory Outline.* Cambridge: Cambridge University Press, 1958.

Ruether, Rosemary R. *Mary: The Feminine Face of the Church.* Philadelphia: Westminster Press, 1977.

Sachedina, Abdulaziz Abdulhussein. *Islamic Messianism: The Idea of Mahdi in Twelver Shi'ism.* Albany: State University of New York Press, 1981.

Schacht, Joseph. *An Introduction to Islamic Law.* Oxford: Clarendon Press, 1964.

Schall, James V. *Reason, Revelation, and the Foundations of Political Philosophy.* Baton Rouge: Louisiana State University Press, 1987.

Schimmel, Annemarie. *Mystical Dimensions of Islam.* Chapel Hill: University of North Carolina Press, 1975.

Schuon, Frithjof. *The Transcendent Unity of Religions.* Wheaton, Ill.: Theosophical Publishing House, 1984.

Shannon, William H., ed. *The Hidden Ground of Love: The Letters of Thomas Merton on Religious Experience and Social Concerns.* New York: Farrar, Straus, Giroux, 1985.

Shariati, Ali. *Fatima Is Fatima.* Translated by Laleh Bakhtiar. Brooklyn: Muslim Students Council, n.d.

Sigmund, Paul E. *Natural Law in Political Thought.* Cambridge, Mass.: Winthrop Publishers, 1971.

———. *Nicholas of Cusa and Medieval Political Thought.* Cambridge: Harvard University Press, 1963.

Smith, Lacey Baldwin. *Fools, Martyrs, Traitors: The Story of Martyrdom in the Western World.* New York: Alfred A. Knopf, 1997.

Smith, Margaret. *The Way of the Mystics.* New York: Oxford University Press, 1978.

Smith, Wilfred Cantwell. *Islam in Modern History.* Princeton: Princeton University Press, 1957.

———. *On Understanding Islam: Selected Studies.* The Hague: Mouton, 1981.

Spellberg, D. A. *Politics, Gender, and the Islamic Past: The Legacy of 'A'isha Bint Abi Bakr.* New York: Columbia University Press, 1994.

Stepan, Alfred. *The State and Society: Peru in Comparative Perspective.*
Princeton: Princeton University Press, 1978.
Tabataba'i, 'Allamah. *Shi'ite Islam.* Translated by Seyyed Hossein Nasr.
Albany: State University of New York Press, 1975.
Thomas Aquinas, Saint. *Summa Theologiae.* Vol. 14. New York: McGraw-Hill,
1975.
Trimingham, J. Spencer. *The Sufi Orders in Islam.* Oxford: Clarendon Press,
1971.
Voll, John O. *Islam: Continuity and Change in the Modern World.* Boulder, Colo.:
Westview Press, 1982.
Von Grunebaum, G. E. *Muhammadan Festivals.* London: Curzon Press, 1976.
Weinstein, Donald, and Rudolph M. Bell. *Saints and Society: Christendom,
1000–1700.* Chicago: University of Chicago Press, 1982.
Weisheipl, James A. *Friar Thomas D'Aquino: His Life, Thought, and Work.*
Garden City, N.Y.: Doubleday, 1974.
Williams, John Alden, ed. *Themes of Islamic Civilization.* Berkeley: University
of California Press, 1971.
———. *The Word of Islam.* Austin: University of Texas Press, 1994.
Woodward, Kenneth L. *Making Saints.* New York: Simon and Schuster, 1990.

INDEX

Ibn Sa'd, 38

Ibn Sina (Avicenna), 18, 100, 101, 102, 103, 104, 113

Ibn Taymiyya, 59

Ibn Tumart, 149 (n. 26)

Ignatius, St. (of Antioch), 64

Ijtihad, 57, 98, 99

Ikhtiyar, 19

Illuminationist philosophy, 23

Imams, 15–17; twelve disciples comparison, 3; suffering and redemption, 7, 46, 65–66; succession, 14–15, 29–46, 79–80; infallibility of, 16, 24–25, 26, 56, 62; disappearance of twelfth Imam, 17, 22, 45, 57–58; truth of teachings, 18; severe restrictions on, 21, 45–46; Babism and, 25; in Paradise, 45; revelation and, 47, 132; Muhammad's link with, 52, 103; intercession by, 55–58, 59, 66, 143; definition of, 56; Judgment Day and, 58; shrines of, 58–59; saints and, 59–60, 80; future resurrection of, 66; nonmilitancy of, 68; as legal interpreters, 97, 98–99, 132

Imamzadas, 58, 80

Immaculate state, 51, 53, 55, 62, 86

Incarnation, 48, 90

India: Twelver population, 4, 5, 6, 25, 151 (n. 40); Catholic mourning ceremony, 70

Individual autonomy, 119, 120

Individual rights, 108, 110, 111, 120–21, 144

Individualism, 13, 83, 119, 137

Inequality, 107, 123–24

Inerrancy, 16, 24–25

Infallibility: of Roman Catholic pope, 10, 18, 26, 62, 111–12, 115,

128; of Shi'i Imam, 16, 24–25, 26, 56, 62

Inheritance law, 22, 98

Inquisition, 69

Intercession, 46, 50–62, 65, 83, 143; passion plays and, 70–71

Interpretation: by conscience over tradition, 12; by Twelver *mujtahid*, 17, 57, 97, 98–99, 132, 133–34; by Akhbaris, 83; by Sunni legal schools, 97, 99; reason/revelation dichotomy, 100–102

Iran: Islamic Republic, 1–2, 5–6, 82–83, 113, 115, 116, 129, 131–34, 136, 137, 145–46; Twelver tradition in, 4–5, 6, 22–25, 81, 112–16, 129–31; Mashhad Martyr's Shrine, 43; 'Ali's importance in, 57; Twelver martyrs in, 67; mourning and passion plays, 70, 72; Sufi strains in, 77, 80–83; modernist/secularist movement, 112–15, 135; women's status in, 114–15, 139–40

Iran-Iraq War (1980s), 67, 133, 145–46

Iranian constitution (1906), 114

Iranian Revolution (1978–79), 5–6, 115, 130–31, 134; Khomeini leadership, 23, 82, 129–34

Iraq: Twelver Shi'ite population, 5, 25, 151 (n. 40); Islamic history in, 31, 33, 36–39, 42–43; mourning processions, 72; Sufi orders, 77; politicized Shi'i *mujtahid*, 130

Ireland, 11, 12

'Irfan, 82, 83

Ishraqiyya philosophy, 23

Islam: view of West, 2; origins, 13–15; affirmation of, 14, 18–19; division of, 14, 35; Christian contacts with, 25–26; early history, 27–46; first male convert, 29–30; sectarian warfare, 33; militancy reputation, 49, 69; state relations, 109–16; pan-Muslim revival, 113. *See also* Shi'ism; Sunnism; Twelver Shi'ism

Islamic law. See *Shari'a*

Islamic Republic of Iran. *See* Iran

Isma'il (sixteenth-century shah), 80–81, 82, 130

Isma'il (son of Ja'far), 16, 42

Isma'ili Shi'ism, 16, 17, 41, 89, 149 (nn. 25, 26), 153 (n. 21), 159 (n. 33); mosque in Cairo, 60

Israeli-Palestinian conflict, 67

Italy, 11, 12, 72; unification, 111

Ithna'ashari Shi'is. *See* Twelver Shi'ism

Ja'far (brother of eleventh Imam), 44–45

Ja'far al-Sadiq (sixth Imam), 16–17, 21, 40–41, 98

Ja'fari school, 21, 22, 40, 98

Jalal ad-Din al-Asadabadi (al-Afghani), 113–14

Jamri, Shaykh 'Abd al-Amir Mansur al-, 130

Jansen, Cornelis, 148–49 (n. 16)

Jansenism, 13

Jesuits, 78, 105, 111, 122, 148–49 (n. 16), 162 (n. 33)

Jesus Christ: views and faith of, 2, 8–10; disciples and apostles of, 3, 12, 62, 68, 140; Islamic view of, 3, 14, 17, 47, 48, 76, 158–59 (n. 22); suffering and redemption, 7, 49–50, 55, 64–65, 66, 74, 138, 144; incarnation of divine Logos in, 9; Protestant view of, 13; Judgment Day return of, 19, 57–58; hidden Imam and, 45; virgin birth, 47, 86; Husayn compared with, 47–50; poverty and, 48, 145, 146; pacifism of, 49, 68; Mary as mother of, 51, 53; humanity of, 51–52; sainthood and, 61–62; original sin and, 64; death and resurrection commemoration, 68–74; as mystical model, 76, 85–86; desert retreats of, 84; nature imagery and, 86; al-Hallaj compared with, 88–91

Jews, 9, 19, 28, 39

Jihad, 14

Joan of Arc, 67

John, St. the Apostle, 3

John of the Cross, St., 83, 85

John Paul II, Pope, 1–2, 86, 106, 112, 127, 128; dialogue with Islam, 1–2, 142–43; social concerns encyclical, 125–26; on Catholic charities, 139; liberation theology and, 145

John the Baptist, St., 84

John XXIII, Pope, 119, 120, 124, 125

Jordan, 149 (n. 24)

Judas Iscariot, 3

Judgment Day, 19, 45, 46, 54, 57–59

Jum'eh, Imam, 134

Junayd, Abu al-Qasim al-, 88

Jurisprudence. *See* Law

Justice, 108, 116, 118, 128; liberation theology and, 122; Shi'i political rule and, 132, 133, 134

Justinian the Great, 8

Karamat, 59

Karbala massacre (681), 3, 37–39, 49, 60, 66, 68, 69; mourning ceremonies, 70–74; desert site of, 84

Kashani, Ayatollah Abu al-Qasim, 115

Kashf al-Asrar (Khomeini), 131

Kazim, al-Musa (seventh Imam), 16–17, 41–42, 43

Kenya, 5, 147 (n. 7)

Khadija, 52, 55

Khamene'i, Seyyed 'Ali, 83, 134

Kharijis, 35, 36

Khatami, Muhammad, 1–2, 6, 134

Khidr (Khadir), 158 (n. 21)

Kho'i, Abol Qasim, 129

Khomeini, Ayatollah Ruhollah, 2–3, 5–6, 57, 82–83, 115, 129–34, 137, 138, 145; philosophy lectures by, 23–24; Imam 'Ali's importance to, 57; Iran-Iraq War and, 67; mystical poetry by, 82, 83; as populist, 132, 133, 145; on martyrdom, 145

Khums, 21–22, 45, 139, 150 (n. 37)

Knights of Columbus, 139

Kufa, 31, 33, 35–36, 37, 45

Kulayni, Muhammad b. Ya'qub al-, 150 (nn. 31, 34)

Kulturkampf, 162 (n. 33)

Kuwait, 77

Latin America: mourning processions, 69–70, 72–73; Catholic hierarchy in, 109; liberation theology, 122, 123–24, 126, 130, 138, 144; populism, 132

Law, 93–104, 136, 137, 143; Sunni primacy of, 17–19; Shi'i foundations, 21, 22, 40; Roman Catholic taxonomy, 93, 94–96, 107, 108, 133; Islamic taxonomy, 97, 98. *See also* Divine law; Interpretation

Lebanon, 4, 5, 67, 130, 151 (n. 40)

Legal schools, 20–25, 97–99

Lent, 68, 69, 79

Leo III, Pope, 148 (n. 11)

Leo XIII, Pope, 96, 105, 106, 116, 119–20, 126, 128

Lesser occultation, 22, 45

Liberalism, 111, 120, 135, 137

Liberation theology, 122–29, 135, 138–41, 144; Shi'ism and, 130, 144, 166 (n. 3)

Lincoln, Abraham, 162 (n. 33)

Little Sisters of the Poor, 139

Livingston, James C., 161 (n. 23)

Logos, 9, 50, 62, 79, 148 (n. 15)

Lombards, 148 (n. 11)

Lord's Prayer, 51

Lull, Ramon, 85–86

Luther, Martin, 13, 59, 61

Madhhabs, 20–21

Madina, 14, 20, 21, 30, 32, 33, 36–37, 39–42, 44, 45, 55

Mahdi, al- (twelfth Imam), 17, 19, 42, 45; continued life of, 46; messianic return of, 57–58

Mahdi, Sadeq al-, 2

Maimonides (Musa b. Maimon), 101

Majlis, 132, 134, 144

Maliki school, 20, 21, 98

Ma'mun, 42, 43

Mansur, 41

Marhab, 30

Marriage, 10, 22, 79

Martyrdom, 3, 61–74, 143–45; Twelver embrace of, 3, 20, 39, 46, 63, 64–67, 80, 144–45; of eleven Imams, 3, 39, 62; Mashhad shrine, 43; of Jesus and Husayn, 47, 49–50, 55, 73; politics and, 66–69; desert experience and, 84; mysticism and, 84, 87; of al-Hallaj, 90–92

Marxism, 119, 125, 126, 137, 145

Mary (Virgin Mary): Islamic view of, 3, 14, 158–59 (n. 22); Fatima parallel, 47, 52–55, 143; as Mother of God, 50, 51–52, 55; immaculate state of, 51, 53, 55, 86; apparitions of, 54; Sufi view of, 86

Maryam al-Kubra, al- (Fatima), 53

Mashhad, 43, 58, 60

Mason, Herbert, 160 (n. 36)

Mass, 68, 87, 140

Massignon, Louis, 3–4, 52, 54, 88–92, 160 (n. 36)

Ma'tams, 39, 70

Ma'tam Bin Saloum, 72

Ma'tam Bin Zabar, 72

Mawla, 15

McSweeney, William, 106

Mecca, 14, 15, 28, 30, 33, 37, 58, 63, 89

Medjugorje, 54

Melkite Catholic Church, 88

Merton, Thomas, 91–92

Messiah: Jesus as, 14, 17, 47, 48; twelfth Imam as, 67–68

Mexico, 54, 126

Militancy, 41, 49, 69

Military orders, 69

Min, Anselm, 125

Minaret, 87

Miracles, 14, 44, 48, 58, 59, 83

Missionizing, 11, 20, 25

Modernity, 106, 111–12, 114–16, 121–22, 127–28, 135, 141, 145

Monarchy, 107–8

Monasticism, 11, 12, 65, 83, 84, 86; mysticism and, 77, 78, 79. *See also specific orders*

Mongol invasions, 23

Montazeri, Husayn 'Ali, 129

Morocco, 15, 149 (n. 26)

Moses, 47, 55, 158 (n. 21)

Mosque architecture, 87

Motahhari, Ayatollah, 66, 131

Mother of God, 50, 51–52, 55

Mourning ceremonies, 69–74

Mourning houses, 39

Mu'awiya, 27, 32–39, 45, 152 (n. 10)

Mubahala (the Ordeal), 29

Mufid, Shaykh al-, 22–23, 43, 48

Muhammad, Prophet, 27–31; traditional Catholic views of, 2; revelation and, 13–14, 19, 27, 99; death of, 14, 29, 31; as prophetic culmination, 14, 47; grandsons of, 15, 36; Sunni legal schools and, 20, 21; inerrancy of, 24; as messenger of God, 27, 132; daughter Fatima, 28–29, 52–55; 'Ali relationship, 29–30; military strategy of, 68; martyrdom and, 70–71; simplicity of life, 76–77; condemnation of celibacy, 78; Virgin Mary compared with, 86; message of, 110. See also *hadith*; Imams

Muhammad (son of Isma'il), 41

Muhammad al-Jawad. *See* Taqi, al-

Muharram, 69, 70, 72

Mujtahids, 17, 24, 25, 46, 83, 97–99; truth of teachings, 18; guidance from twelfth Imam, 46; as major interpreters, 57; tensions with Sufism, 81; Iranian government and, 113, 129–30, 132, 133–34, 145; authority of, 137, 138; monetary controls, 139, 150 (n. 37)

Mulayy Idris, 59

Mu'mim al-Taq, 150 (n. 30)

Muqtadir, al-, 89

Murshid, 78, 80, 81

Murtada, Sharif al-, 22

Patron saints, 69

Paul, St. and Apostle, 65, 79, 83, 95, 107, 121

Paul of the Thebaid, St., 84

Paul VI, Pope, 125, 126–27, 128

Pelikan, Jaroslav, 50

Penance, 10

Pentarchy, 8

People of the Cloak, 29

Persecution. *See* Martyrdom

Persian Gulf area, 4, 24, 151 (n. 40)

Peter, St. and Apostle, 9, 56, 62, 68

Petrine primacy, 10, 11, 112, 147 (n. 5), 162 (n. 35)

Petroleum, 5

Philippines, 72–73, 124

Philosopher-king, 100, 101–2, 103, 104

Philosophy, 18, 19, 23–24, 26, 94, 96, 99–106, 136, 143

Pilgrimage, 14, 54, 55, 58–60, 70–72

Pir, 80, 87

Pius IX, Pope, 106, 111, 112

Pius X, Pope, 11

Pius XI, Pope, 119, 120

Pius XII, Pope, 96, 116, 119

Platonic thought, 102, 103, 143

Poetry, 39, 81–85

Political philosophy, 93–116, 143; Twelver Shi'i, 41, 66–69, 93–94, 97, 112–16, 129–36, 144; martyrdom and, 66–69, 72; Iranian Islamic Republic, 83; mysticism and, 88, 89–90; Roman Catholic, 93, 96, 99, 104–9, 111–12, 118–29; Platonic and Aristotelian, 102–3. *See also* Law

Pool of Kawthar, 46

Poor and oppressed: charity and, 39, 117–18, 136, 138–39; Imam 'Ali

on, 48; compassion of Fatima and Mary for, 54, 55; Roman Catholic/Twelver concern for, 93, 136, 138, 144; religion-state relationship and, 109–10, 115–16; liberation theology and, 123–29, 138, 145; Twelver populism and, 132, 138

Populism, 123, 128–41, 144–46; fundamentalism vs., 132

Populorum Progressio (encyclical), 125

Positivism, 94

Poverty ideal, 86, 91, 117–18, 138

Prayer, 39, 62; Shi'i call to, 22, 27; rosary, 28, 51, 79; directed to Mary, 51, 53; passion of Jesus and, 69

Predestination, 13, 18–19

Press freedom, 111

Processions, 39, 69–70, 72, 88

Prophets, 13–14, 50, 96

Protestantism, 64, 94, 126; Roman Catholicism vs., 12–13; development of, 26; critique of Marian theology, 51; critique of saint cults, 59, 61; distrust of mysticism, 83

Psalms of the Family of the Prophet, 39

Purana, 70

Qadiri, 77, 79

Qahtan (Joktan), 152 (n. 7)

Qajar dynasty, 113, 114

Qarmati movement, 89, 159 (n. 33)

Quadragesimo Anno (encyclical), 120

Quanta cura (encyclical), 111

Qum, 22, 23, 60, 82, 129

Qur'an: on Mary and Jesus, 3, 17, 47, 50–51, 158–59 (n. 22); revealed to Muhammad, 13–14, 27; Sunni view of, 18; Sunni legal schools and, 20, 21; Mubahala incident in, 29; as arbiter, 34–35; Imam as infallible guide to, 56, 62; *batin* aspect of, 60; as Logos, 62; martyrdom commended in, 65; mysticism and, 75; on male and female roles, 78–79, 139–40; paradise depiction, 84; divine law and, 97; *hadith* in, 97; Latin translation of, 102; usury condemnation, 118

Quraysh, 15, 30

Radi, Sharif al-, 22–23
Ramadan, 39, 79
Rationalism. *See* Reason
Rawza, 70
Ra'y (legal school), 20
Reason, 95; Sunni view of, 18; Shi'i view of, 19, 22, 24; reason/revelation dichotomy, 93, 99–106, 135, 136; Thomist emphasis on, 105
Redemption, 7, 49, 63–74, 143
Reformation, 12–13, 26
Relics, 60, 88
Religious freedom, 111
Rerum Novarum (encyclical), 106, 119–20
Resurrection, 66, 69–74
Revelation: Christian Logos, 9; Islamic belief, 13–14, 18, 19, 27, 47–48, 60; immaculate state and, 86; reason/revelation dichotomy, 93, 99–106, 135, 136; of natural and divine law, 95-96, 132; centrality to both Shi'i and Roman Catholic belief, 136
Revolutions, 111, 113; Iranian, as classic, 131

Reza Shah Pahlavi, 114–15
Rida, al- 'Ali (eighth Imam), 42–43, 45, 46, 58; shrine of, 58
Rifa'is, 77
Risorgimento, 111
Roman Catholicism: Twelver links with, 1–4, 142–43; martyrs, 3, 61, 63, 65–69, 144–45; geographical concentration, 6; development in West, 8–12, 20, 25–26; infallibility doctrine, 10, 18, 26, 62, 111–12, 128; Protestantism vs., 12–13; pacifism and, 49, 68; intercession in, 50–58, 61–62, 143; saints, 58–62, 143; martyr vs. confessor, 64; redemptive suffering emphasis, 64–65; mourning ceremonies and passion plays, 69–72; mysticism, 75, 83–88, 91–92, 143; legal taxonomy, 93, 94–96, 107, 133; political and social issues, 93–94, 99, 104–29, 134–41, 144; reason/revelation debate, 100, 104–6; hierarchy in, 108; state relations, 109–16; subsidiarity principle, 120–21, 137; believers' challenges to, 122, 127–28; status quo protection, 127–28; concept of church, 137; charities, 138–39
Roman Empire, 8–10, 20, 25; Christian martyrs, 61, 63, 66, 68
Rosary, 28, 51, 79
Rumi, Jalal ad-Din, 84–85
Ruqayya, 32
Russia, 113, 114, 146, 163 (n. 39)
Russian Orthodox Church, 10

Sacraments, 10, 13
Sa'd b. Abi Waqqas, 32
Sadr, Imam Musa al-, 130

Suicide martyrs, 67
Summa contra Gentiles (Aquinas), 107
Summa Theologica (Aquinas), 118
Sunnism, 15–18; Muhammad's succession and, 14–15, 36; Twelver Imams and, 17, 23, 45–46, 56, 63; *shariʿa* primacy, 17–18; Qurʾan and, 18; legal schools, 20–22, 24, 97–99, 113; as majority, 45, 110; saint cults and, 59, 60; redemption doctrine and, 65; mysticism, 76, 79, 80; Twelver ninth-century challenges to, 89; theological philosophers, 100–101, 102; anti-colonialism, 113; almsgiving, 139
Supernatural powers, 47, 61, 83
Syllabus of Errors (Pius IX), 111
Syria: John Paul II's visit to, 2; Twelver population, 5, 147 (n. 6); Arab conquest, 31; Twelver history, 33–34, 35; Melkite Catholic Church, 88

Tabari, al-, 152 (n. 8)
Tabatabaʾi, ʿAllama Muhammad Husayn, 23–24
Tabriz, 25, 80, 163 (n. 39)
Tahmasb, Shah, 81
Talha, 31–32, 33, 34, 37
Taqi, al- (ninth Imam), 43–44
Taqiyya, 17, 19–20, 24, 40, 42, 45, 115
Tawhid, 110, 115–16
Taʿziyyas, 70–71
Teresa of Avila, St., 83
Terrorism, 67
Theotokos, 50, 51
Third World, 109, 123–24, 132, 141
Thomas Aquinas, 4, 100–106, 111, 136; mysticism and, 75; legal tax-

onomy, 94–96, 107, 136; political philosophy, 107–9, 119; usury condemnation, 118
Tobacco monopoly (Iran), 114
Traditionists. *See* Akhbaris
Trappist monks, 91–92
Trinity, 48
Turkey, 4, 5, 15, 23, 113
Tusi, Muhammad b. Hasan al-. *See* Shaykh al-Taʾifa
Tusi, Nasir al-Din, 23, 101–2, 103, 104, 150 (n. 35)
Twelfth Imam. *See* Mahdi, al-
Twelve, significance of, 3
Twelver Shiʿism, 17–46; Roman Catholic links with, 1–4, 142–43; martyrs, 3, 20, 39, 46, 63, 64–67, 80, 144–45; world population, 4–5, 25, 151 (n. 40); Imams, 7, 15–17, 24–25, 26, 29–46, 56, 62, 124; Muhammad's successor and, 14–15, 31; theology, 17, 18; *taqiyya* by, 17, 19–20, 24, 40, 42, 45, 115; background, 17–20; Sunni comparison, 18, 21–22; philosophical studies, 18, 23–24, 26, 101–2; hidden Imam, 19, 22, 45; free choice belief, 19, 46; as revolutionary movement, 20, 80, 89, 110; law and, 21, 22, 40, 97–104; legal school, 21–22, 23, 24–25, 98; Sufism and, 23, 79–80; minority status of, 25, 110; major personalities, 27–46; Karbala memorialization by, 38–39; mourning rituals and passion plays, 39, 70–74; political and social issues, 41, 66–69, 93–94, 97, 112–16, 129–38, 144; intercession in, 50, 53–58, 143; women and, 55, 114–15, 136, 139–40; saints, 58–60;

redemptive suffering emphasis, 64–65; mysticism, 75–92, 143; as esoteric tradition, 76, 80–83; Massignon scholarship on, 88; *tawhid* concept, 110, 115–16; populism, 128–41, 144–46; liberation theology and, 130, 144, 166 (n. 3); almsgiving, 139. *See also* Iran

Tyrannicide, 107, 113

'Ubaydallah b. Ziyad, 37, 38
'Ubaydallah the Mahdi, 149 (n. 26)
'Ukbari, al-. *See* Mufid, Shaykh al-
'Ulama: Iranian, 6, 109, 113–15, 131, 134, 138; Qum training center, 23–24; mourning ceremonies and, 70; mysticism tensions, 81
Ultramontism, 111
'Umar (third Imam), 21, 30, 31, 32, 35
Umayya clan, 152 (n. 10)
Umayyad dynasty, 39, 40, 42, 109
Umm al-Fadl, 43
Umm Habiba, 152 (n. 10)
Umm Kulthum, 29, 32
Umma. See Community
United Nations, 135
United States: passion plays, 71–72; individual freedoms in, 111; as Iranian Revolution foe, 115, 145–46; Catholic charities, 139
Unity, preemptive importance of, 110, 115–16, 135, 137
Universities, medieval, 26, 86
Urban II, Pope, 12
Usuli school, 14, 24, 25, 83, 98, 99, 113
Usury, condemnation of, 118
Ut Unum Sint (encyclical), 162 (n. 35)
'Uthman, 21, 32, 33, 34, 35, 36, 109

Vatican I, 111–12
Vatican II, 2, 61, 106, 122, 124, 125, 127, 128, 135, 145
Vikings, 25
Virgin birth, 47, 86
Virgin Mary. *See* Mary

Wahhabi sect, 41
Wali. See Saints
Walid b. 'Abd al-Malik, 39
Walid b. 'Utba, al-, 30
Wills, Gary, 127
Wisdom literature, 9
"Withdrawers." *See* Mu'tazila
Witness, giving and bearing, 63, 65
Women's status: Twelver vs. Sunni law, 22; Twelver Shi'ism and, 34, 55, 114–15, 139–40; Qur'an on, 78–79, 139–40; Roman Catholicism and, 122, 126, 128, 140; barriers to authority structure, 128, 136, 139–40
Word of God, 9, 13–14, 50, 62, 79, 86, 148 (n. 15); Qur'an as, 18, 62, 97; Jesus as, 47. *See also* Logos; Revelation
Working class, 106, 119

Yazdegird III, Shah of Iran, 39
Yazi b. Mu'awiya, 27, 37, 38
Yazid, 27, 38, 67
Yemen, 16, 31, 37, 155 (n. 32)
Yunus b. 'Abd al-Rahman, 150 (n. 30)

Zachary, Pope, 148 (n. 11)
Zahir (outer), 75–77, 79, 88, 100, 110, 144
Zahra, al-. *See* Fatima
Zakat, 139
Zanj rebellion, 89

Zayd b. Arqam, 38
Zaydi Shi'ism, 16, 18, 40, 41, 155 (n. 32)
Zayn al-'Abidin (fourth Imam), 39–40, 41, 45

Zaynab, 29, 38, 58
Ziyad, 152 (n. 10)
Zubayr, 31, 33, 34
Zurara b. A'yan, 150 (n. 30)
Zwingli, Huldrych, 13